What the Sig

What the Signs Say

Language, Gentrification, and Place-Making in Brooklyn

Shonna Trinch & Edward Snajdr

Vanderbilt University Press | Nashville

Library of Congress Cataloging-in-Publication Data

Names: Trinch, Shonna L., author. | Snajdr, Edward, author.
Title: What the signs say : reading a changing Brooklyn / Shonna Trinch
    and Edward Snajdr.
Description: Nashville : Vanderbilt University Press, [2019] | Includes bibliograph-
    ical references and index. | Summary: "Argues that the public language of
    storefronts is a key component to the creation of place in Brooklyn, New York.
    Uses a sample of more than 2,000 storefronts and over a decade of ethno-
    graphic observation and interviews to chart two types of local Brooklyn retail
    signage: Old School, which uses many words, large lettering, and repetition,
    and New School, with hallmarks of brevity and wordplay. Presents in-depth
    ethnographic case studies that reveal how gentrification and corporate
    redevelopment in Brooklyn are connected to public communication, literacy
    practices, the transformation of motherhood and gender roles, notions of
    historical preservation, urban planning, and systems of privilege" – Provided
    by publisher.
Identifiers: LCCN 2019031000 (print) | LCCN 2019031001 (ebook) | ISBN
    9780826522771 (Hardcover) | ISBN 9780826522788 (Paperback) | ISBN
    9780826522795 (ebook)
Subjects: LCSH: Signs and signboards – New York (State) – New York. | Street
    art – New York (State) – New York. | Gentrification – New York (State) – New
    York. | Brooklyn (New York, N.Y.) – Social life and customs.
Classification: LCC HF5841 .T76 2019 (print) | LCC HF5841 (ebook) | DDC
    659.13/420974723 – dc23
LC record available at https://lccn.loc.gov/2019031000
LC ebook record available at https://lccn.loc.gov/2019031001

Portions of Chapters 1 and 4 appear in adapted form in Shonna Trinch and
Edward Snajdr, "What the Signs Say: Gentrification and the Disappearance of
Capitalism without Distinction in Brooklyn," *Journal of Sociolinguistics* 21, no. 1
(Feb. 2017): 64–89.
Portions of Chapter 3 appear in adapted form in Shonna Trinch and Edward
Snajdr, "Mothering Brooklyn: Signs, Sexuality and Gentrification Undercover,"
Linguistic Landscape 4, no. 3 (Nov. 2018): 214–37.
Portions of Chapter 4 appear in adapted form in Edward Snajdr and Shonna
Trinch, "Old School Rules: Generative Openness in the Texts of Historical Brook-
lyn Retail Signage," *Interdisciplinary Journal of Signage and Wayfinding* 2, no. 2
(July 2018): 12–29.

In the spirit of Brooklyn's migrations, this book is dedicated to all people everywhere who, for one reason or another, have had to become newcomers.

Contents

Acknowledgments

FOR US BROOKLYN is a special place because it is where we became a family, so we would like to begin by thanking our two children, Charles Snajdr-Trinch and Lucia Snajdr-Trinch, because they were very helpful in our Brooklyn field site. Like most people who migrate from one place to another for work, we used the resources we had to adapt to our new surroundings. We quickly learned how important our children were in this process. They encouraged (and sometimes forced) us to ask questions about, to engage with, and to try to understand what at first seemed a very challenging place for two working parents rapidly approaching midlife with an infant. As this project grew, our children also grew up, inhabiting a household that was part of an active field site, with stacks of photographs, articles, books, notebooks, and laptop computers taking up every available surface in our home. Our children complain that we are always working, and they often recite our questions and comments as evidence. We fear that, to them, we are not merely quirky or curious professors, but rather annoying oddballs constantly collecting data and analyzing the place they always knew simply as their home. We thank them for their patience, their companionship, and their open spirit. Our children are real New Yorkers in ways that we will never be, and we are lucky to live with them for this reason and many others.

We had read books and news articles about Brooklyn, watched films, listened to music, and heard lots of folklore before actually moving here. But none of that really prepared us for what we encountered: the diversity, the disparity, the traffic, the lack of parking, the challenge of finding affordable housing, and of course, very nice, warm Brooklynites, who expected everyone to know what they knew and to be able to go where they went. So, in addition to our children, another valuable resource we had as social scientists, though our whose specializations and field experiences were in quite different and faraway places, was ethnography. Ethnography, anthropology's hallmark method of in-depth cultural submersion, began for us informally in 2003, where we were at first the participant-observers with no prior tangible experience. We began to formalize our ethnographic approach in 2006 by writing grant proposals to study the borough's changes more systematically. In 2010, that goal became a reality, and thus we thank the National Science Foundation's Program in Cultural Anthropology and its program administrators Deborah Winslow, Laura Ahearn, and Jeffrey Mantz, for providing the funding for our data collection (SBE# 0963950).

But if it were not for our son, Charles, just six weeks old upon our arrival, we would never have had friends so quickly and cracking the codes of Brooklyn might have taken even longer than the decade and a half it has taken us to put this book together. Thanks to him, we immediately made friends who helped us navigate our new terrain in ways that only human beings can. These people were lifesavers in those early days. We are so grateful to them for lending a hand, offering their knowledge, and sharing their lives with us. We met many of these people within weeks of our arrival, and we have been through a lot with them. These people are Maureen Landers and Matt Mullarkey, and their children, Max and Leila Mullarkey; Lisa Raymond-Tolan and RJ Tolan; Mooki Saltzman and Stephen Panone; Jana and Joel Turoff; Ivy Epstein and Josh Levine; Barbara Lang; Shira Katz; Sara Silberman; and Alice Saltzman.

All of our kids' milestones continued to provide different degrees of entrée into Brooklyn spaces that, had we not been their parents, would have remained closed off to us: the mothers' groups, playgrounds, preschool, dance studios, kids' creative writing and music groups, youth sports, the public library, and the Brooklyn Arts Exchange (BAX). We are grateful to all the people we met because of our children's early experiences, many of whom are also still with us in one way or another and with whom we have discussed our research in multiple ways. We have much gratitude for you:

Donna Klassen, Martin Brennan and Siobhan Brennan, Meghan and David Andrade, Regina Poreda and Michael Ryan, Karen and David Sheehan, Isabel and Andy Gordon, Mike and Haydee Beltrami, Frank and Michelle Santo, Rob Rossi and Ellie Jones Rossi, Dave Ebert and Cecily Traynor, Jacquie Kelleher and Kirby Pulver, Monsignor Guy Massie, Vanessa and David Aja-Sigmon, Alan Aja and Wendy Trull, Justine and John Allocca, Kristine and Rob Oleksiuk, Nancy and Rob Anderson, Patricia and Larry Sarn, Felicia and Jonathan Geiger, Kariman Jahjah, Rob and Seh Norris, George and Pat Baladi, Stefania Vasquenz and Torin Cornell, Tony Leone, Justin Brannan, Andrew Gournardes, Sharon Locatell and Tim Harris, Alica Mulligan, Rosann Vento, Carol Coombs, Gela Martinez, Yolanda Priego, Rupert Gardner, and Amanda Daglish. Amanda Daglish also read part of an early version of the manuscript and provided us with insightful comments.

We also wish to thank all the teachers, coaches, administrators, parents and children at the public schools our children attended. In these schools, our children made great friends, learned a lot, and became caring Brooklynites and concerned New Yorkers, eager to try to make the world a better place.

We are very grateful to each and every person we interviewed or even just spoke with about Brooklyn, the way it was, the way it is, and the way it is changing. But we must thank our key research participants by name, as this project would never have been possible without them. We are extremely grateful for your time, your stories, and your generosity in sharing your experiences and your work with us: Patti Hagan, Daniel Goldstein, James Caldwell, Bertha Lewis, Daisy James, Justine Stephens, and Jonathan Villaran. We are grateful for the work of Norman Oder who writes the blog *Atlantic Yards / Pacific Park Report*. His meticulous documentation of the Atlantic Yards redevelopment process has been a valuable public resource for us as we chart and interpret Brooklyn's changing commercial landscapes.

We had the honor and good fortune of having Christine Hegel, Luke Cantarella, and George E. Marcus workshop our research in their Ethnography by Design project. This was an intense experience that allowed us to creatively engage with theatrical and musical set designers, graphic designers, and new design anthropologists like Scott Brown (who studied as an undergraduate with both of us at John Jay), all of whom provided new insights into our own work.

Working parents know well that it is difficult to juggle and balance personal and professional life. If not for our John Jay colleagues, this struggle would have been much more arduous. For this reason, and many more, we wish to thank our John Jay friends and colleagues beginning with those in our own Anthropology department. Thank you for your support throughout the years and for the expertise you shared with us along the way that made this a better project: Alisse Waterston, Avi Bornstein, Ric Curtis, the late Barbara Price, Patricia Tovar, Johanna Lessinger, Anthony Marcus, Anru Lee, Atiba Rougier, and our newest colleagues, Emily McDonald, Marta-Laura Suska, and Kimberley McKinson. Also at the College, we would like to acknowledge the contributions of the following colleague-friends: Rich Schwester (for helping us devise our random probability survey), Valerie Allen, Jacob Marini, Susi Mendes, Anthony Carpi and Dan Stageman, Barbara Cassidy (for being a great partner to Shonna on their theater project *Seeing Rape*), Richard Haw, Richard Ocejo, Effie Papatzikou Cochran, Sondra Leftoff, Shirley Sarna, Katie Gentile, former president Jeremy Travis, and former provost Jane Bowers, as well as our current president, Karol Mason, and provost, Yi Li.

In addition to wonderful colleagues, John Jay College also has brought us in contact with great undergraduates from whom we have learned so much. Several of them have also been our research assistants: Akil Fletcher, Shauna Parker, Yance Vargas, Veronica Cortez, Earlynn Bernadin, Patrick Grimes, Loakeisha London, Cheryl Lopez, Stephanie Mireles Cruz, Brandon Dolores, Brittany Muñoz, Samantha Eltenberg, Evy Pettit, Harold Rodríguez, and Angie Dorville.

Colleagues and friends at other colleges and universities who are our life-long friends gave us tons of space to hash out our ideas in conversations, offered readings, and challenged us to think about and articulate our points more clearly. A big thanks for listening and providing feedback to Cotten and Claire Seiler, Mike Monti, Ángel Weruaga Prieto, Marusela Álvarez Rodríguez, Larry Solan, Art DiFuria, Jean Dangler and Ainslee Beery, Aimée Boutin, Linda Pritchard and Mary Osborne, Vicente Lecuna and Pancha Mayobre, Ana Forcinito, and Anadeli Bencomo.

Scholarship is better when peers review it, and we are grateful to those who have strengthened our work by being readers/reviewers, panelists, discussants, or an audience for our paper-presentations at conferences. Our work has benefited from the critical wisdom of great scholars such as Susan Gal, Arlene Dávila, Jeff Maskovsky, Galey Modan, Christiana Croegaert, Gillian Greblar, Lanita Jacobs, Adrienne Lo, Elizabeth Chin, Gary McDonogh, James Wines, Vero Rose Smith, Barbara Johnstone, Jackie Lou, Crispin Thurlow, Adam Jaworksi, Francis Rock, Kellie Gonçalves, Kate Lyons, Frank Monaghan, Durk Gorter, Jasone Cenoz, Robert Blackwood, Jennifer Leeman, Julian Brash, Susan Falls, Susan Ehrlich, Justin Richland, Angelique Haugerud,

Melissa Curtin, Patricia Lamarre, Marijana Sivric, Lindsay Bell Grub, Elana Shohamy, Setha Low, Jonathan Rosa, Greg Matoesian, Rachel Heiman, Mindy Lazarus-Black, and Bill Black.

Some of the material we use in this book was previously published in the *Journal of Sociolingusitics*, *Linguistic Landscape*, and the *International Journal of Signage and Wayfinding*. We are grateful to those journal editors for the work they undertook in finding anonymous reviewers and sifting through reviewer commentary to point us toward the most pressing concerns. These people are Joseph Park, Allan Bell, Tommaso Milani, and Dawn Jourdan. In fact, pieces of this project have had extraordinary amounts of peer review, and while criticism was never easy, we always believed it would make the work stronger, better, and more engaged with the disciplines. We are grateful to all the anonymous peer reviewers who gave their time generously and their expertise for free.

Along these lines, we are indebted to Vanderbilt University Press's former editor Beth Kressel Itkin for being an unbelievably talented, detail- and big picture–oriented editor. Beth knew Brooklyn, and she instantly "got it" when we told her the premise of our project. Her editorial acumen was crucial in the early stages of our writing and structuring of the study, and she found astute readers for it. They were keen in their commentary, and we are so thankful for them. When Beth left Vanderbilt, Zack Gresham took over, and once again we found ourselves in the very competent hands of a skilled and attentive editor. We would also like to thank John Catalano, brother of the late Anthony Catalano, for giving us permission to reproduce a small part of Anthony's extensive and artful photographic archive of Brooklyn life, and we thank Gersh Kuntzman, Tracy Collins, and Robbin Gourley for allowing us to reprint their work as well. Thanks to Evelin Ramírez and Mary Bakija from the New York City Department of Records and Information Services for learning about our project and showing us the wealth of photographic data available to the public.

On a personal note, our hearts also swell with gratitude for our non-Brooklyn family and friends who provided encouragement, resources, and peace of mind. We are forever grateful to Las Religiosas de la Asunción (the Nuns of the Assumption) in Spain, and especially Cecilia Manrique, Pilar Diez Corral, and Toñy Alvarez for providing us with not only friendship and love, but also affordable housing, schooling, and two wonderful places to live while we escaped Brooklyn's summers and put ourselves to the task of writing. We also wish to thank Mercedes Méndez Siliuto, Dolores García Espinosa, and Carmelita Fernández for their kindness and affection. But Spain would never have been a home away from Brooklyn without Nuria Gallego Fernández, Valentín Astorga, Maricruz López González, Amadeo Villareal, Pedro Sáchez García and Asunción Grandoso Cuevas, Marcos Gómez, Olga Nuevalos Santos, Santiago Olmo Diez, Paco Pelicano, and Encina Fernández. The friendship and companionship of these fun-loving, giving people made long days of writing shorter when we knew we had an evening *tapeo leonés* with them waiting for us.

Our very best friends beyond Brooklyn provided everything from love and fun to expertise in things like finance, mortgages, commercial and residential loans, urban development, business, diversity training, website design, architecture, marketing, public relations, workers' rights, health care, and the list goes on. So thank you for always, always being there for everything. They include Kristen and Chuck Hammel and their children Max and Jake Hammel, Jayanne and Gary Matthis, Kelly DaSilva, Kathleen and Dave Wright, Laurie Valkanas, Samantha Swift and Dana Meute, Anne Baldwin, Greg Fisher and Melissa Jones, Jill Morrison and Greg Peel, Colleen Moran, Sharon and Dan Lynch, and Lauren Hauptman.

This book is about family and home as much as it is about anything else. Our own family members have been very supportive of our move to Brooklyn, and we love their enthusiasm for this place. We are grateful for the cross-country treks Sam, Laurie, Lilly, and Jack Trinch have made to be with us on so many occasions. We are also grateful for Paula and Steve Reinhard's willingness to come to the big city to visit. We do not see enough of Christine, Steve, Alexa, Sophia, and Nina Reider in Brooklyn, but we love when they come. Suzanne Snajdr; Elizabeth, Dax, and Chris Hamilton; Pete Poole; and Eric and Nutchana Snajdr all helped us move into Brooklyn in a myriad of ways: from Suzanne's literally unloading the moving trucks and leading sibling painting crews to all their regular visits in the early years when our kids were little. Our siblings and their families would come and marvel at the wonders of Coney Island, the Manhattan skyline, the various languages heard on the street, the beauty in Brooklyn's art and architecture, the local sports, the babkas, pizzas, dumplings, tamales, labné, and so much more that the borough offered. We are indebted to them all for helping us see that there was no place in the world we would rather call home than Brooklyn, NY.

And last but certainly not least, nothing would ever be possible without our parents, Sam and Angel Trinch and Sallee Poole. They share everything they have with us all the time. They give their time, their money, an ear, vacations to relax, space to work, phone calls, letters, love for us, love for our kids, and most of all, constant encouragement. From the very bottom of our hearts, we thank them.

Have you ever noticed which of the street signs, over the shop doors, are the most attractive of attention? . . . the over-largely lettered signs and placards of the street, escape observation by dint of being excessively obvious.

Edgar Allan Poe, "The Purloined Letter," 1845

Introduction: Discovering a Field Site

IN THE SPRING of 2007, a Brooklyn bagel-maker put up a sign for his new store on 5th Avenue near St. Marks Avenue in Park Slope. It read *ARENA* in five large capital letters, above the words *BAGELS & BIALYS* (Figure I.1). The owner said he hoped to link his new shop to the coming sports arena, what would become the Barclays Center, the centerpiece of Atlantic Yards, New York City's largest urban redevelopment project in the past fifty years. The multibillion-dollar plan included the basketball arena and sixteen high-rise office and residential towers in the middle of Brooklyn. The bagel seller soon learned that local residents planned to protest his store's name. They read the name ARENA as an open endorsement of Atlantic Yards, which they were publicly and legally contesting. Local residents disagreed with the plan's scale, and they felt that the developer and the state's partnership was a misuse of public money and an abuse of government power for private profit (Lavine and Oder 2010; Snajdr and Trinch 2018a). Although the shop owner at first told a reporter he was going to ignore the neighbors' threat (Kuntzman 2007), within a month, he relented, and a new, nearly identical, but ultimately very different sign went up: *A.R.E.A. BAGELS & BIALYS* (Figure I.2).

Figure I.1. ARENA BAGELS. In 2007, the owner named his shop in anticipation of the popularity of the new Barclays Center basketball arena, part of the Atlantic Yards redevelopment project, which was to be built down the block from his storefront. Photo by Gersh Kuntzman

Figure I.2. A.R.E.A. BAGELS. The owner changed the shop's name within a month amid pressure from locals who were opposed to the Atlantic Yards arena and towers project. Photo by Gersh Kuntzman

We heard about the wrangle over ARENA/A.R.E.A. Bagels from various informants when conducting our ethnographic study about neighborhood "say" in the Atlantic Yards controversy.[1] For example, we heard about it from Patti Hagan, a Prospect Heights resident and community activist who first sounded the alarm about the plan. Daniel Goldstein, whose property was seized by the state to build the arena and who became the spokesman for Develop, Don't Destroy Brooklyn (DDDB), a grassroots group opposing the plan, also told us about the shop sign incident. But Goldstein explained that DDDB had no position on the bagel shop's name and had never encouraged a boycott of the business. On DDDB's website, a May 18, 2007, post entitled "We're Focused on the Big Picture, Not the Bagel Hole" stated that "We believe that the use of eminent domain for [Atlantic Yards] violates the US Constitution and we have organized and continue to raise funds for a lawsuit alleging just that in federal court" (DDDB 2007). But in fact the discourse of both DDDB and the local press trivialized local residents' concerns about the language of the bagel shop's sign, arguing that there were more important things to fight over than a shop owner's storefront. The *Brooklyn Paper* concluded that

> the opponents of Atlantic Yards are so frustrated by Bruce Ratner and his high-priced pals that they're taking out their aggression on a lowly bagel store owner. . . . So there it is, folks: An immigrant from Punjab—a guy who worked himself up from a dishwasher to a manager to, finally, the owner of bagel stores in Queens, Long Island and Brooklyn—is gunned down in the war over Atlantic Yards. (Kuntzman 2007)

Though we also understand the difference between a small business entrepreneur and a billion-dollar developer, the case of ARENA Bagels shows that the meaning of language in public space, even on the seemingly smallish scale of a storefront sign, can actually play a significant role in the contemporary contest over urban space. Clearly, some neighborhood residents felt they had the right to say something about the bagel-seller's shop sign. And as it turned out, the shop owner, stating that he wanted to fit in with the neighborhood, decided to heed their concerns.

Ten years after the Park Slope ARENA Bagels incident, another group of residents felt they had the right to say something about the semiotics of another Brooklyn shop in their neighborhood. On July 22, 2017, a mere two miles east down the same street as the ARENA Bagels shop, more than two hundred people gathered at the intersection of Nostrand Avenue and St. Marks Avenue in Crown Heights. They congregated to air their concerns about Summerhill, a new, upscale restaurant that had opened up a few weeks earlier. Justine Stephens, a young, African American gentrifier and local resident who had moved into the predominantly African American and West Indian neighborhood a couple of years earlier, had helped organize this gathering. While out walking, Stephens had noticed the restaurant's large plate-glass windows, above which the restaurant's name was inscribed in pale blue script on a stark white background, but she had not yet stopped in for a meal before she began to read about it online. It was then that she learned about the bullet holes.

Shortly before opening, Summerhill's owner, Becca Brennan, a former lawyer and Toronto transplant, had issued a press release to online media outlets

Gothamist and *Eater*. Among other things, the text described the restaurant's interior walls: "Yes, that bullet-hole-ridden wall was originally there, and yes we're keeping it." In Stephens's words, "I was angered by that! I looked at their social media. They have a picture of a cocktail next to this *advertised* bullet holed-wall. Because that's what a press release is—an *advertisement*. . . . And then there are other photos, like with a bartender with a 40 oz. of rosé [wine] in [a display case]." Stephens knew that many people in her neighborhood did not use social media like her generation. Despite a lack of explicit signage, she recognized the establishment as a gentrifying business, and she wondered if local residents, people who had lived in the neighborhood for forty or fifty years, were even aware of the way the restaurant had been marketed to wealthier, and younger, newcomers to the area. She thought that

> people who would go to [local stores], you know, [where] the advertising is clear and up front, who digest information through newspapers and signs on community boards or a lamppost . . . people who have lived here a long time in this community probably wouldn't go to *Gothamist* or *Eater*. So, I thought it was important to open up that dialogue. To see what everyone else thought, too. . . . Because it was their neighborhood before it was mine. And they need to know what's going on. (interview with authors, October 4, 2017)

Stephens and two other people concerned about the use of bullet holes to promote a restaurant then assembled the gathering of Crown Heights residents so they could talk publicly, in front of the establishment, about their feelings regarding the store's semiotics, or the symbols used to imbue the space with particular meanings. But, they said, the owner did not come out to hear them, and they complained that she was slow to respond to their concerns. Although Brennan did eventually cover up the holes, it was only after more protest, a town hall meeting, and a Community Board hearing. Stephens, along with many other residents and community leaders, felt that Brennan was annoyed by their feelings about her marketing ploy. They concluded that she did not truly understand why people were upset and angry.

Both the cases we've described tell important stories about how storefronts and their signage and semiotics can be very meaningful to people. Each case indicates that the impact a public sign may have on people who see it and interpret it can be significantly different from the intended meaning. In this book we examine the way that public language can create place and how place is experienced through public texts in a rapidly changing Brooklyn. The retail shop sign is an obvious but often overlooked type of public text that plays a

Figure I.3. Map of Brooklyn neighborhoods. There are more than forty neighborhoods in this New York City borough of 2.5 million people. Map by Peter Fitzgerald, created July 17, 2009, used under CC BY 3.0, en.wikipedia.org/wiki/List_of_Brooklyn_neighborhoods#/media/File:Brooklyn_neighborhoods_map.png

key role in the definition and experience of place. Not surprisingly, everyone has an opinion about places, but as we will see, everyone's opinion about place may not have the same influence when it comes to defining a neighborhood. And as the two cases introduced here show, shop signs and their other related forms of semiotics matter.

We first noticed Brooklyn's storefront signs when we moved to Flatbush, one of Brooklyn's more than forty neighborhoods, in 2003 (Figure I.3). While shopping along Church Avenue or nearby commercial districts of Windsor Terrace, we were immediately struck by the textual denseness found in most retail signage and then in the commercial space in general. After relocating to Bay Ridge, an ethnically diverse neighborhood in South Brooklyn, we counted more than 1700 storefronts on Third and Fifth Avenues. Each retail-rich street runs through Bay Ridge and neighboring Sunset Park for over sixty blocks, averaging fifteen storefronts (seven or eight on each side of the street) per block. Any given shopping block offers a wide range of small, independently owned retailers including dry cleaners, delis, gift shops, grocers, hair and beauty salons, coffee shops, hardware stores, electronics shops, restaurants, and daycares. Most Brooklyn commercial districts span twenty to forty blocks, creating tightly packed textual landscapes of between two hundred and six hundred storefronts.

It was in this commercial-rich environment that we realized signs on local stores appeared to have all kinds of things to say. They were colorful and had dozens of words on them. Some were hand-painted and contained pictures or photographs. These public texts seemed to announce the commercial and ethnic vitality of Brooklyn, reflecting the diversity of its people and its cultures. At the same time, we also noticed that some newer Brooklyn shops appeared to be very different from the text-rich storefronts found throughout the borough. They had almost nothing on their signs. In fact, their storefronts appeared nearly empty from a distance. This stark contrast pushed us to think about signs as cultural markers and artifacts that operate not just as individual messages or expressions, but together, as social and historical experiences and symbolic systems of place.

As with Summerhill and A.R.E.A. Bagels, there is always a history behind a storefront. Each shop and each block are certainly unique places. But taken together, the collective textual landscape created by neighborhood retail shops also says a lot about Brooklyn as a dynamic place. Our data reveal how language itself participates in the making and remaking of place in complex and multifaceted ways. On the one hand, shop signs may provide messages of openness to others, calling out to anyone to "come in." On the other hand, some signs might not be so "open" to everyone. Importantly, the signs we were noticing also existed in a larger field of urban transformation that included both corporate redevelopment, like the Atlantic Yards project that spurred on the A.R.E.A. Bagels conflict, and gentrification.

Gentrification is not a new phenomenon and many scholars have been working to reveal its processes and effects on place. The term was first coined by sociologist Ruth Glass (1964) in the mid-1960s to describe what she called an "invasion" of the middle class into what were traditionally working-class neighborhoods of London. We like geographer Jason Hackworth's (2002: 815) definition of gentrification as "the production of space for progressively more affluent users." Popular conceptions of gentrification are that it is the result of wealthier and/or more educated individuals merely *choosing* to move into particular neighborhoods, perhaps to find a larger home or to renovate an old building. But both gentrification and redevelopment usually involve broader economic, social, and political decisions on the part of local and state governments. While they may occur simultaneously, residential and retail gentrification has seemed in Brooklyn to precede larger-scale corporate redevelopment in the borough and has occurred in successive waves, as former Manhattan residents arrived in search of more space and more affordable housing (Kasinitz 1988; Lees 2003). The cultural geographer Neil Smith argued that gentrification and redevelopment are driven by the emergence of what he called "the rent gap." Smith defined the rent gap as the "disparity between the potential ground rent level and the actual ground rent capitalized under the present land use" (Smith 1979, 545). Rent gap creations, Smith argued, were not random, but were the outcome of the longer term, purposeful disinvestment and corporate profit seeking that in turn resulted in more decay and an acceleration of the emptying out of American cities. Finally, both gentrification and redevelopment are processes that displace people from a particular place to make room for new construction or the renovation of existing property. Understanding this larger setting of rent gap fluctuations, urban planning, and investment and disinvestment is also critical to considering what it is that Brooklyn signs "say" about place.

To accomplish our reading of Brooklyn storefronts, we think about signs as being more than just features of architecture or expressions of trend or style. To understand shop signs and their meanings in the context of a changing city, we needed to think about them in a geographic, historical, and sociopolitical sense. This way we can investigate them as publicly and *collectively* marking place with aspects of language that have cultural ideologies, or common beliefs and ideas, attached to them. Such an endeavor necessarily demands a combination of anthropological and linguistic perspectives in order to comprehend how texts operate as social practices that help to make particular places in the world and the role those texts serve in changing place. In the next section, we briefly describe some of the work that has been done on texts and the making of place as well as some of the important theory that guides our study.

Reading Signs in a Linguistic Landscape

Beginning with the basics, shop signs are public texts that communicate what stores sell, who store owners want to attract, and what their commercial desires might be (Lou 2016, 2007; Leeman and Modan, 2010; Papen 2012). By *signs* we mean those objects containing words and symbols located on the outside of a building to advertise the presence of a business. People may not give such signs a lot of thought in terms of everyday routines or experiences, but in considering the communicative function of shop signs, especially in dense, urban spaces, signs may very well be the only *perpetually visible* semiotic device of a storefront. For example, even though one might think that store merchandise can be easily seen through shop windows, cityscapes often get reflected on the glass of a storefront and surrounding building shadows make windows dark. Brooklyn storefronts are also usually covered by steel gates at night until as late as 11:00 a.m. People traveling in cars, on bikes, and on buses may not easily see inside shop windows. And finally, pedestrians on opposite sides of streets may rely on signage because windows are obscured by traffic and parked cars. So signage is the key textual device available to communicate to passersby in urban spaces at all times. Additionally, we observed that storefront signage in Brooklyn is often available to passersby who approach businesses from any angle. Brooklyn storefronts tend not to rely solely on signs above the front door; they often incorporate posts that jut out of their buildings at 90-degree angles. Pedestrians on the adjacent sidewalk can read what is on the posts without having to turn their heads to read the larger signs above the door. Corner businesses commonly have signage on both the main street and the side street on which their buildings sit. All of this contributes to a Brooklyn retail district's text-dense character.

Shop signs, moreover, are part of a larger category of public texts that include street signs, public notices, and municipal signage, and they make up part of what language scholars call the "linguistic landscape" (Shohamy, Ben-Rafael, and Barni 2010; Landry and Bourhis 1997). This landscape of texts is composed of all kinds of semiotic devices, with different appearances, frequencies, and purposes. For example, government signage is generally uniform, ubiquitous, and consistent in its functions. Today, most city street signs in New York are generally white lettering on a green background, and they mark the names of avenues and streets, in a sense labelling axes on a grid.[2] Highway signs, another form of government text and also uniformly green and white throughout the United States, show direction toward places as well as identifying a person's location. Municipal signage also serves prescriptive functions, such as indicating the legal speed limit or a one-way only traffic pattern, and proscriptive functions like the "Don't Honk" signs that adorn some of the more exclusive areas of Manhattan's Upper West Side. Sometimes small placards are affixed to apartment buildings with multiple

Figure I.4. Sign posted by a landlord on a residential apartment building restricting certain public behaviors on or in front of the premises.

proscriptions: "No sitting, loitering, ball playing, loud noise, soliciting permitted near the building or on the fire escapes. Do not block passageways to building" (Figure I.4). In rarer cases, one can find city signage that seeks to help people in crisis: standing vigilantly on the edge rails of the Verrazano Narrows Bridge between Staten Island and Brooklyn is a public sign reading "LIFE IS WORTH LIVING," posted to discourage people contemplating suicide by jumping.

Just taking into consideration these examples, one can see that an area's linguistic landscape both delineates and represents the social context in which people find themselves and their languages (Gorter 2006; Shohamy, Ben-Rafael, and Barni 2010). Language itself is a primary mechanism through which people struggle for representation, a tool for making claims to land and land use, and a permit for rights to place in general. Linguists, human geographers, anthropologists, and historians have contributed to understanding both the role of language in place and how place is shaped through language. For instance, historian George Stewart's (1982) study of place-naming in the US reminds us that "names on the land" are determined by the dynamics of conquest as much as by culture and custom. While he recounts the well-known case of the British renaming New Amsterdam, a Dutch settlement in North America, New York, he also tells the lesser-known stories of people naming thousands of streams, valleys, and settlements through their occupation and use.[3] Studies of language often tell us who can speak in a place, how they can speak, and what they can speak about. One example is the establishment of an official language within a state, to which other language speakers must submit or suffer discrimination, marginalization, and the pressures of assimilation (Paulston 1994). Moreover, the manner in which power and capital are inscribed on the land may or may not correspond to the way that people who live there imagine place and community (cf. Anderson 1991).

"Place" is a quintessential, albeit often incidental, object of study in anthropological investigation.[4] In ethnographies that are ostensibly about something other than place-making, we often read about how research participants define place. For example, anthropologist Avram Bornstein's (2002) ethnography of the Green Line, the border that separates Palestinian workers from the land of their gainful employment in Israel, examines how the "location" of the militarized border was created by people's ideas of place as well as the way the Israeli government mobilized those ideas through documents and identification cards. Similarly, anthropologist Alisse Waterston's (1999) ethnography on women with a history of homelessness in New York City considers how humans, in defining themselves, exert considerable effort to create a place of one's own.

These individual and collective struggles of cultural identity and power can be *imprinted* onto place in other semiotic ways: through the images and texts of postcards (Dorst 1989), advertisements (Dávila 2004), and graffiti (Holleran 2017; Caldiera 2012), for example. Imprinting need not rely on formal texts alone and can also be expressed through the materiality of space. For instance, the specific features and qualities of the built environment, such as building facades, lampposts, and typography, can communicate political and economic regime shifts (Gendelman and Aiello 2010) or convey a message of exclusiveness with gateways, panels, and posts (Aiello 2011). From linguistic anthropology we learn how the emotional and political experiences of place become coconstitutive with people's social and cultural identities and are manifested in linguistic forms ranging from collective legal disputes (Forbes 1999) to individual songs and stories about the land. In the absence of written texts, people, like the Western Apache or the tribal Kaluli of Papua New Guinea, give meaning to the land through oral accounts of place and belonging (Basso 1996; Feld 1996). Linguistic anthropologist Keith Basso (1996, 76), for example, shows how for the Apache places become a source of cultural understanding and awareness, a "wisdom" through people's learning of their Apache names (in spoken discourse and in song) and reflecting on traditional narratives that shape and represent them as a group. In other words, language helps to confirm place, or land, as a sociocultural phenomenon that aids in the construction of people's unity and the building of their identity. But, of course, place is a resource, and access to a resource often becomes political and contested as different groups vie for its control.

Returning to our topic of different sorts of signage as public texts, it is important to consider how signs of all types can be *profoundly political* devices.[5] While these devices appear in the landscape in an unexceptional way, they are in fact quite powerful regulators of social interaction, of users, and of usages of space. Viewed diachronically, signs thus reflect a place's historical past and future path.[6] People recognize the importance of signs in their formal and informal efforts to memorialize them for posterity as they do other cultural artifacts that represent their history.[7] But from the perspective of sociolinguistics and anthropology, signs are not just cultural artifacts, they are and always have been formidable and influential *social acts* that mete out and reflect the way power is exercised in and upon the landscape. For instance, signs in specific languages in multicultural societies can indicate a group's explicit political dominance and can also reveal the changing tide of representation and authority among different ethnic and national identities (Barni and Bagna 2010).[8]

In the Jim Crow South, explicit public signs demarcated space according to ideas of racial inequality and openly commanded public behavior.[9] In fact, Elizabeth Abel (2010) suggests that Jim Crow signage did not just restrict space for certain people, it also functioned to reinforce racial theories that justified segregation at a time when science was debunking a biological foundation for race and mounting evidence suggested race was a sociocultural construct. That is, at the same time the anthropologist Franz Boas and his students in the early twentieth century were calling into question racist dogma regarding biological determinism, segregation by public signage upheld and promoted notions of racial difference and ideas of white superiority and black inferiority (Abel 2010, 10–11). Candacy Taylor (2016a, 12) notes that in the mid-twentieth century, small towns along US Route 66 had racist "sundown" rules warning black travelers at their points of entry on the road that they needed to be gone before dark.[10] And, she points out, businesses supported this system by regularly encoding the exclusion of African Americans on their storefronts using names such as Kozy Kottage Kamp or Klean Kountry Kitchen. In these store names, the C in Standard English orthography is replaced with a K, invoking the acronym for the Ku Klux Klan and suggesting to all travelers that they served whites only. Moreover, in addition to telling people whether they could be in a place, Jim Crow signage made places "fit" conventional and local concepts of race, privilege, and power. Signage itself became not only a tool of racial segregation but also a powerful technology of white supremacy.

In contrast to these overtly political manifestations of signage, shop signs mark independently owned small businesses in an urban space and as such are uniquely creative and personal texts. In one sense they are as unofficial or informal as public murals or graffiti, which convey a message of an individual's or family's personal presence or community history. As conveyors of messages, signs may also depict different writing and reading practices that tend to call out to those already there as well as to those who may have not yet arrived. Linguistic anthropologist Susan Philips gives an example of the link between signage, place, and literacy. In comparing the absence of signs in the Indian reservation of Warm Springs, Oregon, with the nearby Anglo-town of Madras, where signs mark businesses, government agencies, and streets, Philips (1975, 370) theorizes that a culture's "communicative needs . . . may be closely related to [their] social needs." Like Basso's (1996) work among the Apache, Philips shows how people can inhabit and give meaning to land without using signs. The small kin-based, homogeneous community of reservation residents learns from elders where things are. Nonresidents rarely appear on the reservation without an Indian escort and non-Indians very rarely become residents. Therefore, there is no need for signage in Warm Springs. Instead, people map social life on the land orally and through routinized practices without having to write on it or having to use any texts at all.

But where signs do exist, reading them requires certain types of interpretive knowledge for geographic mobility and understanding place, and thus, signs are products of literacy. So signage usage in the town of Madras suggests its social structure as well: nonresidents move to town for work all of the time; locals within a sixty-mile radius regularly shop and accomplish tasks there; and strangers, like tourists, campers, and hunters, also pass through often. The cartography of space is partly achieved through reading public texts. Philips (1975) concludes that the existence of signs creates an openness to Madras that allows outsiders, or strangers, entrée. Signage functions as a map of place that people read and interpret.

Words alone, however, do not make interpreting signs completely accessible. While public texts might occur prominently in a landscape, whether they and their meanings are legible to everyone who sees them is another question. Sometimes this textual map can be hard to read if one is not local to a place. For instance, for nonnatives trying to navigate New York City's metropolitan area, interpreting local texts can be a challenge. As both newly arrived outsiders and fifteen-year-long residents who have witnessed other newcomers and visitors, we have seen firsthand how the system of signage in this large urban area with a dense population often appears to be written in a local shorthand. One confronts this curiously abbreviated language whether you are trying to negotiate New York City's intensive network of interstates, bypasses, parkways, and thruways or you are attempting to move through the labyrinthine pathways of public transportation by subway or bus. For example, as one drives north by car heading to La Guardia Airport, just as the traffic flow snakes around a tight curve on the Brooklyn-Queens Expressway near Astoria in Queens, there is a small orange sign, not more than two feet wide, with a black arrow and the letters G.C.P. Blink and you miss this temporary but critical message placed by construction crews directing drivers to the on-ramp of the Grand Central Parkway, which is the *only* route to La Guardia Airport. If this exit is missed, drivers are stuck crossing the Triborough Bridge (officially named the Robert F. Kennedy Bridge in 2008, but no New Yorker we know calls it that) and you are suddenly and hopelessly headed across the East River to Manhattan and the Bronx. Similarly, on regular freeway and parkway signage there are other peculiar local abbreviations. These include the BQE, Harlem Riv Dr, FDR DR, SSP, LIE and MSP—respectively, Brooklyn-Queens Expressway, Harlem River Drive, Franklin Delano Roosevelt Drive, Southern State Parkway, Long Island Expressway, and Meadowbrook State Parkway. In New York, *parkway* is a term that restricts traffic to passenger cars. Trucks and buses are not allowed on these roads. *Expressways*, however, allow commercial traffic and larger vehicles.

On the New York City subway and on busses one also finds similarly unique abbreviations of important place terms. The sides of cars on the R train, for instance, are marked by yellow block lettering on a black field that reads "Broadway LCL." Locals can no doubt read these signs (or do not have to), but we have seen that to visitors and newcomers, it is not clear that LCL is an abbreviation for local, meaning that the train makes all stops on the line. Many visitors to New York have told us that the subway's "Downtown" designations are confounding to them. From everywhere in Manhattan, traveling south the subway signs read, "Downtown & Brooklyn" (with "Downtown" on top of "& Brooklyn" in white text on a black field). Visitors, unaware that most of New York City is designed and spoken about with a Manhattan-centric orientation, often think that these signs are indicating that they could get to "downtown Brooklyn" on that line. New York City residents know that the subway signage refers to downtown Manhattan, but the signage is ambiguous. All these examples suggest that signs and sign makers are quite rooted in the culture of a place and in local notions and practices of reading. The expression of direction in language is deployed through a concept that linguists refer to as *deixis*. Deixis, as we will discuss throughout the book, is a linguistic process whereby the meaning of some words, such as *here*, *there*, *north*, *south*, and so on, depends on the context of the communication and the communicators, for example, who is talking, who they are talking to, and where they are. This context is often referred to as the *deictic center*, or the reference point from which a deictic expression is to be interpreted.

Literary critic and social theorist Michael Warner (2002) argues that all texts, as do all spoken utterances, pick out their publics, meaning that speech and texts are created to appeal to particular audiences. And audiences can certainly vary. In fact, Warner claims that a particular "public" is often created largely through texts. In other words, while we might think of "the public" as everyone en masse, "a public" is actually certain people, called to or constructed by design, often shaped by cultural or political ideology.[11] Publics are generally various competing constellations of community that involve unique cultural worldviews (Staeheli and Mitchell 2007). There can be multiple publics in a given place and many ways in which these different publics are situated, related, and interconnected (Gal 2005; Yeh 2009).

While storefront signs are classic symbols that point to where people can do commerce, they also, as perpetually visible texts in public spheres, are constructed to appeal to certain publics. Signs accomplish this specifying of target-groups through another form of deixis, or their incorporation of what linguists and semioticians call *indexicals* or *indexes*, meaning all those elements in language that point to the things they refer to without necessarily mentioning them explicitly. In language there are two types of indexicals: referential indexicals and social indexicals. Referential indexicals are those linguistic items that stand in for or refer to someone (e.g., I, you, he, she, it) or something (e.g., these, those, this, that) or some place (e.g., here, there, everywhere). And referential indexicals mean different things according to the person who uses them and the discourse and social contexts in which they are uttered. For example, the meaning of the referential indexical "we" changes in the following two sentences: "We are writing this book." vs. "Our children told us, 'We are ready for you to be done writing this book.'" So these referential indexicals have no inherent meaning outside of the contexts in which they are uttered because their meanings shift depending on those contexts (Jakobson 1971). Linguistic anthropologist Michael Silverstein (1976) elaborated an understanding of indexicality by showing how some linguistic elements function to point to or create specific social meanings and/or social contexts. Words, then, in association with ideas, when uttered, Silverstein says, are not just determined by the context, but rather can also create the context. For example, the use of titles such as Mr., Mrs., Professor, or Dr. has the power to create a context of formality between speakers much the way kin-terms, when used by people irrespective of their blood-relations, can create intimacy among them. By considering who and what signs point to or *index* (Ochs 1990; Silverstein 1976, 2003), and how these indices may be read (Bauman and Briggs 2003), we can see how *symbolic capital* plays a part in conferring material and political value on land for a certain public.

Symbolic capital includes texts, images, language, and specific forms of knowledge that are imbued with distinctive status, recognition, and prestige (Bordieu 1984). We argue that symbolic capital, in the form of communicative norms like specific languages or certain literacy practices, is tied to identity and social status (Street 1984; Besnier 1991; Collins and Blot 2003). Symbolic capital, then, gets rendered and recognized on signs through the mobilization of sociocultural *language ideologies* (Schieffelin, Woolard, and Kroskrity 1998; Irvine and Gal 2000). Linguistic anthropologists consider a language ideology to be a set of broad, often implicit, assumptions about the status, use, and role of language in the world. These assumptions about language are intimately tied to other cultural beliefs about people and their nonlinguistic practices. So the meaning and functions of social indexicals that originated in language ideologies—beliefs and ideas about certain norms and ways of speaking that often come about because of their association with the meanings attached to the groups of people who speak them—can be deployed to select and form certain publics. Whole languages, for example, have come to take on stereotypical associations. So, for example, some people come to believe that French sounds sophisticated because it gets associated with French art, literature, and philosophy. Italian may sound romantic to some because it is often associated with romance in general, and to important Italian historical, literary, and artistic figures such as Marco Polo, da Vinci, and Michelangelo. And for some listeners German may sound either imposing and intimidating due to its associations to the systematicity of conquest and oppression during two devastating world wars or exacting through its association with twentieth-century industrial precision. Without being stated explicitly, any of these subjective ideas and stereotypes can be suggested indexically by the incorporation of these languages in certain texts. But language ideologies, we will see, extend far beyond whole languages to their individual dialects, varieties, registers, and even certain types of utterances.

Signage imbued with or constructed with linguistic elements and semiotic devices that index or point to particular language ideologies therefore marks land not simply for a specific language and its users, but more importantly here, for the ways in which different groups of people use language according to their prevailing sociolinguistic standards and values. Shop signs communicate not only what is inside for sale but also who is perceived to be outside; how they tend to communicate, read, and understand; and what they are believed to desire in place.

While owners may not actually be the type of people their signs suggest, the personae indexed locates actors, whether real or imagined, in public space for passersby. Of course, it would be interesting to analyze the intentionality and/or motivations of shopkeepers and sign makers as they talk about and understand the signs they make and put up, but more importantly, we aim to identify and understand the possible meanings of signs because they are available to everyone in the landscape at all times and thus, they are meant to be "public." Linguistic anthropologist Alessandro Duranti (2015, 238–39) argues that intentionality is both culturally informed and dynamic. People go in and out of intentions at an interactional level. But unlike "telling a story" or "preparing for [and participating in] a business meeting" which are temporal and contextual communicative acts, storefront signage has a textual perpetual-ness. In general, we consider the intentionality of store owners only inasmuch as they put up a sign for everyone and anyone to see and interpret, which, in Brooklyn, includes a broad mix of people from different cultural, class, ethnic, religious, educational, and linguistic backgrounds.

While our study is not about reading practices per se (Collins and Slembrouck 2007), literature on literacy informs our analysis of how Brooklyn storefront signs mark the functionality of space for strangers and can demarcate space as a place for certain kinds of people. Therefore, signs can also be viewed as the products of the field of literacy education in which "certain resources are produced, attributed value and circulated in a regulated way" where there is "competition over access" to symbolic capital (Heller 2012, 50). Some signs include differentially valued sociocultural linguistic resources, such as historical references, "clever" turns of phrase, and literary allusions, that function in social contexts to make a certain type of place for a certain group of people. In addition to being geared toward consumers, storefront signs both mark and create the presence of specific markets, residents, and visitors. As linguist Jan Blommaert (2013) notes, shop signs both index and recruit customers. They call to an anticipated audience of consumers— whether from a neighborhood or passing through—who may (or may not) want to buy something at the moment. We concur that signs are vocative in nature, calling to those in place. But by considering how and to whom shop signs make this call, one can also understand signs as highly visible arguments about place and people in place, and therefore, we see storefront signs as unique place-making technologies.

As place-making tools, shop signs, then, are sort of like stories, which sociolinguist Barbara Johnstone (1990) argues function to maintain and reproduce prevailing local ideas about culture. However, stories are usually either told to specific interlocutors and presented in well-defined contexts, or they are read silently by individuals who personally engage the texts. By contrast, shop signs, as always-visible texts, are available to everyone *at all times*, and thus they make their arguments about place out in the open and impersonally, where neither interlocutor is mentioned by name. When these seemingly anonymous texts embody different language ideologies, they come to shape political, social, and economic contexts by conferring differential and competing symbolic and material values on the land. So getting a better understanding of the political, social, and economic context of the contemporary borough of Brooklyn into which we moved was the next critical step to interpreting the story that these signs were telling us.

The Research Setting – Gentrification and Redevelopment in Brooklyn

Each of New York City's semiautonomous boroughs has a sizeable population. While Manhattan (1.6 million) has historically captured the world's imaginary as "New York City," Brooklyn (2.6 million) and the city's other three boroughs (Staten Island, ½ million; the Bronx, 1.5 million; and Queens, 2.3 million) have been known dismissively as outer boroughs, marginal and peripheral to Manhattan, the city's center. For Brooklyn this marginality was reinforced by its role as a home to immigrants, which, during the 1800s, were mainly Europeans—Irish, Germans, Italians, Scandinavians, and Slavs, many of whom were Jewish or Catholic—who came to fill widely available jobs, and who were also joined by a large influx of African Americans who migrated from the southern US (Wilkerson 2010). In the last half of the twentieth century, Asian, Latin American, West Indian, Arab, and South Asian immigrants also settled in the borough.

Although Brooklyn became one of the nation's leading producers of manufactured goods by 1880, its marginality to Manhattan persisted as 40 percent of the workers living in the borough worked in Manhattan. Between 1950 and 1980, this peripheral status intensified as Brooklyn's industrial economy waned, new suburbs lured white families with widely available home loans away from the city, and African American neighborhoods underwent redlining as banks marked certain residential areas high risk, effectively denying residential and commercial loan opportunities for local residents (Hillier 2003). By 1990, Brooklyn's population had dropped by 18 percent, from 2.7 million to 2.2 million.

Over the past few decades, however, Brooklyn has witnessed substantial reinvestment through state- and city-supported corporate redevelopment (Brash 2011), and it has become a destination for upper-middle-class homebuyers, younger hipster renters, Manhattanites looking for new and interesting things, and tourists (Zukin 2010). Brooklyn has been recently considered one of the most expensive cities in the US (Senison 2016), and gentrification is accelerating (Lees 2003; Osman 2012; Susser 2012). For example, average Brooklyn home values have risen 130 percent over the past fifteen years. Some Brooklyn neighborhoods, such as Fort Greene or Brooklyn Heights, have seen increases of 250 percent, with home prices in Williamsburg showing a 600 percent increase between 1974 and 2006 (Furman Center 2006). Along with the rise in home values there has been a growing displacement of working-class, ethnic, and African American populations by white, college-educated residents. As an example, from 1980 to 2000, only 2 percent of Williamsburg residents had a college degree; just six years later, 30 percent of its residents reported having completed college. In terms of ethnicity, the 1980 Hispanic population in Williamsburg/Greenpoint reached 40 percent, but by 2006, this group dropped to only 25 percent, while the non-Hispanic white population increased from 50 percent to 65 percent. In Fort Greene and Prospect Heights, the two neighborhoods surrounding Atlantic Yards, whites constituted 17 percent and 30 percent of the population respectively, while African Americans made up 70 percent and 61 percent in 1990. By 2010, white residents of these areas reached 36 percent and 53 percent of the total population, with the number of African American residents dropping to 45 percent and 31 percent respectively. Moreover, the area averaged five new white residents for each new black resident during each year between 2000 and 2006. Between 2007 and 2010, this ratio doubled to ten white residents for each new black resident. Additionally, after 2000, more than a quarter of a random sample of new residents earned an average of at least $150,000 per year.[12]

While census tract and housing price data make gentrification look linear and easily identifiable, the borough's median household income still hovers around $44,000 per year for a family of four, and in actual neighborhoods the signs of change are complicated and sometimes hard to read. Brooklyn remains extremely diverse. African Americans and non-Hispanic whites each make up 35.8 percent of the borough's current population, with Hispanics at 19.8 percent and Asians at 11.3 percent.[13] While these groups form majorities in certain areas, most neighborhoods are quite mixed in terms of race, ethnicity, religion, and class. As an anecdotal example: our children attended a public elementary school in Bay Ridge where, in 2011, twenty-three different home languages were represented among its some five hundred students, whose families came from fifty-five different countries. And at least 66 percent of these students qualified for the federal free/reduced lunch program.

Both gentrification and redevelopment can be confusing and contested ideas. Not all gentrifiers are white, but in the US many, if not most, are. Not all developers are corporate or large-scale. Some are very locally oriented. Others operate in multiple cities and communities. Not all gentrifiers are wealthy, but again, in the US most either are, or they are not because of professional or lifestyle choices that focus on other forms of privilege and prestige, such as people with PhDs who work as adjunct faculty, or artists and musicians who also may not earn high salaries. Obviously, the idea of choice is also contentious in the US, as most people would not, if they had their way, choose a low wage, even for their labors of love. Finally, as we noted earlier, gentrification can happen in waves, each successive wave being replaced by increasingly wealthier residents, until ultimately what urban geographer Loretta Lees (2003) calls *super-gentrification* has occurred.[14]

Other scholars have tackled gentrification and development on many levels and from many different perspectives (Zukin 1987, 1989; Atkinson 2003; Slater 2006; Freeman 2011). For example, one can find in the struggle for what political scientist John Mollenkopf (1983) has called the "contested city" a host of political sagas about how public space is used and how urban actors shape city areas for certain users. These processes of urban planning, gentrification, and commercial redevelopment (such as state-of-the-art sports venues like the Barclays Center), unfold in an age of neoliberalization (Brash 2011; Sassen 2001; Smith 1996). By neoliberalization we mean a shift in governance, through deregulation, decentralization, privatization, public-private partnerships, and the globalization of markets, that transfers traditionally state or municipal operations to an arena where citizens presumably make personal choices and willingly engage in rational "transactions."[15] Studies have revealed the impact of these processes on racism (Massey and Denton 1993), class inequality (Abu-Lughod 1994; Sieber 1987), and even perceptions of public health (Rotenberg 1993). Within this struggle for place, a range of strategies of resistance have emerged including neighborhood organizing, civic demonstrations, demands for affordable housing, and even squatting (Mele 2000). But some scholars have also found that certain ethnic groups in places like Los Angeles, Washington, DC, and Mexico City participate in a variety of ways in uniquely shaping the norms of use for public space (Davis 2001; Low 1993; Boyd 2005).

In this saga of the movement of capital and neoliberal ideologies, language has not really been a central concern of scholarship on gentrification or redevelopment, but some recent work suggests there is much to investigate. For instance, sociolinguist Galey Modan (2007) explores how residents use language in a variety of ways to claim rights to contested urban areas in Washington, DC. Neil Smith (1996) and urban sociologist Christopher Mele (2000) have demonstrated how conquest-inspired language (e.g., *the frontier* and *pioneering*) has been used to market neighborhoods to more affluent users. Likewise, the oral narratives of neighborhood residents ultimately displaced by redevelopment and gentrification provide affective stories of place. For example, psychiatrist Mindy Fullilove's (2005) informants' accounts of *root shock* record the trauma of losing "home" and consequently the parts of their identity connected to it. Similarly, sociologist Richard Ocejo (2011) captures the nostalgia narratives among early gentrifiers who lament further and future changes to New York's supergentrified Lower East Side, while linguist Kara Becker (2009) has discovered that "white ethnics"—people of diverse European heritages who speak a unique dialect of English—identify themselves as different from both newer nonwhite neighborhood groups (Latino, Asian, African American) and more recent gentrifiers in this same neighborhood. Some scholars have also begun to engage with the theoretical concepts of indexicality and semiotics in understanding the process of gentrification (Thurlow and Jaworski 2011). For example, linguists Adam Jaworski and Simone Yeung (2010) have studied differential frames of Chinese and English on residential signage in Hong Kong that mark elite real estate developments. Linguists Jennifer Leeman and Galey Modan (2009, 2010) and Jackie Lou (2016) have shown how both shop signs and architecture index transitions of economy and power in the redevelopment and gentrification of Washington, DC's Chinatown. And linguist Uta Papen (2012, 2015) has investigated the political and economic transformation of an East Berlin neighborhood, including its recent gentrification, where the various semiotics of shop signs and graffiti both reflect and contribute to these changes.

Our aim in this book is to consider the role that commercial language on small-scale shops has played in marking and making gentrified space. In Brooklyn in particular, we also examine how language on shop signs on the street operated prior to gentrification. Though we cannot provide a complete picture of all processes of gentrification and redevelopment, our analysis seeks to contribute to an understanding of gentrification's complexities through both form and content on shop signs in the context of urban change. If shop signs are sociolinguistic technologies of place-making, one of the key ways that they make place is through their use of specific language ideologies, or those beliefs, feelings, and attitudes people have about how language should be used, which correspond to class or other identity struggles. The language of some shop signs functions in not-so-obvious ways to make distinctive places for the benefit and use of one (more or less) homogeneous group, while in turn serving to gate, to close off, or perhaps even to offend other groups. These processes, we argue, are not so explicitly apparent and perhaps not intentional, yet they conspire with cultural notions of choice and other neoliberal logics to make gentrification seem organic, "normal," and inevitable. At the heart of the matter we not only find the notion of contest—or contested space—but also demonstrate that some signage operates to create and reinforce conflict.

Methodology

Having never even been to Brooklyn before we bought an apartment there, we had no choice but to begin studying it. The changes it was undergoing were astounding. And we quickly learned that we were a part of those changes from the moment we arrived in August of 2003. This complex place of more than two million people, constantly referred to at the time as one of the four outer boroughs, provided challenges in navigating its terrain, reading its codes, and negotiating daily life with its socially and economically diverse population. In that late summer of 2003, one of the favorite pastimes of Park Slope residents was walking along the neighborhood's Seventh Avenue to stop at the various real estate offices' display windows—Corcoran, Aguayo and Huebner, Garfield, and the list goes on—to get a jolt of sticker shock from the steeply increasing prices of homes, condominiums, and co-op apartments. In 2019, as we mentioned earlier, that Brooklyn housing is expensive is a well-known, taken-for-granted fact. But in 2003, the fact that 810-square-foot apartments sold in working-class neighborhoods for more than $200,000, or that Park Slope apartments on 11th Avenue and Prospect Park West sold for more than $500,000, created a truly unbelievable and incomprehensible phenomenon for newcomers and old-timers alike. Gentrification and the skyrocketing real estate prices were all anybody could talk about in Brooklyn.

Our fascination with and documentation of the textual density of Brooklyn's storefront signs also began immediately, as it seemed that we had never seen anything quite like it: words, text styles, languages, symbols, and images were virtually everywhere on the Brooklyn shopping block. We began photographing streetscapes, including storefronts, and other aspects of daily life while living in Brooklyn and working in Manhattan. Eventually, in 2010, we had devised a more formal research project to examine the kinds of "say" people have in defining, creating, and rebuilding the city they live in and call home. This research examines the ensuing conflicts of how redevelopment and gentrification transform urban space (Snajdr and Trinch 2018a). Initially, we combined the approaches of cultural anthropology and sociolinguistics to set our investigative sights on how Brooklyn's Atlantic Yards project, with which we opened this chapter in the ARENA/A.R.E.A. Bagels saga, evolved in the face of community resistance. Opponents of Atlantic Yards argued that the basketball arena and residential and business towers would bring "instant gentrification" to the nearby neighborhoods of Fort Greene and Prospect Heights, despite a promise from the developer, Forest City Ratner Companies (FCRC), to include affordable housing in its redevelopment plan. The project would also displace hundreds of residents and dozens of both old and new small businesses. Our Atlantic Yards research on massive redevelopment and the ways local residents fought against or embraced it provided the rich, multifaceted context from which we could analyze the significance of Brooklyn shop signs.

The field research we conducted for this broader project included interviews with residents, developers, activists, and other stakeholders, digital ethnography of websites and blogs, archival research, and various types of mapping of Fort Greene and Prospect Heights, the two neighborhoods closest to the development site. We also conducted a random probability survey of residents living there in order to learn of their feelings about the development, their changing neighborhoods, and the types of commerce they needed more or less of in their commercial districts. We interviewed small business owners, homeowners and renters, developers, and community organizers, as well as professionals, college students, and government officials.[16] Additionally, we gathered and analyzed US Census data from 1960 to 2017 for both of these neighborhoods, as well as for Brooklyn more broadly.

We grew increasingly interested in how shop signs in particular help to define changing neighborhoods and this became a central part of our research. Over the past fifteen years, we photographed Brooklyn storefront signs, analyzing more than two thousand of them from fourteen Brooklyn neighborhoods, including Carrol Gardens, Crown Heights, Sunset Park, and Bed-Stuy, to name only a few (see Figure I.3). Two of these neighborhoods, Fort Greene and Prospect Heights, border the Atlantic Yards site. Some of our photos also come from Flatbush and Bay Ridge, two neighborhoods where we have lived.

We then systematically examined the signs according to their linguistic and semiotic features. Guided by this notion that city building is a discursive process in which some people have say in defining urban space, our linguistic and anthropological study of the signs followed the methodology of linguists/semioticians Crispin Thurlow and Giorgia Aiello (2007). Ultimately, to arrive at an understanding of what the signs say, our analysis combined a description of what was on the signs, an interpretation of some of the available or potential meanings of the words, and a critical analysis, by which we positioned our descriptions and interpretations within the local ethnographic context of gentrification and large-scale development. While we attend to all the semiotic features of the signs, our focus is on their incorporation of language itself, and our examination is guided by theories of language ideologies, indexicality, and speech as action that we introduced earlier in our theoretical section. Moreover, our interpretations are informed by the many critical issues debated and discussed by informants in our larger ethnography and our long-term field work on urban change. Data from our Atlantic Yards research offered more holistic insights into how residents and business owners engage the urban landscape. While signage was not a prominent issue in our interviews with people involved in the Atlantic Yards conflict, many of our interviewees provided insights into how residents and business owners read the urban landscape and the reasons they engage in these readings. In these in-depth interviews about their history with their Brooklyn neighborhoods and their current relationship to the evolving situation, the Atlantic Yards interviewees discuss small business districts and the texts that mark them as agents of stasis and change that aid in our understanding of how the language on the land is a form of say that has the power to define and redefine urban space as a particular kind of place.

In some ways our methodology and ethnographic experience in our field site are strikingly different from those of many ethnographers who travel long distances to collect data from people whose cultures differ dramatically from their own (see Shostak 1981; Fernea 1965; Snajdr 2008 as examples) or from those ethnographers who tread into institutional settings to study legal (Trinch 2003; Mertz 2007), medical (Martin 1990), or educational milieus and action-oriented social processes (Bucholtz, Barnwell, and Ska-poulli 2012). For us, living in our field site for fifteen years has created a situation in which we are always working, collecting data, talking to people, confirming our ideas of what is happening, and having our ideas challenged by new data from the ever-evolving human happenings and sense-making that is constantly taking place around us. But in other ways our data collection is exactly the same as any other ethnographer's. We selected a cultural phenomenon to study, began collecting tokens of it, identified the relevant stakeholders in that phenomenon to talk to, and began interviewing them. Some of those people emerged as key informants with whom we would meet regularly in interviews or at events. They showed us different things in different ways, such as on walks and at demonstrations or public meetings. Some of the people we wanted to talk to did not want to talk to us, so we needed to read about them or listen to what others had to say about them. And the majority of our interviewees met us once or twice for an in-depth discussion of their history and relationship to Brooklyn. People invited us into their homes, met us at restaurants or coffee shops, and showed us their archives and the artifacts they had collected that made their experience in Brooklyn meaningful. We took field notes and photographs constantly.

But as is the case for any ethnographer, much of our data comes from participating and observing Brooklyn as resident researchers here. This means that every potential encounter, whether in a Brooklyn boutique, grocery store, or movie theater, provides us with information and data about which we make notes, discuss, and analyze as informing and fine-tuning our analysis. We have had many informal, everyday conversations with Brooklynites, many of whom are either gentrifiers or business owners, but some of whom have also been long-time residents of the borough. These have included friends, neighbors, and people with whom we have become acquainted through our children's schools, activities, and sporting events. These interactions also inform our analysis. In these interactions, we were participant-observers in diverse settings such as ball games, schoolyards, or professional functions, and often new and old restaurants and other businesses as well as the general commercial landscape were discussed. People did not talk much about signs per se, but they often recounted and evaluated their experiences in both older and newer businesses.

To see if Brooklynites, both old and new, corroborated our linguistic and anthropological analysis of signs, we conducted a structured email survey among a sample of individuals from our own social networks and from our field research on Atlantic Yards. This was a convenience sample of twenty-five people whom we had come to know very well. We selected them so as to have a variety of people from different socioeconomic backgrounds who had either lived in, worked in, or frequently visited Brooklyn (see Appendix). This survey, which we describe in more detail in the next chapter, asked people to comment on a set of signs from our data and to tell us what they thought the signs meant and why they had their particular forms.

Our ethnographic focus on signage then developed further to include formal and informal, structured and semistructured interviews with various informants about signage in particular. These included open-ended and formal interviews with sign makers, shopkeepers, consumers, and Business Improvement District members, and participant observation on streets, in stores, at community meetings, and in online forums such as a Facebook parents' group where people regularly talked to each other about local businesses.

And, as is the case with most professors, we also discuss our research and work with our students in the courses we teach and with our student research assistants. But unlike many professors whose students travel from their homes to reside at college, we teach at a large, urban public university where the majority of our students commute daily to class from the homes they grew up in. Most of our students are native New Yorkers, many of whom come from the nation's most underrepresented groups in higher education but who are very representative of the Brooklyn neighborhoods we study.[17] Our own insights into gentrifications' complexity are further informed by the communities we both teach and serve, but also to whom we listen and from whom we learn.

We have also tried to contextualize these data in the local history and experiences of Brooklyn's large- and small-scale processes of urban change, including the Atlantic Yards conflict. Where necessary, we incorporate an analysis of data from archival material, media coverage, and government records. We bring all these materials and methods together to discuss the different ways that Brooklyn is defined.

Our Own Positionality, Intersectionality, and Gentrification

We also draw on our knowledge and experience as long-term participant-observers, who now are native anthropologists in gentrifying Brooklyn. As such scholars in residence we balance our objectivity as trained ethnographers and language analysts with our subjectivity as Brooklyn residents and community members. Thus, in many ways, our approach will seem to straddle traditional ethnography and the more innovative approach of autoethnography, because we examine how social forces come to bear on our friends, neighbors, children, and ourselves as well as all of Brooklyn.[18]

As Brooklyn newcomers as of 2003, we fit the common intersectional profile of a gentrifier. We are both white people with college educations and professional jobs and salaries. We were born American citizens, and we speak English natively. And though we both speak languages other than English, we learned them as adults through formal educational experiences both in the classroom and in extended stays abroad in countries where our second languages are spoken. In terms of ethnicity, Edward is of Anglo-Saxon and Czechoslovak descent, and Shonna is of Italian American and Syrian American descent. While we are proud of our heritage and celebrate it with family in the places we came from, neither of us participates in nor orients toward any of those very well-defined ethnic communities in Brooklyn (Syrian, Italian, Eastern European). In terms of our religious backgrounds, Shonna is Catholic and Edward is Protestant, and while we raise our children Catholic and religion is present in our lives, it is often secondary to other things our family might be undertaking at any given time. Ours is not the only gentrifying profile, but it is one of the typical ones.

This process of gentrification is quite complicated. There are, for example, many newcomers to Brooklyn these days from China, Syria, Russia, and Yemen, and these people are not usually considered to be gentrifiers by people we have spoken with whether they consider themselves to be native New Yorkers or whether they self-identify as gentrifiers (who have arrived from other parts of the city or from other places beyond it). This non-gentrifier status for immigrants who live in ethnic enclaves was conveyed by these informants regardless of the fact that recent ethnic immigrants had come with enough money—sometimes in cash—to buy expensive houses. One of the main markers of a gentrifier then is education level *and* the possession of a certain type of cultural capital (Bourdieu 1984). Our data and prior studies on gentrification show how the process is often considered to be driven and facilitated by white people from various ethnic and religious groups (Italian, Irish, Eastern European, Syrian, Lebanese, Catholic, Jewish) who are long-standing residents that grew up in Brooklyn (or in a nearby borough or on Long Island), but went away to college and returned to take professional jobs their own parents (and sometimes their own brothers and sisters) did not/do not have access to. In other words, some gentrifiers come from working-class or lower-middle-class families and their siblings have still not experienced the same socioeconomic mobility. And as we will see, some gentrifiers are also African American, or West Indian, or Arab, or Southeast Asian, whose parents or grandparents may have lived in New York, but they themselves were raised in a wealthier suburb, attended college, and later moved back to the borough to live. A key feature of these individuals is that they orient themselves toward the new and the upscale, whether they still orient toward the traditional enclaves from which they came or lived.

Gentrification is largely about more-affluent users moving into an area to use the land who help to create a new culture and economy on that land. In this sense, even long-standing residents become gentrifiers to the new Brooklyn economy when their college degrees propel them into a new socioeconomic class. While their parents may have owned a small townhouse or a large apartment at a reasonable price, these types of local gentrifiers with lifelong connections to Brooklyn move back after college to purchase a home for ten to twenty-five times the price of their parents' homes.

The gentrification process began in the 1950s, long before we arrived in Brooklyn, and it has been intermittent, sporadic, and relentless ever since. Yet we have no way of knowing when it might be considered complete. Hackworth and Smith (2001) suggest that there have been three waves of gentrification, and their research ties each period (1950–1973, 1973–1989, 1989–1999) to global and national economic trends such as investment, recession, and the degree to which the state participates in the process. By the 1990s, gentrification in urban centers had intensified and expanded past the core places where there was initial investment into other formerly ungentrified areas (Ley 1996). In this study, our informants are representative of these three waves. The first wave of gentrifiers often called themselves or were called pioneers by others, and those who followed them into their neighborhoods intensified the process. By the time we arrived in Brooklyn, Loretta Lees (2003) was writing about how certain neighborhoods in Brooklyn, such as Brooklyn Heights, were undergoing the phenomenon of super-gentrification, where global financiers paid between $500,000 and $1.5 million in cash for the same brownstone in the 2000s that cost its original first wave gentrifiers $28,000 in 1965.

Not having that kind of cash on hand, we ourselves were not super-gentrifiers, and thus our finances did not permit residence in Brooklyn Heights or Park Slope. Our 2003 move to Brooklyn required us to take up residence outside the core areas of gentrification, though we were not the first gentrifiers in the Flatbush neighborhood where we bought our first apartment.

Our presence did, however, probably contribute to the intensification of gentrification in that area. We bought our Flatbush apartment from a single white man from Virginia who had purchased it a few years before for well under $100,000 and then fixed it up before he sold it to us for $210,000. And while our move to Bay Ridge, a fairly affluent, though very mixed-income, mostly white, ethnic, multireligious neighborhood, was not considered by many to be a gentrifying move, the purchase price of the small row house we were able to buy in 2005 had increased in value at least twenty-three times its 1965 price. We bought the home from a white couple, more or less our own age, who had grown up in Bay Ridge. They required more space because an elderly parent needed to move in with them. They had lived in the house for several years, sold it to us at a considerable profit, and moved a few blocks away into a bigger house in a substantially more expensive part of the neighborhood. We do not know whether we were more affluent users of these properties than their former owners, but we do know that the properties are, at the time of this writing, increasing in value at still inconceivable rates. The Flatbush apartment that we bought in 2003 but no longer own is, as of 2019, worth between $500,000 and $600,000.

In general terms, gentrifiers tend to share an intersectional identity that is white, middle-to upper-middle class, college-educated, US-born, and employed in either the professional or the creative sectors of the economy. As we mentioned before, though we have met gentrifiers who are African American, Latinx, Arab, Jewish, Muslim, or atheist, the combination of high levels of education and income, as well as an orientation toward dominant culture and away from ethnic lifestyles, tends to be a primary feature of these otherwise diverse identities. Urban sociologists John Joe Schlichtman, Jason Patch, and Marc Lamont Hill (2017) have recently explored the range of complexities of gentrifier identities in various cities, including their own experiences in the places where they have lived and worked. Similarly to what we have described above regarding our context of experience in Brooklyn, they creatively consider the highly contextualized issues of intersectionality, identity, transitions, displacements, and possible solutions to gentrification's negative outcomes. Our aim in presenting this analysis is to draw from our multiple positions as Brooklyn residents for fifteen years, as gentrifying outsiders, and as trained ethnographers to examine, in a systematic way, how language creates place and contributes to its transformation.

In light of our complex approach, we have noticed that when we have casually asked people in our field site to tell us what they think a certain sign means, they have sometimes appeared distressed, as if we were looking for a "right" answer. For this reason, and because defining the available meanings for signs would not be what anthropologists call an *emic*, or culture-specific, practice, we refrain from simply relying on asking people to analyze the signs for us. This study is not about why store owners named their business a certain way or why they choose to put a lot of words or a few words on their signs, although this kind of information can often be gleaned from the data we collected. Our analysis instead attempts to capture how the signs, once placed, are perceived by passersby and how the semiotic and sociolinguistic features they contain as a set of collective texts help to create a certain type of landscape.

Structure of the Study

Chapter One begins our study with a careful description of examples of two strikingly different types of noncorporate, local storefronts in Brooklyn's retail landscape which, for reasons we will explain later, we call Old School and New School. We first identify the unique and consistent features of each type of sign, because as our opening epigraph from Poe suggests, these features may not be readily noticeable or meaningful at first glance. But we contend that they are very significant in that they reflect implicit practices of place-making that violate New York City's official rules of signage. We then consider what everyday people think of these sign types and show how what they say supports our sociolinguistic interpretation, namely that Old School signage marks and makes an inclusive place. New School signs, in comparison, not only signal the arrival of gentrifiers, but also signify very differently, even exclusively, in the remaking of Brooklyn.

In Chapter Two, we consider how Brooklyn has been historically represented through various written texts, and how it has become a place in which important texts are now produced. In this context of change, we make the case that both Old School and New School signage are linguistic registers of place-making that operate publicly and that function in either the maintenance or the transformation of place. We then take a closer look at how wordplay, a prominent feature of New School signage, operates in processes of gentrification to create intimacy and exclusivity and ultimately, to produce and reinforce cultural and social hierarchy in the landscape.

Chapters Three, Four, and Five present case studies that build on and expand our linguistic analyses in Chapters One and Two. While gentrification is often credited to or blamed on younger people, we show in Chapter Three how Brooklyn, in its transitional state, is a place where women, and especially college-educated, married women who are mothers, play a significant role in redefining the borough and at the same time contribute to redefining cultural norms of motherhood more broadly. And while newly arriving women emerge as key players in the gentrification project, the signs suggest they do so at a price. Thus, we explore how we might read women in a landscape of back-lash as needing to take cover. Some signs suggest women's work goes under the cover of racialized or other class identities because their own identity as women is denigrated and marginalized. In Chapter Four, we look at what we call competing semiotics, which often involves the misreading of both types of signs and other semiotic characteristics of a dynamic Brooklyn. On the one hand we consider how complicated the ethnographic experience of signage can be and present evidence and examples of how people have interpreted Brooklyn's linguistic landscape. On the other hand, we show how persistent and pervasive the process of gentrification has become in the borough and how signage indicates and produces this conversion in some of the most visually complex textual landscapes in the city. Despite the confusing legibility the two sign types create in the urban landscape as they compete for space, both are counter-posed to corporate signage, and we discuss how ultimately the businesses that each type represents are threatened by large-scale redevelopment in Brooklyn.

Chapter Five takes an in-depth look at the issues of intention, impact, privilege, and power in people's struggle to claim space and have a right to define it. We begin by looking more closely at the case of the "bullet holes" on the wall of Summerhill, the gentrifying restaurant in Crown Heights with which we opened the book. We follow the fate of the restaurant owner's engagement with protestors and her attempt to apologize for her actions. Not only are the steps she takes interpreted by people as inadequate moves, but they are perhaps also more damaging than the original incident. We also explore other cases of semiotic conflict between gentrifiers and longer-term residents in place-making that include both cultural appropriations and refus-als to grant space for public tributes to Christopher Wallace (a.k.a. Biggie Smalls), an important member of the community. We suggest how these conflicts contrast with the spirit of Old School signage. At the heart of these disputes lies the issue of privilege and how it impacts the nuances of intent, interpretation, and the integrity of place. However, overshadowing and over-powering these conflicts is the work of corporate developers that remakes place often perhaps without much regard for what gentrifiers or old timers have to say about it.

We close the book by discussing how our findings link to other important issues in American public life that are crucial to understanding how language and semiotic devices work to include or attract as well as to exclude or even discourage certain groups of people. We conclude that, even though they may appear innocuous, peripheral, or irrelevant, the signs say that public language matters.

Since brevity is the soul of wit,
And tedious the limbs and outward flourishes,
I will be brief

Shakespeare, *Hamlet,* Act 2, Scene 2

We're thorough in the borough 'cause that's a must!

Beastie Boys, "An Open Letter to NYC," 2005

1. Reading a "Distinctive" Brooklyn

Noticing Two Brooklyn Sign Types

SHORTLY AFTER MOVING to Brooklyn in 2003, we shared some initial field notes about our observations of the borough with John Jay College undergraduates in an Anthropology 101 class, most of whom were New York City natives. When one of us jokingly complained that Brooklyn was "the kind of place where people cram as many words as possible on a storefront sign," the room filled with the laughter of recognition. The students' chuckles indicated to us that they knew exactly what we were talking about. They told us that shop signs with a lot of words represented a "back-in-the-day-ness" or an "old school" Brooklyn. They explained that *old school* meant "origin" or "of another era," but one deserving "respect." We quickly realized that, with no sign in front of them to read, the students' laughter revealed that they interpreted such signage emically as a textual norm. In other words, it was a feature of an everyday commercial landscape that they recognized and could picture in their minds. Their efforts to explain such signs with a reference to the past also revealed that this norm was in dialogue with a rapidly changing city, one that included the appearance of both the corporate signage of big chains and new shops throughout Brooklyn whose signs were quite different from these old

Figure 1.1. Typical Brooklyn retail block. There are often up to ten storefronts per block on each side of the street.

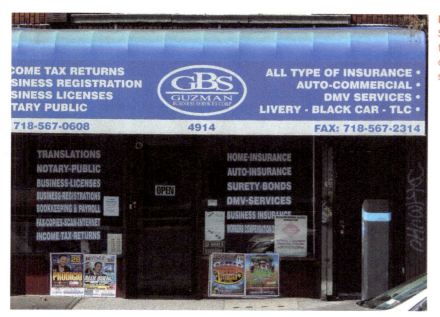

Figure 1.2. The Guzman Business Services storefront has more than forty words, nonstandard forms of English, repetition, and extra signage.

school texts. Linguistic landscape scholars Aneta Pavlenko and Alex Mullen (2015, 114–15) have argued that interpretation of signage is "intrinsically linked to the preceding signs in the same environment and to related signs elsewhere and is thus diachronic in nature." So the student's laughter, and their emphasis on time, also suggested that there was a story that was perhaps worth exploring here about what we had originally perceived to be these wordy, old school signs that represented a back-in-the-day Brooklyn.

In order to get to this story of what the signs "say," we would like to take the reader on a walk down several Brooklyn streets to take a careful look at these text-rich storefronts and consider what features they share. Following this tour of wordy signage, we will take a closer look at newer shop signs which have far fewer or almost no words at all. After noting the shared features of these new signs, we will consider the sociolinguistic significance of the features of each of these two types of signage and also hear from Brooklynites about how they read these different signs.

The text-rich signs, which first caught our eye, are found across Brooklyn. They mark a broad variety of businesses, many of which have been in the area for several decades. For example, Figure 1.1 shows a typical street scene in the Brooklyn neighborhood of Sunset Park. You can see that such text-dense store signs are on all sorts of retail establishments. In some cases, words cover not only the sign but the entire storefront. Reading the street from left to right, we find twenty-nine words on the sign for Kang Yue Inc. Baby Food and Formula Grocery Store. Next to it, on NB Deli Grocery's sign are twenty-two words. And on the sign for GBS Guzman Business Services there are also twenty-two words. We know right away what sort of businesses these shops are because all three signs incorporate this information in their names and provide an explicit list of the goods or services they offer. In Figure 1.2, Guzman Business Services, for example, lists all kinds of business services on its main sign. These range from completing income taxes and registration to providing Department of Motor Vehicles services for various types of cabs (livery, black, and TLC—Taxi and Limousine Commission or yellow taxis). On the display windows below the store's main sign, there are twenty-six more words that both repeat information already listed on the main sign (e.g., "business registrations," "notary public," "auto-insurance") and add new information not previously listed (e.g., "translations, book-keeping and payroll" and "Internet").

Moving over to another neighborhood, this time in Clinton Hill, we see in Figure 1.3 Washington Deli Grocery on the corner of Fulton Street and Washington Avenue. In addition to containing twenty-one words, this store's

sign includes two acronyms (EBT for Electronic Benefits Transfer, which is a state-sponsored social welfare card payment plan, and ATM for automated teller machine). Again, even though the name of the store explicitly identifies its commercial function, the sign nevertheless lists twelve items one would expect to find in a deli/grocery, including the type of phone cards the business carries. Additional smaller signs and advertisements on the storefront below the sign adds to the shop's textual density.

But *textual density* does not mean just lots of words. The term also refers to the size of a sign's letters in its wording. Text-dense signs thus also include those whose words appear in large font-sizes that often take up almost the entire field of the sign, as seen in Figure 1.4. Large font sizes are not reserved for only discount stores. Figures 1.5 and 1.6 show two expensive Brooklyn

Figure 1.3. Washington Deli and Grocery. This storefront includes additional signage, lists of products and services including electronic benefits transfer (EBT), and a sign advertising an ATM machine that dispenses small bills.

Figure 1.4. The Apple Discount sign uses large lettering, nonstandard English writing. An ancillary sign above it repeats information.

Figure 1.5. This Italian restaurant, La Sorrentina, has signage along several storefronts with large lettering, repetition, and pictures of the food that it serves.

restaurants which follow this style, utilizing large lettering not only for their names but also, as we saw in earlier examples, to advertise the food they serve. And they repeat this information with large-font text or pictures or both.

In addition to describing what is on offer and repeating information through words and pictures or photographs on their signs, many text-rich Brooklyn storefronts also accomplish description and reiteration by showcasing the range of their products in abundant window displays (see for example Figures 1.3 and 1.5 above). Some businesses use the sidewalks as well to advertise what they sell by bringing the items out every day and putting them on racks or tables to be viewed by people as they pass by (Figure 1.4). These displays reiterate, with actual examples, the products that are written on their signs.

Another salient feature of many Brooklyn storefronts that we noticed is the presence of nonstandard or nonprescriptive forms of written English. For example, in the GBS Business Services storefront (Figure 1.2), the word TYPE ("ALL TYPE OF INSURANCE") is missing the necessary /-s/, the morphosyntactic plural marker with which the word would occur in Standard English. Notice also that the services listed are nonparallel, meaning that plural and singular forms are mixed: "INCOME TAX RETURNS / BUSINESS REGISTRATION / BUSINESS LICENSES / NOTARY PUBLIC." Language prescriptivists like Strunk and White (2014), who provide examples of standard American English, would require, where appropriate, all plural or all singular nouns. In the Washington Deli Grocery sign in Figure 1.3, the word cold cut is missing an *s*, with which the word always occurs in Standard English. In Figure 1.4, while most 99-cent stores advertise that items cost "99 cents and up," Apple Discount elides the "and" and reads as if something is missing: "99¢ UP INC." Other examples of nonstandard spelling and syntax will occur in text-dense sign examples throughout this book.

Figures 1.7 and 1.8 depict signage in Brooklyn that incorporates languages other than English. Juanita's Bridal Shop not only explains that it provides "Souvenir for All Occasions," but it lists them in Spanish as well. Sometimes, as is the case with the bridal shop sign, the translation to English is slightly off. The word *souvenir* is likely to be a translation of the Spanish word *recuerdos*, a

Figure 1.6. Chadwick's is an upscale restaurant in Bay Ridge with large lettering and a list that indicates the types of food that it serves.

WHAT THE SIGNS SAY

Figure 1.7. Juanita's Bridal Shop's storefront has both English and Spanish text, lists its products and services, and includes ancillary signage.

Figure 1.8. The signage for Alex International Food includes Roman and Cyrillic alphabets and large lettering.

term used to refer both to small trinkets one purchases on a trip (i.e., *souvenirs* in English) and small tokens of appreciation given by hosts to their guests as thanks for attending their event (*mementos* or *favors* in English). It seems Juanita's Bridal Shop means *mementos* and not *souvenirs* in this case. Similarly, the translations of the Spanish words "Encajes, Cintas, Organzas" (meaning laces, ribbons, and organzas) do not map onto the English glosses that follow on the sign, which are "Ribbons, Laces, Plastic Items," and they are listed out of order. In Figure 1.8, on the Russian deli called Alex International Food we find non-Roman script accompanying English words that refer to what is sold there.

Figure 1.9. Note on this storefront the painted images of a cow and a ram as well as a nonstandard phone number, explicit religious references, and information in English (Roman script) and Arabic (Arabic script), as well as a sign for an ATM.

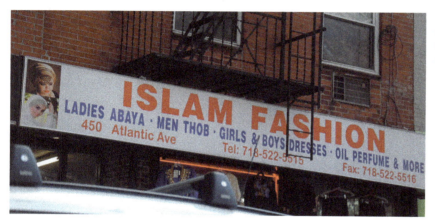

Figure 1.10. This sign includes an explicit reference to religion and images of women wearing head-scarves.

In addition to large fonts, nonstandard English, and languages other than English, some text-dense signs make direct references to religion. In Figure 1.9, Fertile Crescent, a grocery in Boerum Hill, makes several explicit references to Islam in English and in Arabic, and also pictorially, including words such as *kutub a'rabia* (Arabic books); *milabes Islamia* (Islamic clothes); *al-hilal al-khaseeb* (fertile crescent); *lhoom halal* (halal meats); and *baqalat shar-qia* (eastern groceries).[1] A crescent moon, an emblem of Islam, inhabits the background of the main sign, and ancillary signs running up the sides of the second floor windows contain Islamic arches with English words advertising "Islamic clothes," "Prayer rugs," and "Islamic posters." Likewise, the sign for Islam Fashion on Flatbush Avenue (Figure 1.10), includes a large picture of two women wearing head-coverings in addition to explicit text. A sign for Little Lords, Little Ladies in Bay Ridge explicitly advertises children's wear for

Figure 1.11. Michael's Holy Land Gifts reiterates that it sells Christian religious items.

Figure 1.12. Meir's Hemishe Bakery has large lettering with both English and Yiddish (in Roman and Hebrew script) as well as a list of beverages one can purchase inside.

the Christian rituals of communions, weddings, and christenings.[2] Similarly direct religious references can be spotted in Figures 1.11 and 1.12 on signs incorporating Christian and Jewish words and iconography.

Brooklyn has been known as the borough of churches because its cityscape includes multiple church steeples. But its storefronts have also been converted into houses of worship, or "storefront churches." The Reverend Herbert Daughtry, the pastor of House of the Lord Church on Atlantic Avenue near downtown Brooklyn, told us of how his family moved north as part of the migration of African Americans from the South in the 1930s. He said they rented a storefront to start their church because buying or building a church was prohibitively expensive. The same might be true today: many religious groups rent commercial storefront space to create new places of worship or religious fellowship. The signage of these religious places (Figures 1.13, 1.14,

Figure 1.13. (above) This sign for a storefront church includes symbols, large lettering, and the names and titles of clergy.

Figure 1.14. (left) This sign for a Brooklyn mosque on Church Avenue in Flatbush includes English and Arabic text.

Figure 1.15. This sign for a Jewish Center includes large lettering, ancillary signage, and another explicit reference to religion.

and 1.15) has features similar to the signs of the stores that surround them, including multiple words and graphics and languages other than English.

Some storefronts blend religions or ethnicity, what we call *syncretism*, in their signage. One example is the sign for a Boerum Hill Chinese restaurant called No Pork Halal Kitchen (Figure 1.16). The owners of this restaurant are of Uyghur descent, an ethnic group from Western China and other parts of Central Asia that has been Muslim for more than a thousand years. So while it is true that the owners themselves are Muslim Chinese, in the Brooklyn context the restaurant calls to all Muslims and anyone else who wants Chinese take-out on their way home from work. In a similar vein, a sign for Garden Tortills & Chinese Express in Dyker Heights explicitly (and with a non-standard spelling of *tortillas*) calls to customers interested in the food of two different ethnic groups with the words "Tex-Mexican & Chinese Food." And in Figure 1.17 we find syncretism in the Famous Gourmet sign in Sunset Park that announces a variety of ethnic foods—tacos, rotisserie, and Chinese—suggesting that it serves the tastes of various ethnic groups or of any customer interested in this ethnic fare.

Ethnic and religious syncretism can also be found at a variety of Brooklyn restaurants that identify themselves on their signs as "kosher." On Avenue U, for example, there is a kosher German restaurant called Holy Schnitzel. This sign has a tag on it that playfully reads, "Keepin' it kosher." The sign for a pizza shop in Borough Park contains an image of a pizza overlaid with the words "Authentic Kosher Italian Food." A *New York Times* feature story on the nearby Brooklyn neighborhood of Midwood, which has a large conservative Jewish community along with sizeable South Asian, Latino, and West Indian

Figure 1.16. An example of syncretism or cultural blending: no pork, halal Chinese food.

Figure 1.17. Famous Gourmet. Another example of syncretism: Chinese and Mexican food.

populations as well as residents of Irish and Italian descent, reported that also on offer in the area are "Kosher Chinese" and "Kosher sushi" options (Fiorvante 1996).

Finally, text-dense storefronts often include additional or *ancillary* signage. For example, many Brooklyn storefronts have smaller signs reading, "ATM ONLY 99¢" as shown in the window in Figure 1.17 of Famous Gourmet. The Washington Deli and Grocery sign (in Figure 1.3) has ancillary signs that notify passersby that its ATM dispenses small denominations ("$10. BILLS"). Additionally, in Figure 1.3 one can see signs announcing "EBT," alerting the public that this store serves people on this social welfare program. One might assume that only delis advertise that they will do business with people whose finances are restricted, but that is not the case. Many restaurants, grocery stores, and wine and alcohol vendors include the words "free delivery" on

Figure 1.18. This law office clearly provides clients with limited means an opportunity to use its services.

their storefronts. We also find signs on law offices that suggest attorneys will work with people with limited means. In Figure 1.18, the first words on the sign for these law offices are "FREE CONSULTATIONS," indicating that people can consult an attorney about "REAL ESTATE / ACCIDENTS / DIVORCE / CRIMINAL" without being charged a fee.[3] The storefront for Peña's Food Market, a small grocer on Vanderbilt Avenue, included the sorts of ancillary signage described above. Inside, however, we also found dozens of white slips of paper taped to Peña's cash register with "IOU" and monetary amounts written on them. The Dominican American owner told us that some customers need things they cannot afford and his IOU slips show shoppers his willingness to do business with people who have no money at the moment.

Borrowing from our students' use of the phrase *old school*, we call the type of signage described above *Old School Vernacular*. As a linguistic term, *vernacular* refers to the native, spoken dialect of a codified or uncodified language that is associated with a particular place or a particular people. Often understood as counterpoints to learned or literary language, vernaculars are conceptualized as informal and colloquial and have been known historically as the commoners' parlance. Though textual density is the most salient feature of Old School Vernacular, these signs also systematically share some of the following key features:

1. store names that refer to location, surnames, type of business, and/or products or services;
2. reiterations and repetitions through words and/or complementary symbols and pictures;
3. nonstandard, written English forms;
4. languages other than English in Roman transliteration and/or non-Roman scripts;
5. explicit references to religion, ethnicity, national origin, race, and class; and
6. ancillary signs.

In contrast to these Old School signs, we also noticed that the storefronts of many new neighborhood businesses throughout Brooklyn tended to be textually very sparse. In fact, they often did not advertise their wares or explicitly indicate the services they provide on their signage. Sometimes, not only did these newer shops have minimal text, they were also cryptic. For example, in Prospect Heights the awning of a new restaurant contains the single word "james" (Figure 1.19). Similarly, a sign on another building in the same neighborhood reads "Wink," which turns out to be a hair salon. Another sign nearby reads "Beast" and adorns a bar. In the adjacent neighborhood of Park Slope, there is a new storefront with the word "Seed" overhead advertising a restaurant, and then there is a small, rectangular signboard protruding from another storefront that reads "bird" (Figure 1.20). It is difficult to tell from the sign itself that this business sells upscale casual women's clothing.

New small businesses like the ones mentioned above are appearing with more frequency every year. While many of these new retail shops are "trendy cafés," "small boutiques," or "fancy" or "funky ethnic" restaurants, as they have been described in the gentrification and sociolinguistics literature (Zukin and Kosta 2004; Zukin 2010; Papen 2012), their laconic signs—like their Old School counterparts—mark a *full range* of stores from garden shops and jewelers to clothing stores, salons, and grocers. We term this new style of sign *New School Distinction-Making Signage,* or simply New School. As we look more systematically at their characteristics, we notice that these signs tend to share many of the following textual and linguistic features:

1. one word or a short phrase written in a reduced font-size;
2. the use of all lowercase letters;
3. languages other than English that index sophistication and worldliness;
4. erudite historical and literary references; and
5. polysemic or cryptic names.

Figure 1.19. (right) james: one word in small font and all lowercase.

Figure 1.20. (above) bird, a women's clothing store that also uses one word for its name and its storefront signage.

Closer readings of these New School signs indicate that their one- or two-word descriptors often incorporate polysemy, or many meanings, and wordplay. That is, new signs are often witty and even impudent and irreverent. For example, while perhaps not well known to most Americans, the word *bird* is British slang used somewhat derogatorily to refer to a woman. In Bay Ridge, the wordplay on a sign for a children's boutique, "hipsqueak," is phonetic, lexical, and intertextual. *Hipsqueak* indexes smallness and coolness and remakes a negative term for a child (pipsqueak) into an endearment suggesting fashion-forwardness. Likewise, on a shop selling locally made ice cream in Prospect Heights one finds "Ample Hills Creamery." The phrase *ample hills* comes from the 1865 Walt Whitman poem "Crossing Brooklyn Ferry." The shop's owner explained that Whitman's poem made reference to the connections different types of people make with each other (Wharton 2012). But as Whitman also probably intended, the words *ample hills* also allude to women's breasts, making a playful connection back to ice cream's key ingredient, milk.

Throughout our field research, we would often hear Brooklyn newcomers speak with enthusiasm about new establishments and engage a bit on what they think a new store's name meant. Upon hearing of a new restaurant in Bay Ridge called Brooklyn Beet while at a child's birthday party, one of our informants, a newcomer who grew up in a lower-middle-class Manhattan housing project and who recently purchased a multimillion-dollar brownstone in Park

Figure 1.21. This restaurant's sign is in French; *le gamin* means the kid, and in its adjective form means mischievous.

Figure 1.22. This famous Brooklyn restaurant is named *al di lá*, an Italian prepositional phrase meaning literally "beyond," but used to indicate "above and beyond."

Slope, asked, "Is that b-e-a-t? Or b-e-e-t?" At another Brooklyn newcomer's birthday dinner, celebrated at a new restaurant called Walter's in Fort Greene, diners noticed with delight a wall of black and white photographs of famous celebrities named Walter (among them, Hollywood actor Walter Mathau, CBS newscaster Walter Cronkite, NBA basketball player Walt Frazier, and famous Brooklyn poet Walt Whitman). From the restaurant's website, we learn that Walter is also the name of the owner's dog.

Sometimes New School signs appear cryptic simply because they are in a language other than English. But upon closer inspection, when translated into English, the sign still retains an ambiguous and playful set of meanings. For example, the text on a sign for an upscale bistro in Prospect Heights, "LE GAMIN" (Figure 1.21), plays with French instead of English. *Le Gamin* is syllabically, orthographically, and phonetically similar to *le garçon*—a commonly known French word among English-speakers meaning "the boy" or "the waiter." But if pushed for a translation, the reader would note that the meaning of *le gamin* is not obvious and thus may also invite a curious person to look it up. While on the street, an inquisitive passerby might google it, and a search for "le gamin" reveals the following: "French: kid, mischievous, playful, or childish." Both the multiplicity of meanings as well as the meanings themselves suggest that someone wants to play.

Similar non-English-language wordplay on a New School sign can be found on one of Brooklyn's most popular restaurants, Al di Lá Trattoria (Figure 1.22). This restaurant opened in 1997 and, in some circles, it is credited as pioneering Brooklyn's foodie movement (Vaughn, Vaughn, and Turkell 2010, 4). When we asked several people who had begun living in the borough around that time what the name Al di Lá meant, they told us that they did not know. One informant joked, "I never thought of the words as meaning anything other than the food . . . at that restaurant where I could *never* get a table!" But for those who know Italian, or who take the time to look up the name, more wordplay becomes evident. *Al di lá* is an Italian expression meaning "beyond" or even "beyond this life," which could be interpreted as "heaven," "out of this world," or simply "something that is more than the usual."[4] But English speakers might associate it phonetically with the phrase *la di da*, used more in spoken than in written speech to mean pretentious, hoity-toity, or affected, all of which also entail a notion of something "beyond the usual." Ultimately, as with Ample Hills or Walter's, the phrase *al di lá* as the name of a restaurant suggests an effort to be clever both intellectually and intertextually.

This awareness of and involvement in wordplay, whether in English or in some language other than English, suggests one of the ways that these New School signs both mark and encourage the process of neighborhood change. Gentrifying newcomers often say they are eager to try new places and to patronize them so that they will stay in business. Furthermore, these newcomers seem unperturbed by the ambiguity of their signs' meanings. These new Brooklyn shop signs, despite their sparseness of text, can be characterized as being, in a way, quite rich in meaning. At the least, they seem to be saying something very different from the text-dense and explicitly worded Old School signage.

When we began comparing these sign types, they appeared to mark or represent in some way two quite different Brooklyns. But we also wondered how official laws, policies, or regulations might influence the features of Brooklyn signage. Although it turns out there are many regulations governing signage in New York City, it seems that such laws have had very little effect on the appearance of most signs. So before comparing what these two different sign types seem to be saying about Brooklyn and its residents, we will discuss how sign making practices in the borough violate the city's rules of signage. Quite notably, sign makers and shopkeepers seem very willing to break the rules laid out by the city in order to make their points.

Rules and Norms: Some Sign Makers' Views

When we talked with sign makers, we first learned that there are lots of different types of signs, at least materially. We also learned that there are different rules for different sign types. The simplest signs are painted sections of a storefront exterior wall, directly above the building's first floor windows. An installed sign is a separate entity, perhaps a wooden board, a metal sheet (flat panel signs), or a piece of molded plastic, for instance, which might have lights above, underneath, or within it.[5] Blade signs—also known as shingle signs— hang from a frame perpendicular to a store's building.[6]

You must have a permit to put up most sorts of signs.[7] Awnings, marquees, and flagpoles also require permits. But sign makers point out to us that, in addition to requiring permits to install or hang a sign, there are lots of other rules governing signage in New York City.[8] Most of the rules governing signage pertain to its size (it must be no larger than three times the street frontage of a building's ground floor), whether it has lights (if so these need to be properly installed and maintained), and what commercial zone your business is in. Other basic rules state that signs cannot project beyond the street line or be attached to a fire escape. In a brochure published by the Department of Buildings, the city admits that "sign regulations are complicated" and advises that one "should consult an architect or engineer and find out what zoning district one's business is in." For example, if a sign is smaller than six square feet, not illuminated, or simply painted directly on a building's exterior wall, it does not require a permit, but according to one of the city's official brochures, it still must "comply with local zoning regulations for signs." These zones are also complicated, but briefly, there are three categories of zones—commercial, residential, and manufacturing—and within commercial zones there are eight district types (five of which in some way include small retail shops, whether as primary businesses or along with other types of commercial operations). There are twenty-four signage codes which differentially apply according to the commercial zoning district one is in. For example, in commercial zone district 1 (C1), which includes retail and personal services establishments for local shopping, only eleven of the twenty-four codes apply (e.g., signage may not be higher than twenty-five feet above curb level). Moreover, the rules and guidelines for making storefront improvements and information about permitting are not all located in the same place. Some are on the Department of Buildings' website; others can be found on the site for Small Business Services (both available online at nyc.gov). We will discuss these guides and their relationship to our two sign types and to gentrification in Brooklyn a bit later. But suffice to say that official resources regarding the rules and the laws covering signage are publicly available.

Among all these rules for retail signage, however, there is an important exception: a sign's text. While local law establishes the regulation of commercial signage, state law governs that "municipalities can regulate signs attached to businesses provided the law does not regulate viewpoint" (New York State Division of Local Government Services 2015).[9] In other words, the language and semiotic devices on a sign, from a legal standpoint, are protected at the level of free speech rights.[10] Two prominent Brooklyn sign makers, both of whom have been in business for over thirty years, reiterated this fact in an interview:

ED: There are no rules about the lettering on a sign?
SIGN MAKER 1: The sign? No.
SIGN MAKER 2: A commercial sign? No.
SIGN MAKER 1: The sign, you can put as much lettering as you want. The sign's *a sign!* (interview with authors, June 29, 2017).

But we also learned from these sign makers (and after consulting the various city government guides and guidelines) that not all Brooklyn signs are signs! If you look closely at many of the examples of Brooklyn signs we provided earlier in this chapter, you will see that one of the most common types of signs is what sign makers call a fixed awning. An awning is a retractable piece of canvas on a roller and folding metal frame that one can pull out or pull in toward the building. But a fixed awning is a nonretractable metal frame, attached to the building, covered with a material (e.g., canvas, vinyl, cloth). One sees these fixed awnings on storefronts all over Brooklyn. Figures 1.2, 1.4, 1.5, 1.7, 1.8, 1.11, 1.12, and 1.16 all show fixed awnings. Figures 1.21 and 1.22 are examples of retractable awnings.

The sign makers also told us that awnings of any kind also need permits to be installed and, surprisingly, there actually is a legal restriction on what text can appear on them. A 1961 New York City regulation prohibits the inclusion of anything more than the name of a business and a street number on awnings, whether retractable or fixed. Images, including corporate logos, and additional text are not allowed on awnings and subject to fines.[11] Local government typically has not proactively enforced the awning code, but occasional crackdowns occur. For example, in 2003, during Mayor Michael Bloomberg's administration, the city slapped businesses with illegal fixed awnings with fines as high as $5000.[12] In an op-ed piece criticizing the crackdown, one city planner noted that then City Council Speaker Gifford Miller estimated "that over 90 percent of [New York City] awnings [were] in violation of the code" (Gerend 2003). Many of our sign photographs included here support this estimate, a fact that the sign makers also pointed out. They would immediately refer to one of our sign images as depicting what they called an "illegal awning." The sign makers also suggested that some sign shops might not be officially licensed to hang or install signs. They might be licensed to have a business, for instance, but a license for sign-hanging requires a substantial amount of training and must be renewed annually.[13] So one thing that our own photo data show is that, in general, many store owners do not follow official city rules when it comes to creating and hanging signs on their storefronts.

The city's 1961 ordinance is somewhat puzzling in light of state regulations determining that the contents of storefront signs are not and cannot be regulated. In coverage of the 2003 awning crackdown, however, historical preservationists and urban planners characterized text-rich awnings as "visual clutter" (Peyser 2003), "a blight on the quality of street life" (Hartocollis 2003), and "the ugliest signage in the world" (Gerend 2003). Some of these commentators volunteered their own theories of why so many awnings had so many words. For example, Gerend (2003) suggested that this practice is the result of an "awning 'arms race'" where one "merchant will put up a large flashy awning and block the view to the other more modest signs on the block." Others surmised that such a "bigger-is-better attitude has been driven by sign manufacturers" (Hartocollis 2003). Retailers of course countered that the fines for violations were unfair and that the city was enforcing the regulation simply to generate revenue to close budget gaps. Several merchants we spoke with during our fieldwork had heard about the regulation but had not yet been fined.

Sign makers, of course, have their own professional tastes regarding signage and these seem to be different from the linguistic and semiotic characteristics of both the Old School and New School signs in our data set. Note the following exchange we had with the sign makers as we showed them an Old School sign for a barbershop:

SIGN MAKER 1: It says Fresh on 4th. . . . And who are they trying to reach? . . . He's not getting me.

SHONNA: Who's his clientele?

SIGN MAKER 2: I would say young.

SIGN MAKER 1: Young *males*.

SIGN MAKER 2: [only now recognizing the store's function] It's a barbershop! See Fresh on 4th I thought it was *food*! Is that a razor? That's a razor!

See that's why. The word "barbershop" is not *big enough!*

SIGN MAKER 1: Third Street Newsstand and Deli. Who's he trying to reach? He doesn't know . . . if you are a newsstand AND a deli, pick out ONE. "Newsstand." Obviously you're gonna have candies . . .

SIGN MAKER 2: [overlapping] and newspaper, and cigarettes . . .

SHONNA: And that's an awning, right?

SIGN MAKER 1: Yeah that's an awning, so that's a hundred percent illegal. *Too much wording!* (interview with authors, June 29, 2017)

In the above conversation, besides being obviously concerned about official sign regulations and rules, both of these sign makers suggest that there is a particular number of words that are "just right." Too many, and a sign is too cluttered, too chaotic, and not focused on a particular clientele. Too few, and people do not know what the store has. Their critique implies that there is some number of words that explicitly states who you are, what you sell, and what you do. But for them *too many* words overwhelm the customer or make them think that the business does not do much of anything well.

Many photographs of both our Old School and New School signs exemplified, for these sign makers, unsuccessful departures from this semiotic and visual balance. In the next excerpt, one of the sign makers we interviewed tells a story of a shop that requests what we would probably consider to be a New School sign:

SIGN MAKER 2: I had a client . . . it's my favorite story. It was N. N! "I want 'N' on my sign." And I'm like . . . capital N? Really? You're a men's suits, men's fashion [store]. "I want N on the sign." And I said, "Really? . . . Can we please say 'Menswear'?" Nope! "I want 'N'" [the client said.] I said [to the client] "You are NOT McDonalds, this means NOTHING to me as a customer." I always, that's how I sell a lot. I go in as a customer. What is going to make me go in as a customer? He said, "Everyone will see me." We walk out into the street and look at [his] building. I can't see the storefront because [the street] is filled with cars and vans and trucks. BUT, the customer's always right. Ok, against my better judgement, fine! Six months later, I get a phone call. He's like "I'm dying here! Please come and put 'Menswear' on the sign!" Ok! Several months after that I [asked] "How's it going?" and he was like "Wow! What a difference!" It's just a matter of trying to tell the customer what *professionally* you see is the right way . . . and [with] thirty years [experience], I tell you *my* opinion, I don't pull any punches. (interview with authors, June 29, 2017)

In the story above, the sign maker pushes for what he considers to be a tried-and-true professional norm, but he ultimately acquiesces to the customer's wishes. In the end, it seems that regardless of the law and professional, experienced sign makers' suggestions, retailers appear to follow informal, unwritten rules of text-making.

Our data set indicates that, in general, older Brooklyn signage appears to follow an Old School style, containing a combination of the characteristics we outlined. Some new businesses, however, still put up Old School signage, even in gentrifying areas. But we have observed that new, more expensive shops appear to select signage that we have classified as New School. And interestingly, occasionally some Old School shops convert their signage to New School, while others put up new Old School signs. We contend that these two patterns mark two very different Brooklyns. They tell two very different stories about the place and what is happening to its neighborhoods and residents. What the signs say goes beyond the simpler story of deviation from the expectations of professional sign makers or whether a store owner is following or violating city signage rules. As we examine more closely below, one way to read the features of Old School signage is to see them functioning to create a certain kind of public space.

Old School Signs: Capitalism without Distinction

In order to assess what different people thought about the sign types we were seeing in our data set, we conducted a survey of a sample of twenty-five individuals. This sample represented people from various socioeconomic backgrounds with differing lengths of time living in, working in, or visiting Brooklyn (see Appendix for full demographic information). They were students from immigrant families, developers, newly arrived business professionals, and longtime neighborhood residents.[14] We asked these informants to look at three examples of each of the two salient sign types that we discovered and to tell us what the signs said to them and about the stores.[15] When people gave responses about what we considered to be Old School shop signs, there was significant agreement in their interpretations, regardless of their diverse identities and the length of time they had lived in the borough. One lifelong Brooklynite in her twenties from a working-class background noted that Old School signs are "very descriptive in regards to what services they provide to the public." An upper-middle class woman who moved to Brooklyn in 2002 concurred, saying the abundance of words functions primarily to sell goods and services. But she also added that such signs targeted the poor, saying, "stores that deal with lower-income communities want you to know directly that they can meet your basic needs, so they put it all out there on their signs and in their windows." It is interesting that this informant associated Old School stores with lower income clients, even though the Old School establishments we photographed sold goods at a wide range of price points. One young working-class Brooklynite offered a more general proposition about the text-rich signs we showed her. She concluded that, "if [these] storefronts did not have a description of what services they provide, how would they encourage the public to visit their shops?"

An upper-middle-class Brooklyn transplant felt that these text-dense signs were "locally owned . . . by small-business entrepreneurs" who were "friendly." He thought they had "many words to remind locals of multiple services [they] can provide, so as not to spend their money on . . . chain [stores]." A wealthy urban developer who visits Brooklyn frequently told us that these signs "make *everyone* feel welcome" because of their straightforwardness. In other words, she read them as saying "'no matter what you want, we'll be able to help you.'" A middle-class man in his late sixties, who has lived in the borough for over fifty years, agreed with this reading. He described the textual density of these Old School signs as meaning that the businesses were "*open* to everyone."

Interpretations of these signs by Brooklyn residents and other readers are certainly important, and we will return to peoples' impressions throughout our examination. Our data set of thousands of signs also allowed us to take a more extensive and thorough look at the specific systematic features that Old School signs possessed. From a sociolinguistic perspective, or what language philosopher John Austin (1962) would characterize as interpreting what the words on a sign actually "do" in a social sense, we can see how the different linguistic elements of Old School signage work together to communicate a message of openness. Linguist Michael Silverstein's (1976) finding that social indexicals both carry and create meanings that are separate from what they semantically refer to helps to explain how the features and not the words themselves create the sense of "open" and "accommodating" to other groups of people in the Old School Brooklyn market place. Additionally, these indexical features are produced within the context of a specific language ideology.

First, this openness is evident in how Old School signs use language literally and explicitly. In addition to clearly listing what it is they sell, often in more than one language, some shop signs include the word "friend" in their names (Figure 1.23). Or they display explicit statements of openness such as "All Nationalities Welcome!" (Figure 1.24). But even if they do not use

Figure 1.23. This market includes the word *friends* in its name, along with other information such as that it is open twenty-four hours.

Figure 1.24. The slogan on this barber shop is explicitly and emphatically inclusive: "All Nationalities Welcome!"

such terms, they often include literal and explicit references to ethnicity, race, religion, or class. Explicit, in this sense, means "we are what we are telling you we are" or a "what you see is what you get" honesty. Thus the specific identity markers that we observe on Brooklyn Old School signs, like religious icons or concepts (such as in Figures 1.9 through 1.12), or images of particular hair types (Figure 1.25) or certain kinds of food, are *directly* and *intentionally* referred to in order to communicate to people who maintain such identities.

These explicit identity references with direct and literal terms of racial or ethnic designations are often *balanced* with an equally explicit reference to a presumably non-ethnicized entity. In other words, if a sign calls out to a

Figure 1.25. This shop includes an explicit and sincere reference to race using an image of a woman's hairstyle.

specific ethnicity, it also makes an appeal to anyone who may want that product or who may also desire non-ethnicized items as well. For example, phrases like "Pakistani and American Food," "African and American Cuisine" (Figure 1.26), or "American and Mediterranean" food (Figure 1.27) are among the many we find. This communicative balance also extends to the larger category of language itself. Thus, when languages other than English, such as Chinese or Hebrew, appear on Old School signs, the text is usually also translated into English, which appears next to or beneath the non-English words.[16] Just taking into account these four features alone—that is, numerous words, explicit references, various languages, and how these languages are represented together— we can begin to see how Old School Vernacular signage produces a particular language ideology. The belief instantiated in the use of these features suggests that words should not be limited, language should not be restricted to only English, and that one can be literal and explicit. This overwhelming directness not only gestures toward *anyone* interested in buying what a shop is selling, it also projects the message that a business *does not discriminate*.

Another arguably ideological feature of Old School signage that underscores this nondiscriminatory message is the manner in which English is commonly used *nonstandardly*. Nonstandard English, such as the use of singular forms for words that in Standard American English are frequently referred to in plural terms (e.g., "cigarette" or "flower"), nonparallel constructions, and even repetition, might elicit critiques from grammarians as incorrect, redundant, or wordy. But we see them operating, especially as they are displayed out in the open on fixed signage for any passerby to see, as reinforcing a stance that is free from the hegemony of prescriptive grammar rules and standard language practices.[17] Linguistically and anthropologically, the "standard" form of a language is simply one of a variety of actual forms. The standard is the form of the language that is taught in school, associated with the written rules of formal grammar and usually marks prestige. Linguists do not consider nonstandard dialects to be deficient communicative systems in any way.[18] Still, irrespective of linguistic expertise, many scholars have shown that people across cultures come to believe that speakers whose linguistic norms more closely approximate the formally taught rules of writing and speaking are "better" at speaking than those who do not. Most people, linguists included, believe that an agreed-upon standard form of language is necessary for the functioning of a complicated democracy.

The nonstandard elements of Old School signs suggest that sign makers and shopkeepers do not need to rely on Standard English in the way that the US educational system prescribes as necessary for people to communicate adequately through texts. And given the quantity and variation of nonstandard forms, it also seems that many Old School store owners do not seek the advice or input of native English speakers or grammarians. We have found signage where languages other than English are also written without regard for standard or codified rules of writing, so in some cases the source may be a lack of formal education on the part of the business owner or the sign maker. In other settings and contexts, standard (or prescriptive) language practices have been shown to make "social class[es] . . . races, and nations seem real . . . and elicit feelings and justify relations of power, making subalterns seem to speak in ways that necessitate their subordination" (Bauman and Briggs 2003, 9). But in Brooklyn, Old School signs make a place where nonnative English and nonstandard writing practices are acceptable in public, and thus the signs seem to say that one communicative system does not have dominance over any other in the Brooklyn marketplace.

Finally, whether in English, a language other than English, or in nonstandard forms of either English or another language, the repetition we find on Old School signage of the numerous words that are placed there suggests a make-no-mistake approach. Along these lines, perhaps *all* the words on these "wordy" Old School signs are necessary to ensure that their shop's message and their social indexing of openness get across.

Taken together, all these linguistic features of Old School signs signal an aggressively democratic and tolerant system of commerce, marking a place that performs what we call *capitalism without distinction*. We use *capitalism*

Figure 1.26. The sign for Adama Restaurant indicates that it offers both African and American food.

Figure 1.27. The Lutheran Halal Café sign announces both Mediterranean and American food plus other offerings. *Lutheran* is not a reference to religion, but a location: the shop is blocks away from Brooklyn's Lutheran Hospital.

instead of *commerce* here because Brooklyn's small business economy involves more than a retail market. Commercial districts often integrate labor with production, investment, and distribution of goods. After the health care industry, the small business sector is Brooklyn's largest for-profit employer. By *distinction* we mean, following Bourdieu (1984), both the contrast between similar things and an evaluation of those things as having qualities that mark variation in cultural capital. Capitalism without distinction thus denotes tolerance and inclusivity despite differences in people's identities, bank accounts, educational levels, and religious beliefs.

We find this spirit of capitalism without distinction also extends to more upscale establishments that have been operating in neighborhoods with Old School signage for decades. These places, like Gargiulo's Italian Restaurant, a Brooklyn institution for more than one hundred years, are expensive, elaborate, and extravagant. Even today, people can go to Gargiulo's and feel luxurious as it offers a lavish environment. A local website describes the establishment as a "circa-1907 banquet hall–style eatery" where "tuxedo-clad waiters serve old-school Italian fare."[19] But despite its elegance and expensiveness, it still seems quite open to everyone. Brooklyn middle schools often hold eighth grade dances there, and many public high schools choose the restaurant for their functions. We attended a Brooklyn high school's football awards banquet with our son, his team members and their families, and the coaches. So, while people go there for special events, one does not get the sense that only special people can enter. In fact, Gargiulo's business model and advertising suggest that no matter who you are, they will make you feel special. Moreover, many Old School establishments have products worthy of distinction. It is important to emphasize that capitalism without distinction refers to the clientele and not necessarily to what a business offers. In an Old School Russian food store in Bay Ridge, one could buy one ounce of high-quality black caviar for only $40, whereas caviar of similar quality at Petrossian, in Manhattan, would sell for $129. As another example, Di Fara's, an Old School pizza shop in Midwood, attracts customers from throughout New York City, who stand in line for a distinctive but inexpensive slice of pizza.

Evidence that Old School signs resonate favorably with some people comes in the way of admiring reviews of recently published coffee-table books featuring photographs of Old School storefronts. In one volume, they are described as "New York originals" (McDonald 2012). In others, they are described as having "vibrant canvas[es]" that represent "countless ethnic groups" offering "unique" but "humble" signs that "capture the neighborhood spirit of familiarity, comfort and warmth" (Lacy 2008; Murray and Murray 2011). This ideal imaginary of a canvas of ethnic diversity and neighborhood warmth cultivated in these commemorative books also appears to invoke Jane Jacob's (1961) classic notion of neighborhood "vitality," where a diverse population would, ideally, use urban space throughout the day for a variety of purposes.

We recognize that signs on storefronts cannot, by themselves, create a utopian neighborhood. Racial, ethnic, and religious discrimination existed and still exists in Brooklyn (see Purnell 2013; Wilder 2000; and Bayoumi 2008). For example, Spike Lee's film *Do the Right Thing* depicts the complicated and contentious relationships among different ethnic and racial groups who share and vie for control of a Brooklyn neighborhood's urban space. And small business establishments are not inherently fair-minded and equitable, as an accounting of the exploitative labor practices found by immigrant rights activist and scholar Peter Kwong (1997) and of the unfriendly and antagonistic relationships studied by linguists Benjamin Bailey (2000) and Rusty Barrett (2006) between different ethnic groups interacting in the contexts of these types of sites can attest. So, what is behind the sign may be quite different from what it says out front.[20]

Sociolinguistically, we see the idea of openness enacted on multiple levels. First, most businesses suggest that they are open to people from any background. And second, if a business seems to target a narrower customer base (a Norwegian food store or a Mexican bakery), its explicit reference to this group strongly suggests that the area is "open" to them, or that there is a place on the street for them, next to and nearby others. We read these explicit references to different identities as a way to say that the presence of others in the community is neither ignored nor assimilated into dominant culture. Instead, the presence of these groups is brought into the open and asserted. These literal and sincere multicultural identity references comport with sociolinguists Andrea Smith and Anna Eisenstein's (2013, 2016) finding that residents living in Syrian Town, a multiethnic neighborhood in Easton, Pennsylvania, always used explicit ethnonyms (Lebanese, Jewish, black, Italian) to refer to one another. In their study, the elderly research participants of all backgrounds insisted that, before their neighborhood was demolished by an urban renewal project, they lived harmoniously as a "close-knit," "happy family" (Smith and Eisenstein 2016, 63). In fact, the participants said they lived "thoroughly mixed," and yet they continually referred to themselves and each other with ethnic labels or what they themselves called "nationalities" (Smith and Eisenstein 2013, 1).[21] When Smith and Eisenstein first heard their informants talking like this they thought it sounded "jarring," "old-fashioned," "old-timey," and even "outdated." They asked themselves, "At first, upon talking with these men and women about the old neighborhood, we were stumped: Why would people constantly describe a world as close-knit across ethnic lines while constantly labeling the ethnicities of the subjects of their stories in a fashion that by today's criteria would seem judgmental or even racist?" (Smith and Eisenstein 2016, 104–5). Yet their informants insisted that there was clearly an accepting and peaceful coexistence of Otherness in this community (Smith and Eisenstein 2013, 1).

When we first moved to our Flatbush apartment, and then to our home in Bay Ridge, we noticed that people constantly referred to others by mentioning their ethnic and racial backgrounds as well.[22] Smith and Eisenstein explain their research participants' usage of ethnonyms through Bakhtin's notion of chronotope—in order to talk about time and space, people use language from that (in this case) previous time and space. They say, "These past terms in turn carry their own power to help conjure up the physical space and time, the former context, in which they were telling, acting on both the speakers and their listeners in the present day chronotope" (Smith and Eisenstein 2016, 105). And while we do not disagree with this theory for narrative storytelling in the past, it left us wondering about people's usage of this linguistic feature in contemporary Brooklyn.

Another way to interpret these explicit references is by considering them to be expressions of what anthropologist John Jackson (2005) calls sincerity. "Sincerity is an attempt to talk about racial subjects and subjectivities" (17). For Jackson, sincerity is an expressive stance from which a person can claim racial identity from a subject position. Jackson counters sincerity with the objectifying processes involved in designations of authenticity. "Authenticity theorizes difference as an unbalanced relationship between the powerful seer and the impotently seen, the latter being a mere object of the seer's racial gaze and discourse" (17). For Jackson, concepts of authenticity are deeply dependent upon positions of authority, and domination. Rather than objectify an identity and subject it to the scrutiny of others' evaluations of veracity, Jackson suggests that sincere expressions of identity, such as race, operate on the level of a "subject-subject interaction" creating a "liaison between subjects" (15). And this approach, argues Jackson, is "an attempt to talk about racial [or other identity] *subjects* and subjectivities" (17). Jackson's theory of sincerity sheds light on Brooklyn's past, current, and persistent use of ethnonyms and other representations which seems to balance relationships between all groups of people in the commercial landscape (See, for example, Figure 1.25).

Such signs, then, with explicit and sincere references to race, ethnicity, national origin, religion, and the like, fly in the face of dominant cultural values such as assimilation and monolingualism. Unlike conformist ideologies that obscure or erase intersectional identities, Brooklyn's Old School shop signs articulate and proclaim the presence of diversity at every turn. This proclamation is carried out in a sincere subject position that need not be usurped by nor hidden from the dominant group. The signs' sincere references to the organizing principles of race, ethnicity, national origin, class, and languages other than English, seem to suggest that a group's right to expressions of difference is dependent on every other group's right to express unique differences as well. In other words, such a right can only be achieved if every other group in the space is offered the same due respect. So, the signs seem to say, there is a place for everyone on the street, not irrespective of ethnic differences, but because of them.

The multitude of this collective sincerity shows other groups of people that there is a place for *everyone*. And as each such sign becomes a place marker on the street that makes up the commercial district, the multi-everything of Old School signage marks the *logos*, or the local logic and reason, of an area where all different types of people can be. It is in this diverse communicative context that Old School Vernacular signage conveys a message similar to the Civil Rights Act of 1964 and the consequent nondiscrimination policies found throughout US institutions. On the street, Old School features create a public textual strategy for people who speak English and languages other than English, who use nonstandard varieties of English, and who cannot read. There are repetitions and reiterations for those who might doubt, and long lists of what is inside for those who might wonder. Old School signage, then, is an indexical system that, in removing barriers to communication, signifies inclusion and openness. At the same time, this system that signals capitalism without distinction speaks of an idealized nonclassist, nonracist, and non-ethnocentric commercial area that epitomizes notions of democracy in diversity and a free market, where there is a place for anyone and everyone.

New School Signage: Making New Distinctions in Place

When we asked people in the survey about the sparsely worded New School Brooklyn signage, they attached very different meanings from those they associated with Old School signs. For example, the upper-middle-class woman who moved to Brooklyn in the early 2000s told us that she interpreted the one-word signs as "modern" and thought they indexed "expertise." And the urban developer who told us that Old School signs were welcoming thought that our New School examples incorporated a "simplicity" that was "elegant" and "sophisticated." But it was not just "modern" and "elegant" that people were seeing in these signs. For instance, one Brooklyn newcomer, an upper-middle class male, read a "notion of mystery/aspiration/clubbiness" in New School Brooklyn signage. Others interpreted this notion of mystery positively and linked it to upscale fashion and consumption. For instance, an upper-middle-class newcomer told us that "stores [with one-word signs] are selling a lifestyle and attitude . . . you don't *need* to buy a shirt from Bird or dinner at James, you do because you like what it says about you." Notably, the cryptic nature of the name *Bird* confused almost all our informants. Several lifelong residents thought Bird was a pet store or a bird store. And even Brooklyn newcomers wrongly guessed Bird sold upscale children's clothes. But they were right in thinking that, whatever it sold, the items were relatively expensive. Not surprisingly, many gentrifiers to whom we showed our sign examples read the ambiguity of New School signs as far from being open places or welcoming, but seemingly targeting a specific type of customer. One newcomer, an upper-middle-class woman, thought that this targeting was accomplished in the very way that such signs used language. She described the one-word signs we showed her as having "an intriguing story to tell," using language as "a strategy to pique interest, almost like it's insider information . . . 'exclusive.'"

These readings from residents and other observers clearly show that people see New School signage as saying something different from their Old School counterparts. But taking a closer look at the specific features of these signs allows us to discover the underlying language ideology governing this New School sign style. To begin with, picking up on one Brooklynite's reading that the textual sparsity of New School signs is a "modern" aesthetic, we see this same idea in both governmental and large-scale corporate signage and advertising. The notion that messages should be sent through simple, "clean," and "uncluttered" text is a "modern" language ideology that has prevailed since the late 1950s and is exemplified by the development of Helvetica, a typeface without flourishes or serifs (Hustwit 2007). When it appeared on the design scene, Helvetica was thought to express a direct simplicity unencumbered by prior meanings and thus suitable to mass marketing. Rising in popularity alongside the global advertising revolution, people liked the typeface because it was not associated with any particular group. Its lack of associations appealed to governmental and corporate messaging that sought to communicate to all people everywhere, regardless of their local identities.[23]

But these minimalist trends in typography, text-making, and branding of corporate advertising are supported by a much more long-standing language ideology. This ideology, evidenced in the writings of Locke (Bauman and Briggs 2003) and encapsulated in the time-honored Shakespearian aphorism, "brevity is the soul of wit," places a premium value on *concision*.[24] This premium is reinforced throughout professional writing guides, such as Strunk and White's *Elements of Style*, first published in 1959 and a veritable authority on good composition. "Vigorous writing is concise" states the guide's fourth edition, listing a number of principles and suggestions to support this view:

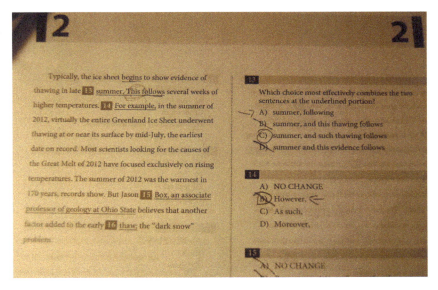

Figure 1.28. The ideology of concision in writing is reinforced in this and many other questions found in study guides US high school students use to prepare for the ubiquitous college entrance exam, the Scholastic Aptitude Test, commonly referred to as the SAT.

"Omit needless words" [Principle 17]; "Do not overwrite" [Suggestion 6]; "Do not overstate" [Suggestion 7]; "Do not explain too much" [Suggestion 11] (Strunk and White 1999, vi–vii). The promotion of textual brevity is also quite clear in pedagogical materials for students pursuing education degrees, as one popular textbook proclaims that "concise expression, particularly in writing, is considered one of the basic goals of teaching the English language" (Buczynski and Fontichiaro 2009, 7). We also recently came across this ideology of concision while helping our son prepare for the Scholastic Aptitude Test, the college entrance exam colloquially known as the SAT that most students take in order to apply to universities in the US. In *The Official SAT Study Guide*, published by the College Board (2017), we came across a practice test question on grammar that touted concision for concision's sake. The question asked how two sentences at the beginning of a paragraph could best be combined into one. The correct response turned out to be the shortest choice among several others. According to the *Study Guide* this response is correct because "as trained test-takers, we know that if the shortest answer choice is grammatically acceptable to the College Board, then the College Board will credit it as the correct answer." Notice in Figure 1.28 how the answer key drills into the College-bound test-taker the idea that repeating words is unnecessary, and thus not preferred or valued. Such questions are peppered throughout the practice exams, presumably so the test taker can acquire the rule that brevity is "correct."[25] In contrast to this ideology, Brock and Walters

(1992, 4–5) note that other cultures may very well value redundancy and verbosity, as these features are meant to show a good command of a language.

Taking a closer look at the form of New School brevity, we see another reading alongside this idea of conciseness, which is quite different from corporate or government language. Against the text-dense Old School signs, sparsely worded signs operate on the principle of what linguists Ron and Susie Scollon (2003, 113) call "low semiotic intrusion." Linguists and anthropologists studying urban and public space have found that an absence of dense public textual display signals an elite geo-semiotics. One can see this aesthetic reinforced in "livable cityscapes" promoted in architectural books and represented by a lack of signage in upscale urban areas such as Washington's Georgetown, Spain's public plazas, and nineteenth century Viennese arcades (Scollon and Scollon 2003). This aesthetic has even been legislated through a "clean city" campaign in Sao Paulo (Caldiera 2012). Correspondingly, anthropologist Arlene Dávila (2004, 189) notes that gentrifying avenues of the predominantly Latino neighborhood of East Harlem appear "clean and demure," an aesthetic she likens to that of Manhattan's wealthy Upper East Side, where few, if any, advertisements exist. Dávila quotes an advertising executive who says people in more upscale neighborhoods "would be bothered by the ubiquity and ordinariness" of such advertisements (189). And this aesthetic is not limited to urban spaces. Jaworski and Thurlow (2009, 207) find that newspaper and magazine ads use a text-sparse "discursivity of elitism" to attract upscale consumers to travel destinations, which are depicted as landscapes of silence and emptiness.[26]

In a way, this elite, and arguably elitist, language ideology enacted on New School signage, which looks minimal and unelaborated, contrasts with the abundant reiterations, long lists, literal and obvious meanings, and nonstandard grammar and punctuation found on Old School signs. Therefore, it is not surprising that the developer among our informants who visits frequently and who saw sophistication in New School signs also told us that, while Old School signs had "something for everyone," they also had "so much random information blaring." She argued that their "unrelated and redundant" texts sent "a message that they are not confident in their expertise." For her, "details create clutter and clutter equals unsophisticated and messy." Likewise, the critics in the illegal-awning crackdown of 2003 characterized the textual density of Old School shops as "visual clutter" and "ugly."

But minimalism and its elitist referent are only part of a sociolinguistic analysis of New School signage. Taking an even closer look, we see that New School signs quite consistently take up the other half of Shakespeare's famous adage "brevity is the soul of wit." Brevity also calls for the use of words in pithy and entertaining ways, and this ideology is rife among the formally educated intellectuals trained in writing courses in US high schools and college classrooms and by grammar books (Milroy and Milroy 2012). Poe's character Dupin, in "The Purloined Letter," denigrates the largely lettered shop signs because they are too ordinary to call one's attention. Poe's proto-detective takes this negative position on these texts for being too literal, common, and ultimately, mundane. Thus, in contrast to the Old School signs, which use explicit and literal references to location, products, services, and customers, New School signage often utilizes erudite and playful references to history, literature, and culture to reframe a nondistinctive outer borough, once marginal to Manhattan, as a Brooklyn with distinction. These place-based references also take a stand against the homogenizing nature of big business and corporate branding, an influence that people complain much of contemporary Manhattan has been subjected to. For example, a Fort Greene restaurant called the General Greene lexically alludes to the old-fashioned grocery nomenclature of "the general store" but substitutes the word store with Greene, simultaneously indexing the Revolutionary War general Nathaniel Greene and both his namesake fort and neighborhood. Similarly, the sign for Cornelius, a Prospect Heights oyster bar, playfully combines history, place, and placement in a single word (Figure 1.29). When one reads the adjacent street sign on the corner, "Vanderbilt Av," the two texts together reveal a clever homage to Cornelius Vanderbilt, the nineteenth-century New York steamship magnate. Likewise, Knotting Slope, a Park Slope retail knitting shop, evokes the London neighborhood Notting Hill or the 1999 feature film of the same name. At the same time, the name makes an orthographic pun to sewing, knitting, and creating knots for making rugs. Finally, in replacing *Hill* with *Slope* the nomenclature makes a strong reference not only to the name of its Brooklyn neighborhood but also to its topography.

These historical, cultural, and geographic references are suggestive of reading practices common in middle- and upper-middle-class homes. Shirley Brice Heath's (1982) classic ethnography of reading shows how middle- and upper-middle class families constantly relate written texts to other texts and to real world contexts when reading to and talking with their young children. Such literary practices continue to be lauded by educators for providing a foundation for school literacy, which is "taken as the standard . . . marginalizing other literacy practices" (Street and Besnier 1993, 551). So, as high-brow literary references (Whitman's ample hills), history lessons (Cornelius, the General Greene), and even linguistics (Bird, or a yogurt shop called /eks/—written in the international phonetic alphabet and perhaps suggesting "x marks the spot") exist writ large on the gentrifying streets of Brooklyn, both the text on and the reading of New School signs certainly seem to be inspired by the literacy of formal education. For college-educated gentrifiers, such signage might foster a familiarity in place and a sense of being among like-minded neighbors. And thus literacy as manifest in these types of signs may create an inter-subjective economy of affect (Besnier 1991, 582) that emotionally and existentially links readers with each other and with place. For those who notice these playful references, the signs provide a semantic operation that can feel like an experience of intellectual exclusivity.

So it is not just in the act of purchasing an expensive shirt or meal that separates a buyer from everyone else, it is also one's awareness of these references that indexes a distinctive group of people "in-the-know" who trade in specific forms of cultural capital. Likewise, non-English words on New School signs are rarely if ever translated into English the way they are in their Old School counterparts. Instead, non-English signs such as "LE GAMIN," "al di lá," or "palo santo," for example, fall in line with what Heller (2003) describes as the normative use of languages other than English to call to a clientele with foreign tastes and global sophistication. The use of these languages is meant to look foreign or exotic and not to index any local group with native fluency in these languages. As was the case for many Brooklynites we asked, we were also unaware of the meaning of the words *al di lá* until we began doing research for this book. But long after it became one of our examples, we learned that Shonna's Italian American mother knew the song only as she began to sing along with it in a bistro in Rome during her first visit to Italy to celebrate her fiftieth wedding anniversary. She said people used to dance to the song "Al Di La" at all the Italian weddings she attended in her youth. She did not know what the words *al di lá* meant, but the phrase had great sentimental meaning to her, though we had never heard anything about it before. As the above data point suggests, meaning is highly contextual. The store owner put up a sign that breaks with the literal norms of Old School signage in ways that clearly allow for novel, personal, and contextual interpretations of their meanings.

Storefront signs that playfully point to higher education in history, literature, and culture rewrite the meaning of Brooklyn precisely for those gentrifiers who hold college degrees and who work in professions requiring such credentials, marking the place as unique from the nondistinctive commerce of their immediate neighbors/predecessors. Old School explicitness indicated that one should neither risk meaning nor make assumptions about other people on the street. These text-dense signs were and still are, as the Beastie

Figure 1.29. Note the juxtaposition of the street sign for Vanderbilt Avenue with cornelius, the one-word name of this oyster bar, to create an allusion to the nineteenth-century shipping magnate Cornelius Vanderbilt.

Boys suggest in a line from their 2005 song "Open Letter to NYC," "thorough in the borough" of necessity.[27] After reading the signs, we do not think it a coincidence that the Beastie Boys and Smith and Eisenstein's (2013) informants use the word *thorough* as characterizing a way of being in multiethnic urban communities. In contrast, with their lack of information, New School signs convey numerous assumptions: that customers can deal with any price point, that they do not need halal or kosher food, and that they speak English, have foreign tastes even if they are not fluent in any language other than English, and understand what the signs mean. New School Distinction-Making shop signs typically do not include URLs, but our participant-observation reveals that gentrifiers presume new stores will have a web presence, and they will google them for their websites, for reviews about them, and other types of information, such as stories about them in the media. In our fifteen years of living as participants, observers, ethnographers, and analysts, it has been a rare occasion when a New School business did not come with a website. Most Old School businesses do not have websites, yet most now do have a web presence through Google Maps and social media platforms such as Yelp.

Figure 1.30. These shops on Fifth Avenue in Park Slope are all in the New School style.

Signs as Tools of Gentrification

New School signs are encroaching on blocks with Old School signage at a steady pace. In some cases, entire sections of certain Brooklyn neighborhoods contain only this new form of signage. Figure 1.30 depicts a section of a shopping block in Park Slope; it shows three of five storefronts in a row that together have a total of only ten words on their signage. In this case, each of these storefronts is a restaurant. The names are, from left to right, Two Boots, Blue Ribbon, Calexico, and not visible in the picture, Bonnie's Grill and Naruto Ramen. With the exception of Bonnie's Grill, which sells $16 hamburgers and an order of large fries for $9, each of the other restaurants is inspired by what would be considered in the US as an ethnic or regional cuisine.[28] But our experience as participant-observers indicates that each of these restaurants is largely designed to serve the gentrifying community, which is middle to upper-middle class. As a place-making technology, New Brooklyn signage literally broadcasts—to everyone—a message that, from a sociolinguistic perspective, appears to be clearly aimed at a particular audience.[29]

If we compare an Old School block (Figure 1.1) with this New School stretch of shops, Scollon and Scollon's (2003) notion of semiotic intrusion gives way to what we will call *semiotic exclusion*. Simply reading the signs from the street may not provide enough information to know what is inside, or it may actually give you the information that you might not be welcome to come in. In fact, while new one-word signs evoked sentiments of exclusivity for gentrifiers, they produced feelings of exclusion for those on the other side of the gentrification equation. For example, a life-long Queens resident from a working-class background who now works in Brooklyn told us that one-word signs are "almost like a secret club. And if you don't already know what's inside . . . then you don't need to know or belong there." The middle-class, long-term Brooklyn resident who saw Old School signs as "open" concluded that "one-word sign names mean a selective group." Even some gentrifiers saw this exclusionary function in New School signage. An upper-middle-class male said of the sign for James, "you have no idea what it is from the signs. One word and it's someone's name. You need to be 'in-the-know' to even approach." And another working-class Brooklyn resident explained that not knowing what was in a store made her uncomfortable. For her, New School signs "do not welcome the public." She added, "as a Brooklynite, I think it is offensive."

Rather than being "the humblest of literacy artefacts" (Collins and Slembrouck 2007, 349), commercial shop signs are in fact very powerful public texts that constitute, communicate, and have the power to change social, economic, and political life. At the same time, one can see that signs are clearly and uniquely integrated into the human fabric of urban neighborhoods. In the following chapters, we examine why people may be offended by these New School signs, what other linguistic features are involved in their role as place-making tools of gentrification, and how other ethnographic realities are engaged in Brooklyn's distinctive and dynamic linguistic landscape.

His face with smile eternal drest,
Just like the Landlord's to his Guest's,
High as they hang with creaking din,
To index out the Country Inn.
He looked just as your sign-post Lions do,
With aspect fierce, and quite as harmless too.

Robert Burns, "Versicles On Sign-Posts" (1789)

The world was to me a secret which I
desired to divine.

Mary Shelley, *Frankenstein, or,*
the Modern Prometheus (1818)

"Everyone is trying to figure out a different way
to write 'Brooklyn'"

Brooklyn sign maker, 2017

2. Deep Wordplay
Registering, Belonging, and Excluding

TO UNDERSTAND HOW ideas about Brooklyn have changed over time, we found we needed a crash course in geography and literary texts. Much of how we began to try to understand Brooklyn came from how it was being written about. But we also learned about it from how people related it geo-discursively to Manhattan. Beginning with geography, one quickly notices that so much discourse about "place" in New York City occurs in terms of local geographical coordinates and landmark references. Typical conversations among New Yorkers sound like the following: "I ran into Bridget's sister at Union Square last week. I said, 'Do you live around here?' She said, 'Yeah, 26th between 5th and 6th.' I said, 'I used to work on 19th and Broadway. Do you ever go to Pipa?'" Note that this utterance contains a reference to a place with a New School sign: it's rather cryptic, it sounds like a non-English word, and we cannot tell from the name alone what sort of place it is.[1] Compounding the outsider's confusion is the fact that certain areas of New York City are usually referred to directionally: one encounters, for example, neighborhoods such as the East Village and the West Village, and transportation, including uptown trains and crosstown buses, without explicit reference to a deictic center.

Deixis, as we mentioned earlier, is a linguistic indexical term that refers to words and phrases that point to or indicate spatial or temporal relationships but that require context to be understood. One cannot understand the meanings of deictic references such as *here*, *there*, *this*, or *that*, without more complete knowledge of who the interlocuters are, where they are located, and how the terms relate to what is known, in linguistic shorthand, as the *deictic center*. The implied context for these New York City place references in the above example is Manhattan, irrespective of the fact that there are 5th and 6th Avenues and 26th and 19th Streets in Brooklyn as well.² This geo-discursive privileging of Manhattan—the place the world collectively recognizes as "New York, New York" or "New York City"—marginalizes the relevance of the city's other four boroughs: Brooklyn, the Bronx, Queens, and Staten Island. Arguably, these boroughs have been historically and culturally peripheral to The City, as Manhattan is often referred to by natives themselves.

For Brooklyn, however, this has all been changing for the last decade and a half, as mainstream media, many popular and nationally important fiction and nonfiction writers, and academics have become fascinated with the place as an object of their reporting, writing, and study. No doubt, beginning with Whitman's poem "Crossing Brooklyn Ferry," the borough has always been an intriguing subject of the American imagination. From H. P. Lovecraft's disparaging short story "A Horror in Red Hook" (1927) to Betty Smith's aspirational immigrant novel *A Tree Grows in Brooklyn* (1943), the gritty coming of age film *Saturday Night Fever* (1977), and Spike Lee's intercultural conflict parable *Do the Right Thing* (1989), writers and artists have long engaged with Brooklyn's dynamic but inevitably marginalized status. Notably, Brooklyn's marginality has been characterized in these works as making it an unexplored place, relatively unknown to the larger world. This sense of being unexplored is a major theme in James Agee's ethnographic report *Brooklyn Is* (1968), whose subtitle, *Southeast of the Island—Travel Notes*, again makes Manhattan the center, the place from which Brooklyn is "visited." Brooklyn's marginality also has served as a kind of metaphorical hiding place; for example, in William Styron's 1979 novel *Sophie's Choice*, the neighborhood of Flatbush serves as a refuge for a grief-stricken victim of tyranny and oppression.

But Brooklyn's deictic status has quickly shifted from the peripheral "there" of literary subjects that writers have explored to the "here" of a place where writers themselves now live and work. The borough is now home to award-winning authors including Jennifer Egan, Jonathan Safran Foer, Nicole Krauss, Jhumpa Lahiri, and Amitav Gosh, to name only a few. As sociologist and gentrification scholar Sharon Zukin recently described it, Brooklyn has morphed from a place people come *from* in order to go somewhere else, into a destination people would go *to* in order to live. In other words, Brooklyn has become "cool" (Zukin 2010, 35). And this coolness, Zukin has noted, has emerged in conjunction with how the borough has been rapidly repackaged and marketed for new consumers in a symbolic economy, not merely as a destination, but as a distinctive way of life. For example, in 2007 the hipster guidebook *Lonely Planet* shifted the traditional center of New York City from Manhattan to Brooklyn: "Brooklyn's booming. . . . Any New Yorker worth their street cred knows the new downtown lies just across the East River" (quoted in Zukin 2010, 35). To give an idea of how quickly such attention to the borough came about, a popular 2002 guidebook that we used in preparation for our move to Flatbush did not name Brooklyn at all, referring to it collectively in the last chapter along with Staten Island, the Bronx, and Queens as "The Outer Boroughs" (Zenfell 2002). Less than a decade later, Brooklyn attracted the attention of the highbrow traveler set with Conde Nast billing it in 2011 as one of "The 15 Best Places to See Right Now." The website's beckoning portrait finishes with a resounding endorsement of the borough's new status: "Because there's nothing cooler than being among the first at the hippest spots in the city—way before the tour buses pull in" (Payne 2011).

One of those "hippest spots" in Brooklyn is Fort Greene, and a quick browse through this historic neighborhood's Greenlight Bookstore suggests that, at least in print, Brooklyn has truly become a place unto its own. Book titles range from *Brooklyn in the 1920s* and *Brooklyn Dodgers* to volumes dedicated to Brooklyn neighborhoods like *Bay Ridge* and *Crown Heights* (from the Images of America series) to new parent guide *City Baby Brooklyn* by Alison Lowenstein, children's books like *Knuffle Bunny* by Mo Willems, and novels such as Jonathan Lethem's *Motherless Brooklyn* or simply *Brooklyn*, by Colm Tóibín. And we find that this rapidly growing notion of Brooklyn "coolness" has certainly spread beyond the place itself. In 2011, Anthony Lane wrote in the *New Yorker*: "At Pixar, as in New York City, Brooklyn is the place to be," referring to the name of one of the buildings on the film giant's sprawling campus near San Francisco. In Europe we have seen kids sporting Brooklyn Nets jerseys, smokers buying a brand of cigarettes called Brooklyn in Spanish tobacco shops, and, most recently, in Luxembourg in 2017, we found a bar called Brooklyn. Such texts in the global linguistic landscape indicate Brooklyn has shifted out of its status as one of Manhattan's outer-boroughs and into an internationally known "place to be."

Now, residents, journalists, and bloggers who helped make it such a place have become protective of its new status by referring to any further transformations of the borough as the soulless "Manhattanization of Brooklyn." For Zukin (2010, 2) "Manhattanization signifies everything in a city that is thought not to be authentic: high-rise buildings that grow taller every year, dense crowds where no one knows your name, high prices for inferior living conditions, and intense competition to be in style." The implication, of course, is that Manhattan is no longer itself, but rather has been heavily transformed through redevelopment, gentrification, and global tourism. A favorite example among Manhattanites is to note what they term the *Disneyfication* of Times Square, with its corporate chains, gigantic digital ad boards, and annoying film characters jockeying among a throng of tourists to charge them for photo snaps.[3]

Brooklyn's coolness is no doubt a complicated thing. Zukin's own analysis of "How Brooklyn became cool" focuses on the way ideas about "the authentic" figure in the current consumption trends in Brooklyn, a process that is intimately connected to both redevelopment and gentrification (Zukin 2010). But as we pointed out above, its fashionableness is intimately tied up in how language constructs the borough's density and diversity and its current demographic changes. Brooklyn's transformation has been marketed and carried out through writing: in commercial advertising, in blogs, in journalism, and in both popular fiction and nonfiction. Such writing makes clear that Brooklyn, departing from its long-term marginality to Manhattan, now stands up to The City in the creation of its new identity by new residents. And though these new residents seem to embrace "the authentic," they may fail to recognize their impact on this multiethnic, multiclassed, and multireligious space.

We may be quite familiar with how a novel, a history, or even a magazine article can represent and market a city, but less obvious is how shop signs assert cultural value and establish and communicate social hierarchy. The multiple meanings that are available in New School storefront signage raise questions about authenticity and sincerity and the new order of place-making in Brooklyn. Our analysis of New School signage in this chapter highlights some of the broader implications of the seemingly innocuous practice of the laying out of "names on the land" to advertise a business. In addition to creating, promoting, and changing place, New School signage establishes a social hierarchy on land where, we argue, no obviously definable hierarchy had previously existed.

Place Registers on the Land

Register is a linguistic concept that refers to the functionally appropriate style of language and linguistic devices necessary for a given situation. As a form of social indexicality, register also varies according to the context in which it is used. A particular register signals meaning and at the same time creates a context for that meaning to come into being. Registers usually occur in predictable places, because speakers have, as part of their sociolinguistic competence, the ability to choose, from among competing or available forms, one that is appropriate to the meaning-making at hand (Agha 2001, 212). You would not, for example, talk to your boss in the same way you address your closest friends. But introducing language you would use with your friends into a conversation with your boss might function to change the relationship you have with her. This new language use or style reconfigures the "sense of the occasion, indexically entailing that the associated social practice is now underway" (Agha 2001, 212). Registers are usually highly context specific and are defined by contexts or place in addition to the specific relationships between people. For example, *medicalese*, *legalese*, or *academese* are registers associated with particular professions and their unique settings (Biber and Conrad 2009). The courtroom, for instance, requires legal actors such as judges and attorneys to use legalese that entails not only particular terms but also titles and honorifics. So, while a judge and the district attorney might call each other by their first names when greeting each other on the street, the context of the courtroom requires the use of legal terminology and formal forms of address such as "your Honor," "Counselor," and the like. These elements of the legalese register help to then create the context of the court as much as they are required by its context.

As social and political instrumentalities of ethnographic contexts (Hymes 1974), registers both express ideologies and are directed by them. And this relationship between function and context is important not just for spoken language, but for texts as well, as more recent work on register shows (Agha 2011). The way things are written as texts and where they appear, such as "wine notes" (Silverstein 2003), slogans on souvenirs and t-shirts (Johnstone 2009), or the words and images of postcards and tourist pamphlets (Dorst 1989), situate, mark, and represent certain contexts. Appearing in certain forms (lexical, grammatical, syntactical, etc.) and styles, such texts also help to create and recreate place for us, and thus, we might consider these types of texts as different *place registers*.

Place registers are a type of social indexical that gains intersubjective prominence in peoples' minds where it functions to create an identity that can be claimed for themselves and others from the same place. A place register is thus deeply engaged with the regulation and representation of a space's use and users. And like other elements of an area's linguistic landscape, different place registers are employed to create texts that appeal to certain users, or following Warner (2002), specific publics. One might describe government signage as a formal place register that, as we mentioned in the Introduction, uses textual features to de-localize place and to make all places within a jurisdiction of power semiotically uniform.

Register usually tends to operate in a straightforward way as people recognize it as either appropriate or inappropriate language for the context, often without thinking much about how it operates as a defining characteristic of the very context that it in fact functions to create. Arguably, Old School Brooklyn signage, with its word-rich, repetitive, and descriptively sincere texts, helps manage a place of tremendous diversity by taking a nonstandard but egalitarian stand on communication, people, and place-identity. The features of Old School signage literally say that they configure a market where there is a place for all, irrespective of differences. Such differences, incidentally, are never erased, avoided, or ignored in the Old School landscape. Instead, at least with respect to what is written on the signs, the community's differences are openly referred to and presumably tolerated if not whole-heartedly accepted. In contrast, the features of New School signage function to redefine Brooklyn's neighborhoods as hip, cool, fashionable, and stylish. But in addition to examining how New School signs operate to attract newcomers to place, we want to explore more closely how some of its features stratify social groups and create hierarchy among them in a way that starkly and dramatically diverges from the meaning and message of place creation of Old School signage. Although several elements of New School signage operate to create these feelings of social, economic, and cultural distinction, in the remainder of this chapter, we will specifically examine New School's reliance on wordplay in its function as a register of place.[4]

Linguist Eva Kittay (1987) defines wordplay as "purposive ambiguity." Studies have shown that ambiguities and vagaries in language help to keep things interesting and fun for all sorts of linguistic contexts. Rather than immediately trying to resolve ambiguity, people purposefully retain the undefined nature of some linguistic elements in order to keep the human brain excited. People in conversation often play with ambiguity and polysemy in order to enhance or electrify the context of interaction (Nehrlich and Clarke

2001). At the same time, to be successful and meaningful, play with words also involves indexing its readers' social group membership and the insider nature of their knowledge. As we have seen earlier, to understand some references on New School signage may require deciphering a code that relies on either specialized education or research that goes beyond the sign itself.

Wordplay in New School signage exists at every linguistic level: (1) at the lexical level where simple yet provocative words such as *Beast*, *seed*, and *Dirty Precious* adorn new storefronts; (2) at the morphophonological level, where sound similarities are used in puns such as *Baked in Brooklyn* for a bakery in Greenwood Heights, or *Pork Slope* for a charcuterie and *Pup Slope* for a pet grooming business in Park Slope; and (3) at the orthographic level on a sign for a frozen yogurt shop called /eks/ in Prospect Heights. The name is represented in a phonetic transcription from the International Phonetic Alphabet, which linguists are trained to use to represent the sounds of any spoken language. Not surprisingly, wordplay is not a common feature in Old School signage.

Once we noticed the pervasive play as an integral feature of New Brooklyn signage, we found that contemplating their meanings was fun and interesting to us. We could take any sign and see how far we could go with reading the range of its available meanings. Indeed, some reviewers of our work have suggested that we have read "too much" into some signs' possible meanings. But we also hasten to point out that our search for possible meanings is not unlike the work of literary critics who do a close reading or critical interpretation of a text. Literary criticism often takes shape because of the deep contextual knowledge the analyst has of the work in time and place. And while this is our aim in our own analysis, the reader will decide whether we have "gone too far" (or not gone far enough) with the potential or available meanings of these signs.

Additionally, when we present available meanings as possibilities, we take the concept *available* to mean accessible to any possible reader. Unlike a novel or a poem, storefront signs exist in public, so they could at any moment be read by anyone, that is, any type of person from anywhere. That some readers strive to suggest that one sign or another does not "really" have the meaning that we identify as a possible one restricts the concept of available meaning that is itself an important language ideology. This stance reveals an assumption based on that reader's own positionality, that what the sign really means and what the shopkeeper's intention was can be safely concluded. We make no claim to knowing any shopkeeper's intention, and when a sign is ambiguous, we cannot assert that any specific meaning takes prominence.

We will, however, suggest that New School shopkeepers probably did very little, at least in comparison to their Old School counterparts, to resolve ambiguities on their signage. And we make this claim based on the data we find in the signs.

Below, we provide a reading of the possible meanings of several examples of New School signs. Our analysis focuses on how the ambiguity of these texts functions in dialogue with place on multiple levels, leaving them open to all sorts of possible interpretations. We then probe more deeply into the available messages of these polysemous signs and their implications for place-making.

Play with Words: Making Intimacy on the Street

Our first example of wordplay is a sign for a maternity store in Park Slope that says "bump" (Figure 2.1). For us, this four-letter word conjures many associations, some funny, some mundane, and some taboo. For starters, we find journalists often speculating as to whether celebrity women might be pregnant by writing about the possibility of "a baby bump." So the rounded belly of a pregnant woman is one available interpretation for *bump*. In this case, though, the word *baby* is missing from the sign, and the word *bump*, therefore, remains ambiguous. For us, it also summons to mind other meanings, such as in the common phrase "things that go bump in the night," which refers to frightening supernatural beings. Here, we might further suggest that pregnancy presents somewhat terrifying life changes for parents (a "bump in the road" toward certain plans). And *bump* can also stand in as a slang term for the taboo referent *sexual intercourse*, as in "when we go bump in the night" or the phrase "to bump uglies," meaning "to have sex." The word *bump* plays not only with the idea that pregnancy causes women to have a *bump* but also that babies are made by a *bump*.[5] The ambiguous sign all at once euphemizes and emphasizes women's bodies, the sex act, and the creation of family, as well as the long, sleepless nights that come with newborns.

A second example is Big Nose, Full Body, a Park Slope wine store. The words likely refer to the taste, texture, and smell of wine as they are commonly discussed in wine notes. But taken more literally, the words can be interpreted to be an impolite remark about physical appearances, a reference to art, or a metaphor for the art of winemaking. The juxtaposition of these two

<figure>

Figure 2.1. A one-word sign for an upscale maternity store.
</figure>

corporal features could index heteronormative sex, where a *big nose* is phallic/masculine and a *full body* is voluptuous/feminine. Big noses are also suggestive of Picasso's paintings and full bodies of the work of Rubens.[6] The arguably elite allusion to wine notes coupled with the more taboo meanings helps to produce a place where passersby can cognitively engage in a particular sort of meaning-making exercise that allows them to also imagine and foster the particular type of place in which they live.

As we mentioned earlier, both gentrifiers and old timers told us that the appearance of these polysemous or cryptic signs meant neighborhood change. Sparsely worded storefronts with wordplay on their signs indicated that rents were on the rise, home values were increasing, and wealthier people would be moving in. But how such signage facilitates gentrification is a sociolinguistic function of the very ambiguity and playfulness of their texts.

For many early gentrifiers, Brooklyn was constructed as a "real" or "authentic" albeit "gritty" place to be. Our research suggests that in this context, wordplay on local New School storefronts could create a sense of

Figure 2.2. This restaurant's name, The Farm on Adderley, appears only on the storefront's plate glass window.

togetherness. This message of togetherness is especially important to gentrifying newcomers who tell us that moving into economically depressed neighborhoods seemed risky to them. The inside jokes of such storefronts might have helped to indicate that there were people like them in the landscape, both in terms of shopkeepers and in terms of other patrons. While gentrifiers may not have seen a lot of people like themselves on the street, the textual and compositional playfulness of New Brooklyn storefronts can act as an index for newcomers that there were others who shared their reading practices, education, and cultural knowledge in the area. In other words, wordplay on New Brooklyn signage signals a specific public at the same time it helps to create one.

Though gentrification is well underway, beyond the reality of rising rents, the process does not always look complete in many still extremely diverse Brooklyn neighborhoods. At one end of the spectrum there are neighborhoods like Brooklyn Heights, an area that has ultimately experienced the super-gentrification of the top 1 percent (Lees 2003). Even so, those top earners live relatively close to areas like Gowanus and Red Hook, both of which show substantial signs of gentrification, but which continue to struggle to provide what gentrifiers perceive as adequate public schools and other services that they deem necessary.

Moreover, there are some neighborhoods where there are still very poor people living literally next door, often in the same building, with very wealthy people. So New School signage becomes a linguistic resource, a place register that also communicates to newcomers that there are people around with whom they have things in common. Wordplay, alongside New School's other essential features of brevity, pithiness, erudition, and polysemy, has the power to create feelings of not only familiarity, but also of intimacy, with anonymous but probably like-minded, similarly educated and employed readers. Store names such as Big Nose, Full Body, and Bump permit readers to engage with private topics in public with their new imagined community, which in turn can provoke sentiments believed to be enjoyed by other friendly shoppers in public spaces with whom one might share an affinity or rapport. By merely reading public texts in this playful register, gentrifiers can feel privy to inside jokes, see their linguistic and intertextual reading practices in the landscape, and consequently picture themselves and others like them in place. One can then feel "at home" in a place that is full of possibility and full of meaning, but because of clear income disparities and cultural diversity, in a place that is, at the same time, seemingly risky.

This sense of risk is sometimes expressed through playfully cryptic New School signage that functions as quite subtle expressions of uneasiness in place. Take for example the signage found on the Ditmas Park restaurant The Farm on Adderley (Figure 2.2). There is no overhead sign with words to advertise its presence on the street; only a small signboard projects perpendicularly from the building façade on a metal post. On it there is a simple pencil-grey sketch of a barn and a silo. Etched in script on the front plate-glass window in lowercase letters are the words "the farm." Below them, in smaller font, and in all capital letters are the words "ON ADDERLEY."

At first glance, the name seems to fit right in with other public texts in the neighborhood, as many of the surrounding Flatbush streets have traditional upper-class British names: Westminster, Stratford, Argyle, and Marlborough. In the late 1800s, amongst the bucolic farmsteads of this area, Victorian malls were built and then lined with large single-family Victorian homes. But the restaurant is not on a street named Adderley but rather on Cortelyou Road, a main commercial district running through the mostly residential blocks of Ditmas Park. The name *The Farm on Adderley* alludes to another place, not in Great Britain, but in South Africa. The restaurant's owners, a South African married couple, revealed in an article in *Edible Brooklyn*, a locally oriented food, wine, and spirits lifestyle magazine, that the name of their establishment comes from a South African saying, "When there is a farm on Adderley!" (Matsumoto 2012). In this expression, the word *Adderley* refers to one of the busiest streets in Cape Town and thus, it would be highly unlikely to find a farm there. So the saying is used when conditions or facts are implausible to the matter or context at hand. The equivalent idiomatic expression in American English might be "When pigs fly!" or "When hell freezes over." And since the restaurant's playful name is auto-referential in more ways than one, we can imagine how the owners themselves might struggle with—and at times delight in—the fact that they and their business are located not just in New York City, but in a part of Brooklyn that has not had upscale farm-to-table restaurants in its recent history.

The irony "in play" in The Farm on Adderly's name is also in dialogue with the area's rapid changes and lingering economic disparities. While many of the Victorian houses lining the British-named streets of Ditmas Park have been restored from multiple occupancy dwellings to single-family homes, this transformation occurred in fits and starts. Even in the early 2000s, when other parts of Brooklyn were already heavily gentrified, the *New York Times* still wrote about the area as a "best kept secret" (Wilson 2003), despite the fact that thousands of people have always lived there. But the neighborhood's value continued to increase, and quickly. When we were selling our Flatbush apartment, Brooklyn real estate guru Roselyn Huebner came to our home and told us about the Victorian home she bought on Stratford Road that became

Figure 2.3. An example of polysemous wordplay using the word *Brooklyn* in the store's name.

WHAT THE SIGNS SAY

newsworthy. She had restored it in 1999 then sold it to a "young family" for $1.02 million in 2005. The *New York Times* reported it was the first home in that neighborhood to sell for over a million dollars (Wilson 2005). This million-dollar house on Stratford Road, however, was also just one block away from a stretch of Westminster Road between Caton and Church Avenues labelled by Columbia University urban geographers as a "million-dollar block" (Kurgan, Cadora, et al. 2015). The million-dollar threshold in this case, though, indicates the amount of money that the state is spending on incarcerating the residents of a single city block and indicates it has one of the *densest* populations of formerly incarcerated persons.

Thus when it was established in 2007, the name *The Farm on Adderley* pointed to the oddity that there was now something like a "farm" again in the middle of Flatbush, Brooklyn, but it was really a restaurant selling upscale food, sourced from animals that were carefully raised on local farms (but not necessarily farms in Ditmas Park!). So The Farm on Adderley captured the irony of its own existence as an exquisite dining experience amid a low-income and at the time still racially segregated neighborhood right on the sign. But cracking the sign's coded meaning required the reader to solve a puzzle that involved reading far beyond the sign (a literary practice much like the ones identified in Heath's (1982) study of middle- and upper-middle-class families).

In addition to this story in *Edible Brooklyn*, we found another version of it in a best-of-new-Brooklyn-restaurants-for-foodies cookbook called *The New Brooklyn Cookbook* (Vaughn, Vaughn, and Turkell 2010). But many new Brooklyn restaurants and other retail establishments also tend to have websites where they link to favorable press and media coverage of their businesses. A Google search for "The Farm on Adderley" would of course also bring up the stories written about it in *New York Magazine*, the *New Yorker*'s "Tables for Two" feature, and the like. While curious readers could always hunt on the Internet for more information about businesses with New School cryptic names, not everyone rushes to know what the name of a place means. For some people, it seems, not knowing what a name means may help to keep the place interesting.

New School signage also seems to make bold claims about place. Take for instance "brooklynbread," found in Park Slope (Figure 2.3). Orthographically, this storefront contains a compound word made up of two nouns: the place *Brooklyn* combined with the bakery item *bread*. But the two words also create a polysemous term that encodes other meanings. First, brooklynbread ostensibly refers to an establishment that makes and sells "bread" in Brooklyn. But it is still ambiguous. Does this mean the bread was "made in Brooklyn," just sold there, or crafted in a Brooklyn style? And the word *bread* also has synecdochal

Figure 2.4. This wordplay invokes Brooklyn with a textual format akin to what is found in a dictionary entry.

meanings of basic human economic and spiritual subsistence, as in "Man does not live by bread alone," or in the line of the Lord's Prayer, "Give us this day, our daily bread." *Bread* is also slang for money, and thus the sign could also be interpreted as a crass remark about capitalizing on the Brooklyn brand. But interestingly, the word *bread* in the store's name is a homophone for the perfective form of the verb *to breed*. So now the sign becomes a *specific* type of claim to Brooklyn. Here, *bred* refers to place of origin and/or to being brought up in a place. Therefore, who or whatever it is indexing was supposedly "born and raised in Brooklyn," making a legitimacy claim to the land through the cultural concept of birthright and upbringing. With this interpretation the sign engages in a spirited dialogue with current debates about what it means "to be from Brooklyn," simultaneously entailing issues of authenticity and rights of belonging.

Interestingly, Old School shop signs in our data set hardly ever incorporate the borough's name. Old School register, instead, focuses on the local, the neighborhood, and often the exact coordinates (e.g., street, nearby cross street, or neighborhood name) where a place of business can be found. For example, bakeries with Old School signage such as 4th Ave Bakery (in Bay Ridge) or Northside Bakery (in Greenpoint) are literal about locating placedness. Through such features of this place register of signage, we see how Old School businesses are disposed toward an intra-borough, or even an intra-neighborhood commerce. The register suggests no intention of attracting people from other boroughs or other places.

Our sign maker-informants also noted how other new businesses attempted to incorporate the term *Brooklyn* creatively into their names, obviously drawing on its fashionableness and marketing cachet. When we showed them a photograph of "['brook·vin]," a wine store in Park Slope (Figure 2.4), one of the sign makers said, "'Brook-vine,' you know, it's a wine store." When we pointed out that it was written in a faux version of a dictionary entry, the sign maker remarked that "everyone's trying to figure out a different way to write 'Brooklyn.' That's another latest craze!" (interview with authors, June 29, 2017).

With New School signage that boldly claims the entire borough as its own, we see the indexing of the emergence of an inter- versus intra-borough shift in Brooklyn commercial life. This shift was first ushered in by a few enterprising locals and was followed by a wave of newcomers. Notably, these first moves to place-claiming were met with initial skepticism. For example, the *New York Times*, in 2008, wrote skeptically about companies branding with Brooklyn as part of their name with the following opening paragraph about Steve Hindy, a former war correspondent and Brooklyn native who cofounded the company Brooklyn Brewery: "There was a time, decades ago, when Steve Hindy's friends couldn't believe what he and his partner wanted to call their new business. Brooklyn Brewery? Why, people wondered, would you name a beer after that place?" (Mooney 2008). Hindy started brewing in the late 1980s and opened Brooklyn Brewery in 1996 with the intention of selling beer not only in Brooklyn but to places outside of it as well. Twenty years later, the beer maker does over $23 million dollars in sales.

In 2015, the Brooklyn website *Brownstoner* amassed a list of all things that use *Brooklyn* in their names. While not all the nearly one hundred entries are small business storefronts (for instance, the list includes the Brooklyn Bridge, the Brooklyn Museum, the Brooklyn Nets), nearly half of them are New School businesses ranging from Brooklyn Gin and My Brooklyn Baby to Bklyn Larder and the Brooklyn Watch Company (Eldredge 2015). By 2018, one Forest City Ratner executive observed in an NYU Schack Institute interview that the Brooklyn name practically sells itself (NYUSPS UrbanLab 2018).

How this came to be, we argue, was a contextual process intimately linked to gentrification. As businesses that fancied themselves distinctive began to open in Brooklyn, using the name of the borough in a store's name distinguished it from stores like it in Manhattan. As more artists and artisans began to create a "small-batch" production style in Brooklyn itself, the use of the word moved from marking these endeavors as distinctive from others to marking them as distinctive in general. Brooklyn is now branded as local and not local, meaning the use of *Brooklyn* signifies localness to its residents at the same time it orients Brooklyn to the outside as a commodity for sale.

The word *Brooklyn* in a business's name is thus evidence of its centrality in many people's minds. Many of the New Yorkers we have talked to, especially our academic colleagues who were born in Brooklyn, state that they wanted to get out of the borough and move to Manhattan (or out of the city altogether). But first and subsequent waves of gentrifiers began to redefine Brooklyn as a place that was different from other New York City boroughs. Assuming the borough's name for their new businesses could be about paying homage to the historical role of the borough in nation building, wearing it as a badge of honor, or claiming to have an "authentic" product. Presently in Manhattan, there are restaurants and diners with Brooklyn in their names like Brooklyn Diner and the Brooklyner. And as we find Brooklyn elsewhere, even globally, it is clear that the name has become worthy of claiming, confirming Zukin's contention that Brooklyn is now a destination.

This centering of Brooklyn in contrast to Manhattan is whimsically represented by the New School sign Brooklyn Industries (Figure 2.5). This sign not only proudly lays claim to the entire borough but also puts Brooklyn in a direct semiotic dialogue with Manhattan. In the foreground is a Brooklyn rooftop-scape in black silhouette with the iconic Manhattan skyline in the background. The composition privileges Brooklyn but joins the two boroughs in a nod to the recent reverse migration story of many new Brooklynites who came from Manhattan. Its website tells us that the skyline on the sign is a view from Williamsburg—the once über-industrial zone now teeming with New York City's twenty-something creative types (Susser 2012).

Urban scholars have noted how post-industrial urban "productivity" is presently exemplified by small-scale soap, jewelry, and pickle making or the proliferation of creative service careers of artist, musician, designer, or chef (Florida 2012; Zukin 2010; Ley 1996). Brooklyn Industries is one of the retail stores that capitalized on this wave of artisanal production. The company began as a manufacturer of messenger bags made from recycled billboards and evolved into a designer clothing store. The nostalgic use of *Industries* in

Figure 2.5. (right) The sign for Brooklyn Industries is a banner on a metal pole. Note the Brooklyn skyline in front of Manhattan's more famous silhouette. The Empire State Building is adjacent to a water tower, a common symbol for Brooklyn.

Figure 2.6. (above) Brooklyn Industries' slogan, on the exterior side wall of one of its Park Slope shops, above open garbage cans.

the name props up manufacturing as part of Brooklyn's origins through the concept of industrial-heritage (Benito del Pozo and Alonso González 2012). The company's slogan, "LIVE, WORK, CREATE," is prominently stenciled on the side of one of the Park Slope store's buildings, right above open garbage cans (Figure 2.6). Appearing as a graffiti-tag, this slogan epitomizes the new Brooklyn order of things where (soon-to-be) affluent people can work at their "craft," create their art, and establish their way of life in an urban space once thought of as marginal to Manhattan.[7] The industrial aesthetic itself not only gets reverently repurposed in the transformative uses of the materials associated with Brooklyn's factory age, but it also gets taken up as a clothing style. Brooklyn Industries proposes what appears to be a simultaneously nostalgic and progressive attitude on fashion by reclaiming industry and grit as in vogue. Its signage helps to redefine the borough as a place with the possibility of fabricating a cool way of life for newcomers to be productive.

From 2000 to 2003, however, Brooklyn lost over eleven thousand manufacturing jobs. Domino Sugar closed its Williamsburg refinery in 2004, and the Pfizer corporation closed its chemical plant in the same neighborhood four years later, in 2008. With semiotic humor, Brooklyn Industries both appropriates and exploits the motif of mid-twentieth-century industry, but absent the factories and working-class jobs. Thus, to some, the nostalgia may appear as a taunting celebration in light of the departure of large-scale manufacturers from the borough.

Appropriations of the borough's name, along with joking and ironic references to class identities and historical forms of American labor, are not the only ways that new Brooklyn businesses assert themselves in place on signage. Lifestyle, home, and family are also prominent themes. For example, just three blocks from The Farm on Adderley is a sign for a restaurant called Picket Fence (Figure 2.7). This two-word sign is composed of green lowercase letters on top of white fencing material on a yellow background. On an ancillary sign is a phone number and two more words, also in lowercase letters: "comfortable food." Their website states that the shop's name refers to Ditmas Park's history as a bucolic, affluent, and suburb-like area. *Picket fence* is a phrase that indicates homeownership and the rights and privileges it engenders. Another association with *picket fence* is an idealized American lifestyle of privacy, economic stability, and the ability to control an otherwise unencumbered area. Accompanying this control of space is the idea of movement up the socioeconomic ladder, mainly accomplished by physically moving out of the city and into the suburbs. However, we read other insinuations in the sign as well.

On this sign, although the word *white* is absent, the elliptical construction "white picket fence" is readily available to American English-speaking passersby. Linguists define an elliptical construction as a phrase that is inferable from context alone. And *picket fence* often collocates in American English with the word *white* as a modifier—thus "white picket fence." One could read this sign as a cheekily confrontational text, where a symbol of white suburban middle-class comfort and security hangs prominently on the street in the middle of a working class and poor, nonwhite neighborhood. The section of Cortelyou Road upon which *picket fence* sits straddles two zip codes: 11218 and 11226. Each

Figure 2.8. Note the silhouette of a child in a yellow taxi apparently headed for the destination "brooklyn." The words urban and monster invoke a range of meanings.

has very different socioeconomic demographics. To the northwest of Corte-lyou lies the neighborhood of Kensington, with a largely middle class, white (60 percent) and increasingly more Hispanic (20 percent) and Asian (19 percent) population of thirty-seven thousand. To the south and east of the area is a largely working-poor Flatbush population of about one hundred thousand people, where one in four residents lives on a salary below the poverty line.[8]

The words *comfortable food* also have many available meanings. First, there is an elaboration of the "comfort food movement" trendy in the 2000s. *Comfort food* refers to home-cooked, family-style Americana dishes such as fried chicken, mashed potatoes, and macaroni and cheese, food that is meant to console the ailing, lonely, or heartbroken. But here, the sign reads "comfortable food," which might beckon to patrons needing solace because they might feel uneasy, awkward, or nervous. On one level, both the phrases *picket fence* and *comfortable food* can be interpreted as minimizing what discourse analysts Charles Briggs and Richard Bauman call intertextual gaps (Briggs and Bauman 1992). Intertextual gaps are gaps between the contexts of texts. While the texts *picket fence* and *comfortable food* index idealized, "down home" values of small-town America, they do so in a strikingly different context. The terms try to close the gap between the suburban or idyllic and the diversity and complexity of city space. But the words could also be read as maximizing the contextual gap between constructs of stereotypical wholesome, white, middle-class values, and stereotypes of vice-ridden communities of working-poor and racialized people living in the "inner city." Viewed in this way, the sign marks a place where newcomers may feel like they can escape their anxieties of not fitting in with and perhaps even feeling threatened by the communities of the neighborhood to which they have moved. Of course, *comfortable food* might also suggest that anyone and everyone can feel cozy and pleasant while eating there. But to some longstanding community members, this establishment might appear to be literally putting up a "fence" that marks itself as apart from the neighborhood and perhaps unwelcoming to the people in it.

Another sign in our data set with themes of home and family in dialogue with underlying issues of belonging and displacement, uses a supposedly humorous invasion motif. Brooklyn Urban Monster, an upscale children's clothing store on Atlantic Avenue (Figure 2.8), includes a prankish phrase and an equally mischievous image of a taxi being driven by a baby with the word *Brooklyn* on the car's roof. In black silhouette, the child has just four straight hairs standing on end, and thus, might very well be white.[9] Conceptualizations of monsters in the urban context come into our American imaginary with King Kong (in New York) and Godzilla (in post–World War II Tokyo), the monsters in old movies shown on television of the Saturday afternoons of our youth. But here, *urban monster* could also be read as a play on the two-word epithet *little monster*, another common American English collocation, meaning "unruly, bratty little children."[10] The phrase *little monster* is an ironic disparaging term of endearment used by many American English-speakers to lessen the importance of either their children or their imperfect behavior. In terms of this sign, the substitution of *urban* for *little* not only marks the store for newcomers, but it also distinguishes them from their suburban counterparts. *New York Magazine* described Urban Monster as "part store, part community resource . . . the go-to spot for hip Brooklyn moms" (October 4, 2005). The semiotics of this sign, its wording, and its reference in a major weekly magazine all suggest that these urban monsters are the children of gentrifiers most of whom, though not all, tend to be white.

For decades the term *urban* had been used in media and municipal policy-making and by the larger public as a euphemism to refer to poor inner-city populations that, because of redlining, tended to be predominantly African American or Afro-Latino. At John Jay College, where we work, for example, there is a program called the Urban Male Initiative. This program's mission statement begins by saying "The Urban Male Initiative (UMI) is a program for all students on campus, particularly, men of color."[11] Modan (2017) suggests that the term *urban* has been re-appropriated or reclaimed by gentrifiers. In some ways we see this re-appropriation as a self-congratulatory term used by gentrifiers to signify their hipness because of their own residence in urban space. This particular meaning of hipness is made possible because the term *urban* retains some of its original meanings of crime, decay, and poverty. From our field research in Brooklyn, however, we would like to add that the meaning of *urban* for gentrifiers also entails ideas such as "complex," "complicated," and "diverse." For many gentrifiers, homogeneous spaces and places are ostensibly simpler and presumably easier to figure out than are multicultural urban spaces.

The sign "brooklyn urban monster" indexes different groups of people both directly and indirectly (Ochs 1990). First, the term *monster*, as an ironic endearing reference to a child, could indicate a commonality of class experience between urban gentrifiers and their suburban counterparts and thus serves to minimize another sort of intertextual gap (Briggs and Bauman 1992)—in this case, the out-of-place-ness that the image indexes. At the same time, the substitution of *urban* for *little* also maximizes the contextual gap between the newcoming, rich urbanite children who tend to be white and poor urbanite children who have historically been thought of as either black or Latino, and

WHAT THE SIGNS SAY

who, in fact, had been already living in the city. Plus, we argue that the term *urban monster* probably would not succeed in being "cute" to anyone if it were meant to refer to African American children en masse. This sign is also ironically self-referential because the modifier *urban*, defined in this case as "gentrifying," points to the group "gentrifiers," and therefore presumably white children, as a new and newsworthy demographic in the social life of the city. In fact, the entire array of *available* meanings "at play" in this sign possessively lays stakes as an intriguing cultural signpost for gentrifiers.

Media coverage on Brooklyn corroborates our reading of this sign. During the first three years of the 2000s, the *New York Times* reported that the number of white children in the city "increased by 11 percent, with the biggest increases found in gentrifying Manhattan and Brooklyn" (Roberts 2011). By mid-decade, the *Times* reported, the population growth of white children was accelerating. Driving the growth were "wealthy white families . . . [whose] ranks expanded by more than 40 percent from 2000 to 2005. For the first time since at least the 1960s, white children now outnumber either black or Hispanic youngsters in that age group in Manhattan. . . . As Manhattan becomes the wealthiest area in the country, middle income whites are following the urbanization trend and moving . . . into Brooklyn" (Roberts 2007). New School signs of gentrification, like Brooklyn Urban Monster and other examples we have shown thus far, make apparent a new population lives in the city. This population claims its place through all sorts of semiotic, linguistic, and reading practices that appear on storefronts. In this way, the playful language of new Brooklyn shops is used both as a home-making tool and as a way to make one's self at home. At the same time that it connects some people and attracts more newcomers in a seemingly good-natured way, the wordplay employed can also operate in a more threatening manner. We now turn to a more in-depth study of this phenomenon.

Catchy Exclusions

Occasionally, people with whom we shared our ideas—whether living in Brooklyn or outside of the city—suggested that we were reading too much into the signs. In fact, one woman who lives in a small town about a two-hour drive from New York City said she thought store owners "just wanted something catchy" for their shop names.[12] While we agree that "catchy" is one purpose for ambiguity, we argue that there are sociolinguistic reasons why some language usages are catchy and others are unremarkable. For example, the use of *urban* to modify *monster* works as catchy because it heightens people's awareness that something is amiss, interesting, and unusual. That children nowadays live in the city is not remarkable because children always have. The sign for Urban Monster makes visible the presence of newcomers and their children who are mostly white and affluent—the opposite of what urban children were thought to be decades ago—without actually saying so. Through its intertextuality, Urban Monster manages to simultaneously use and render invisible African American and Latino children who were already in place. Similarly, returning to the example of the maternity store Bump, in Figure 2.1, one might argue that the word *bump* is a verb that means to move something or someone forcibly if unintentionally out of a space, which interestingly, is one of the common definitions for the word *gentrification*. While store owners might not have meant this particular definition of *bump*, once readers catch on to the way this New School register works, there is, of course, no reason they might not arrive at this meaning.

In addition to signaling upscale exclusivity, signs that employ wordplay such as Picket Fence and Urban Monster may also come off as coarse, boorish, and even offensive with respect to populations already in place. Another example is a sign for a garden store on Atlantic Avenue that has one short word in lowercase letters: "dig" (Figure 2.9). The sign is small, hanging from a post perpendicular to the building. The words *outdoor* and *indoor*—also in lowercase letters—occupy each corner of a black awning. At first glance, the word *dig* (both as a noun, "a dig," and as a verb, "to dig") obviously refers to the work that goes into making a garden. But *dig* has many possible meanings, ranging from "to stand firmly" to "a tease or taunt."[13] Sociolinguist Geneva Smitherman (2000) identifies *dig* also as an African Americanism in, for example, "They really dig our music," (meaning "enjoy"), or "Do you dig?" (meaning "understand/like"). These usages can be found in Zora Neale Hurston's fiction, first published in the 1930s, and in the popular 1970s television comedy *Good Times*.[14] The polysemy and the play this word packs is interesting in the Brooklyn context where space and place are being appropriated and changed. Arguably, urban gardens have been a practice for all socioeconomic classes, but this sign seems to beckon to people who have economic resources, land, and leisure time.[15] As applied to gardening (e.g., "I dig gardening"), the word *dig* expresses zeal and passion for the hobby. It looks imperative, perhaps, to say, "Dig gardening indoors and outdoors." But in a poor area, an upscale garden store can appear threatening, a dig as in a jeer, a kind of "in-your-face" performance of the newcomers' wealth.

Figure 2.9. This garden store, called just "dig," can be read as making an ironic reference to race through the linguistic appropriation of the word's meaning "to like," which originates in African American English.

Another garden store nearby to Dig, and also on Atlantic Avenue, is called Botanica, and it sells high priced potting plants, cactuses, and succulents (Figure 2.10). Once again, we have a storefront with just one word on it whose meaning is ambiguous. In general, the word *botanica* comes from Latin and means botany, or the scientific study of plants, their physiology, environments, and classification. In this way Botanica indexes and calls to those who have an esoteric knowledge of plants, maybe even of their Latinate names. The word *botanica* also seems a root for the more common *botanical* in English, often used to refer to gardens, teas, or shampoos with plant extracts. Linguists suggest that context usually acts to disambiguate words with multiple meanings. However, in this case, context creates the ambiguity in meanings, because in Brooklyn, a place where 20 percent of the borough's population is Latino, the word *botanica* commonly refers to a shop that caters to the Latino community, selling herbal and other traditional remedies, charms, incense, and candles used for religious or spiritual purposes.

Following the work of linguists Jane Hill (1998) and Geneva Smitherman (2000), we see words such as *dig* and *botanica* as linguistic appropriations or *mock* forms of other languages or other dialects of English. Hill (1998, 2008) argues that mock forms of some languages and dialects, like Spanish or

African American English, are used by nonnative speakers to perform a casual or informal *stance*, or the way in which speakers position themselves in an interaction (see Jaffe 2009). Hill's research focuses on mock forms of Spanish as used by people who are typically white and not Hispanic. An example of mock Spanish would be when a white person who speaks very limited Spanish uses the Spanish word *mañana!* to say "Good-bye!" even though no Spanish-speaker would ever use just this word in a leave-taking context. The instances are numerous, and new forms of mock can always be generated.[16] Hill concludes that using mock forms has become a sociolinguistic practice of whites for other whites, and its intended meanings may fail for, and even offend, Latinos/Spanish-speakers.

In our data, the indexicality of mock conspires with polysemy: these uses of *dig* and *botanica* directly index casual, cool urban informality, but only because they *indirectly* point to negative or quaint stereotypical conceptualizations of the groups of people who speak these languages or dialects. In this case, *dig*

Figure 2.10. Here is another upscale garden store; this one uses a word that is either Spanish or Latin for plants.

WHAT THE SIGNS SAY

can be considered a mock-like term because it rather ironically marks "race." In comparison, consider Mitchell's Soul Food (Figure 2.11), which makes a straightforward reference to race, in a way that Jackson's (2005) theory of racial sincerity would deem as a sincere racial term. The use of *dig* by and for white, nonnative speakers of the African American dialect in order to be catchy is also quite coy. Similarly, *botanica* on an upscale garden store is used without any regard for how the local Latino/Spanish-speaking community in Brooklyn might interpret it. In Figure 2.12, there is an example of a typical traditional *botanica* that serves Brooklyn's Latino community. Perhaps the available ethnic and racialized meanings on both these garden stores make the words on these signs more exciting and more interesting than they are without them, but they easily could be read by some as unsettling linguistic appropriations by white, upper-middle class people who want to appear unstuffy or laid-back.

Another example is a restaurant and bar called Don Chingon, on Flatbush Avenue, directly across from the Barclays Center. Its meaning could be translated

Figure 2.11. On Mitchell's Restaurant is a sincere reference to race: "Soul Food."

Figure 2.12. A traditional botanica in Sunset Park with text in Spanish and English.

from Spanish as a masculine figure who is a badass or a "badass motherfucker" in either a good or a bad way, depending on tone or affect.[17] We discussed this term with Hispanist linguists and anthropologists and with native Spanish speakers from Puerto Rico, the Dominican Republic, and Mexico, and found many different interpretations ranging from very positive to very negative. Most people concluded, however, that there would be some speakers within their ethnolinguistic group—such as parents or grandparents—who would consider having "Don Chingon" on a sign inappropriate for public space. Among other things, mock forms allow speakers from dominant culture to use taboo words that they would be far less likely to employ in these contexts in their own languages.[18]

Both Hill (2008) and Smitherman (2000) find that many African Americans see linguistic appropriations like this as a type of theft because the appropriators have not paid the same emotional or social dues to use them. In doing fieldwork, we have found that many urban newcomers believe they have "paid dues" of some kind because the neighborhoods they have moved into have been neglected by landlords, city maintenance, and commercial and individual investment. For example, gentrifying Prospect Heights residents living near the Atlantic Yards project footprint told us that they organized "community clean-ups" in the area around their newly purchased condos, which were valued at over a half a million dollars in 2003. These clean-ups included gathering with their neighbors to pick up trash and remove unsightly abandoned items around the railyards such as cars, washing machines, and refrigerators. Additionally, other informants have also suggested that they had to endure living in crime-ridden neighborhoods with robberies, drug deals, and shootings.[19]

When we asked a couple of store owners about the possibility of their signage being in some way derogatory, they claimed it was not their intention and that no one ever complained about it. Arguably, whatever the shop owners say, their intentions are still impossible to know. In fact, their intentions may also be irrelevant to the feelings of those possibly offended. But an intention to offend was never admitted to by any shop owner we spoke with.

Unintended offense and appropriations are also probably not uncommon. Take, for example, a 2015 case about a cocktail named Strange Fruit served at a Cambridge, Massachusetts, bar. A Boston University medical student asked the server why the bar had a drink referring to the lynching of African Americans in the US as memorialized in the 1939 Billie Holiday song with the same title.[20] As it turned out, the server, the bar owners, and the person who made up the cocktail list all said they had been unaware of the phrase and the song as a reference to lynching. The owners said the bar had a history of naming drinks after banned books and the name of the drink was intended to refer to the 1944 novel *Strange Fruit*, written by Lillian Smith, about an interracial romance (Levy 2015). Smith's book was banned in Detroit and Boston. The owners and the cocktail designer said that they should have known the reference to Billie Holiday and lynching and admitted to being embarrassed about not knowing it (Hoppenfeld 2015). In another case, the writers of a blog and vegan cookbook called *Thug Kitchen* (2014) came under scrutiny for their use of the word *thug*. One of the cookbook's authors, Matt Holloway, was quoted as saying: "Where I grew up [in Texas] thug was a bad mother who looked out for No. 1." The authors argued that *thug* was shorthand for "We're not going to apologize for eating healthy. We're not going to serve you shots of wheat grass" (Green 2015). And the *New York Times* writer Penelope Green paraphrased their explanation in the following way: "The language, they say, is about poking fun at the preciousness of veganism, and claiming it for folks like themselves, which is to say people on a budget" (Green 2015).

In both instances, when people suggested that Strange Fruit and *Thug Kitchen* were offensive, those responsible said they meant no harm. The *Thug Kitchen* authors' response, however, suggests that people knew that they were doing something communicatively critical with words, but they might not have understood how polysemy can work sociolinguistically to also allow for the emergence of a racist interpretation of their word choice. When one of us introduced the story of *Thug Kitchen* to our African American and Latino students at John Jay College, one of them knowingly stated, "Oh, so they wanted to black it up?" The verb *to black up* is a reference to white performers using dark makeup to paint their faces as black people for the purpose of entertaining an all-white audience with exaggerated racial stereotypes. This tradition, known as minstrelsy or blackface, has a long racist history in American culture, reaching back to the early nineteenth century (Lott 2013).[21] The students' suggestion of a linguistic minstrel show gets at how the use of *thug* here complicates attempts to make veganism look less severe, less special, and less rare or exquisite than the popular nonvegan audience might consider it.[22]

Deep Wordplay: Asserting Hierarchy on a Landscape

At the heart of the difference between the two registers we find on Brooklyn's storefronts is the issue of risking meanings. As we have shown, Old School signs mark the land and its users as nondistinctive, nonhierarchical, and undifferentiated in terms of status. Given the historically diverse socio-economic composition of Brooklyn neighborhoods, the ubiquity of this place register seems rational. It leaves no meaning at risk. In contrast, New School seems to risk a lot. But, as anthropologist Clifford Geertz (1973) would predict, the issues that long-time residents, shop owners, and gentrifiers all face as they make a place for themselves "on the street" are symbolically and socially embedded in the meanings of their signs. In Geertz's classic reading of the Balinese cockfight, he interpreted this common cultural event as a paradigm in which the higher and more equal in status the challengers are in a match, the larger the bets placed on the contestants. Therefore, such matches (where the odds are "even") garner ostensibly irrationally higher wagers from an economic perspective, or what Geertz notes the English philosopher Jeremy Bentham would call "deep plays." But according to Geertz, these wagers make perfect cultural sense. He argues that such bets are not irrational at all, but rather incorporate and enact the normative hierarchies of Balinese society. As everyone bets on high status opponents, they may have only a 50 percent chance of winning, but there is a 100 percent chance of condoning the social hierarchy. Ultimately, wagers risk nothing culturally and reflect and reproduce normative meanings of Balinese authority and social stratification.

In contrast to the Balinese system, the social calculus on the streets of Brooklyn is economically and culturally a bit more complicated. Both gentrifiers and long-time residents read and use public texts to trade in the commodity of place (see Agha 2011). Viewed as Geertzian deep-play bets on one's status value, all shop signs are at once an explicit and potentially risky move to "lay one's public self (allusively and metaphorically) on the line" (Geertz 1973, 434). As Geertz reads the cockfight as a local activity that can be interpreted as a text about maintaining social and cultural relationships, we see Brooklyn signs as local texts that can be read as engaged in either maintaining or transforming place. Thus, Old School signs seem to make linguistic moves that avoid risky plays with words. Using explicit language, indexical sincerity, repetition, and symbol to limit misunderstandings, Old School signs protect meaning and attempt to keep any iterations of hierarchy or notions of status inequalities at bay. Consider, for instance, the response of Zarina, the wife of the owner of an Old School storefront, Nio's West Indian Restaurant and Bakery, a shop that has been open in Flatbush for more than thirty years (Figure 2.13). When asked about how they chose their sign, she said, "Well because our background is West Indian so the name of the owner is Nio, and we named it as Nio's West Indian Restaurant. And we do baking, so we add on the bakery to it" (interview with Akil Fletcher, Student Research Assistant,

February 16, 2017). When pressed to provide more information, Zarina admitted that they had previously had another name for the store:

ZARINA: At first, we had it named Nio's Roti Shop, then we have it as Nio's West Indian Restaurant and Bakery, so we just kind of change it up a little bit and put like West Indian.

AKIL: Just to broaden it up so everyone can know that they can come in?

ZARINA: Right. . . . *Even the white people they come in and they buy West Indian food* because you know they see we sell the roti and stuff. . . . Because we introduce the food to them and they love it. (emphasis added; interview with Akil Fletcher, February 16, 2017).

Though the question, with its explicit statement of "broadening the meaning" of the sign to include everyone, certainly helps to shape Zarina's answer, the fact that she without prompting included "white people" in her reply speaks directly to the idea of capitalism without distinction, a goal to sell to the widest possible range of customers. Zarina also suggests that once introduced to quality roti, anybody would like it. The product sold is "distinctive," but the business is not. When asked why they displayed so many ancillary signs listing the food items one would encounter inside, Zarina replied:

We display it so people have a better option of what they want, you know? We display all the meats so they can see what meat they looking for, you know. If you don't display it, they don't really . . . sometimes you want to buy something and if you don't see it, you don't know what you really want, you know? But if you look at it and you see it, you might say well, ok, well I want this, you know? And I forget to tell you that we also have fish and shrimp! (interview with Akil Fletcher, February 16, 2017).

Along these lines, we received the following feedback from an anonymous reviewer about an earlier draft of our work that appeared ideologically to favor the wordplay of New School signage: "The new [school] stores, . . . have clearly put much more thought into the shop sign as a branding strategy, a statement of not 'what we can offer you' but 'who we are.'" After Shonna shared this comment with John Jay College students in a Language and Culture class, a Dominican-American student later came to her office to talk about her studies, but added, as she was leaving, "Oh, and I wanted to mention, my family has a pharmacy in the Dominican Republic, and we spent so much time trying to come up with an appropriate name for it. Finally, we settled on Farmacia

Express, because we thought it best represented who we were and what we had to offer" (Student, Spring 2016). When asked to explain a bit further about the naming of her parent's shop, she said the following:

> My parents put a lot of thought into the sign because they wanted something new, to stand out from others. In the Dominican Republic, most businesses are named after people's names, and my father thought it was a little cliché to name our pharmacy the same way. The other thing is that, in the Dominican Republic, speaking in any other language, especially English, is cool because our culture admires American culture. . . . That being said, my parents settled for the name Farmacia Express, because they wanted people to know that we worked fast, especially since we had delivery services, and they thought *express* sounded better than *rápida*. Also, adding an English word to the name seemed modern and cool back in 1999. The last thing is that my parents wanted to attract all types of customers, but most of all middle and upper-class customers. (interview with authors, January 10, 2018)

The reviewer's commentary aside, the student's story brings to light the ideological meanings entailed in New School signage. The notion that people with new Brooklyn storefronts put "so much more thought into the shop sign as a branding strategy" is impossible to prove. And while sparsely worded signage might be rich in meaning, whether the sparse words are "well-chosen" depends on who you ask. And the process this student's family and the owners of Nio's West Indian Restaurant and Bakery went through to come up with an appropriate name to suggest what they did, who they were, and what kind of customers they wanted entailed quite a bit of thought and thoughtfulness.

So, for Old School signs, risk is clearly calculated, and the resulting linguistic move is metaphorically shallow: literal, definitive, and thorough in meaning. It reflects (and promotes) a language ideology of sincerity and open inclusivity, and, arguably, it makes a "deep play" for equality in place.

In New School signage, polysemous terms coyly play with words. But New School wordplay can also make mocking references to the people of nondominant groups. There is, for example, a store named Trailer Park that sells high-priced, repurposed furniture; the name taps into and possibly makes fun of working-class and working-poor people who cannot afford a traditional home or the land on which to put it. We also find an upscale restaurant whose sign reads "Shelter" and could be making an ironic joke at the expense of those in the area who are actually homeless.[23] As we pointed out earlier, women, gender, and sexuality are a frequent theme of New School wordplay. For instance, along with our earlier example Bird, we find the phrase The Bad Wife on the

Figure 2.13. Nio's West Indian Restaurant and Bakery. Note, though, that the word *restaurant* does not appear on this Old School sign, but *roti* and *Trinidad* are included as well as the flag of Trinidad and Tobago.

sign for a corner grocer, a waffle shop called Sweet Chick, and a bar named Plan B (possibly referring to a controversial form of birth control). The name of women's clothing store Habit could be making a playful reference to women's consumption and shopping habits, and thus indexing gendered stereotypes of women's "bad" habits. But Habit could also be poking fun at Catholicism, since the religious female clergy of this non-Protestant denomination of Christianity has historically worn a *habit*, or modest clothing that distinguishes them from others. Likewise, we find other playful references to Catholicism as in a Park Slope bar called Parish. The word could refer to the traditional community boundary of a Catholic church or perhaps the local political territories of some American cities, such as New Orleans.

A final example of hip irreverence to other people's categories and experiences is a café called Outpost. This upscale coffee house opened in the long-standing African American neighborhood of Bed-Stuy (Bedford-Stuyvesant). It looks like a saloon and thus suggests a "Wild West" kind of setting. *Outpost* has connotations of both military encampment and imperial conquest. It is also used to refer to a settlement on the frontier of civilization. So this coffee shop's colonial meanings in the context of place-making technologies are also certainly available for gentrifiers who feel they are in the middle of territory uncharted by their people. Outpost is an example of Neil Smith's (1996) classic analysis of the *urban frontier* in Manhattan's Lower East Side neighborhood, generalizable to other parts of the city—particularly where large populations of working poor and people of color lived—that constructs these neighborhoods as a *wilderness*. The people in this wilderness were seen as uncivilized because they, and the conditions in which they lived, were constructed as "natural" to the physical environment of an urban area in decay.

An audience member at a talk where we presented Outpost suggested that the bar's wordplay was really a coded reference to the fact that it catered to a gay clientele. It was a *post*, that is, a place, in which people could be *out*. Still, the name of the bar remains problematic as it retains a colonizer meaning in addition to any other possible meanings. The polysemy inherent in Outpost makes it very different from, say, the Big Gay Ice Cream shops found in Manhattan's East Village and Greenwich Village neighborhoods. Or take, for example, Kiki Queer Bar, not in Brooklyn but found by a friend in Reykjavik, Iceland, in 2017. Arguably, both of these signs are in an Old School register with their sincere references to nonheteronormative sexuality that make a place on the street for LGBTQIA people.

We are not suggesting that shop signs in a New School register sell only to people from the dominant cultural group (i.e., white, Anglo-Saxon, Protestant, affluent, hetero males). Our argument is that their shop names use direct and indirect indexicality to make statements about people belonging to all other categories—women, children, and people with nonwhite identities. Whether or not a nondominant person is offended depends. Many women for example, may claim that *bird*, though a British derogatory term for woman, does not personally offend them. This language use seems to bank on the idea that people who share at least one intersectional identity with the dominant group will claim not to be offended by it.

So, along with fostering exclusivity and exclusion, New School signs also erect and maintain the linguistic architecture of cultural hierarchy. It is precisely because people claim not to be offended that this linguistic architecture of domination can be insidiously built. That an individual is unoffended is both relevant and irrelevant to the system of oppression. It is irrelevant because the system gets built whether people find it offensive or not. It is relevant because the more unassuming people are about the power of words, the more cunning their ability to create a system of valuation and dominance. The New School register imposes dominant culture's ranking over all other groups, but its clever depth of meaning can bury any suggestion of offense or intentionality beneath its layers. This is a very different way of placing "names on the land," as Stewart's (1982) classic study of place-naming in American history described it, but the function of domination is the same.[24] Analogous to Geertz's use of irrational economic gambles that make cultural sense, the publicness of "deep" wordplay on new Brooklyn signs may risk meaning "on the street," but their establishment of dominant culture's authority in the context of rent gap opportunities is a conservative bet. Thus, as Warner (2002, 8) contends that public discourse is inherently risky, "commit[ting] itself, in principle to the possible participation of any stranger," the wordplay of gentrifying signage remains confident in its message to a "given audience." And New School's polysemic register can act as an implicit code to communicate dominant culture's supremacy at the same time its ambiguity makes it ostensibly unaggressive, and therefore not always overtly or directly confrontational.

Hill (1998, 2008) suggests that mock forms of Spanish produce and uphold the "elevation of whiteness" because they indirectly point to negative stereotypes of Spanish speakers as lazy, dirty, and even sexually loose. We find that the linguistic resources common to New School signage, particularly wordplay, serve also to elevate the other dominant organizing principles of American culture that include heteronormative gender (male) and sexuality (straight), religion (Protestant), income, and education (elites with financial and social capital). But wordplay on New School signs casts a wider net in its mocking forms: in using these words ironically *and* ambiguously, newcomers hedge their bets with privilege, a problem we examine in detail later. With polysemy, any risk of animosity toward others can be countered by denying intentionality and professing to have meant one of the socially more innocuous meanings.[25] And such assertions of unintentionality would be all fine and good, but of course, that rationale is not what makes the sign "catchy."[26] Without the other socially more incendiary meanings, the language on the sign would be less alluring and less interesting.

Linguist Asif Agha (2004, 30) notes, "discourse associated with a particular register makes certain personae recognizable through speech," and the new signs index a new group of users of space. Occupying Brooklyn's multicultural and economically diverse neighborhoods, new Brooklyn signs use a specific register to signal the upscale transition of place, to suggest the transition is organic, informal, and nonthreatening, and to make it complete. The Farm on Adderley's "irony in place," its message of "Hey, we also are surprised to be *here*!" is joined by other artful yet ambiguous claims to birthright, belonging, and authenticity. In one sense, we see playful signage as a linguistic strategy used to soften the reality of revanchist takeovers of other people's space as well as a means to express unsettled feelings about living among people different from one's own culture. And finally, the language on the signs can make the project of gentrification seem lighthearted, unplanned, surprising, and even fun or exciting to gentrifiers.

Indeed, many gentrifiers, though not all of them, suggest that one-word signs are inviting to them as patrons and to other gentrifiers looking for residential space. When shown a one-word shop sign, one such gentrifier in Bay Ridge said, "looks like someplace I'd like to live." And for those in danger of being displaced or of seeing their communities displaced, the signs also carry far more menacing meanings, like "there goes our neighborhood." When asked to respond to what one-word store names like Bird and Cornelius meant for the neighborhood, one old-timer, a black male resident, said:

> Bird—another sign that the community is changing. This appears to be a business that's reaching out to young upscale families. [And] Cornelius—an upscale bar that serves oysters and fine dining, owned by a successful Russian businessman. This building was once owned by a black family as early as ten years ago, [but they] sold the building because [they] couldn't afford upkeep.

While "catchiness" may seem to be remarkably risky on one level—offensive, politically incorrect, uninterpretable, even bad for business—as one of the tools of gentrification, the New School place register makes clear to everyone that some people can afford to risk meanings as they also make economic moves that revalue the land as distinctive, desirable, and exclusive.

Similarly, while one could make the case that New School signs appear to be full of meaning, and maybe even very thoughtful, or "full of thought," in how they are constructed, as some gentrifiers and even some academics have suggested to us, at another level, they could be, and have been read by several of our African American, Latino, and some white gentrifier informants, as being very "thoughtless" with regard to people's feelings. In these cases of potentially offensive wordplay, there are usually several different responses.

People often claim to own a meaning other than the one the aggrieved have assigned to such words. Hill refers to this position as a personalist language ideology (Hill 2008, 89–90). Sometimes there is an excuse—either of ignorance of reference or ignorance of how the reference works—but rarely is there any reckoning that such signage might be wrong. In fact, those who complain about (or analyze) such signage in these ways are often accused of reading too much into things or of being too sensitive or being too politically correct. We argue, however, that rather than being too sensitive, it may be that those who can read the offense into the meanings are just plain aware of (and of course, then sensitive to) the racial and racialized socioeconomic, cultural, and historical inequities in place, as well as aware of how the linguistic norms seem to maintain them. Perhaps those who create the signs are not so much insensitive to other people's experiences, histories, and realities as they certainly are unaware of them. Sociologist Joe Faegin (2000), however, has noted that white people are curiously unconcerned with hurting black people's feelings. African Americans perceive this type of white behavior as lacking in respect for their history and experience.

The exclusionary and potentially offensive humor of these New School signs, and the cultural hierarchy that they ultimately impose and uphold, is reinforced in the way media, literature, and gentrifiers themselves continue to disparage Brooklyn's past identity. For example, revisiting the upscale promotional efforts of *Conde Nast*, one finds the imprudent belittling of Old School Brooklyn. It reads:

> Brooklyn's tide has been rising for the better part of a decade as hipsters, chefs, writers, and artists have fled Manhattan in search of more affordable . . . everything. As these stylish immigrants have filled the borough's old neighborhoods, they've transformed lowly bodegas into Michelin-starred restaurants, dive bars into wineries, abandoned warehouses into playhouses, and a gothic bank building into a massive flea market. (Payne 2011).

The description of *Gimme Shelter*, an autobiographical book about one writer's hunt to purchase an affordable home in Brooklyn, includes the phrases "ugly houses" and "cruddy neighborhoods" (Williams 2009). And real estate bloggers and media outlets have referred to the borough as Manhattan's "ugly stepsister." [27] Such data suggest that gentrifiers' relationships to their new homes differ from those of other immigrants to Brooklyn in terms not only of their perception of the area as substandard, decrepit, and decaying, but also in their willingness and need to go on record and say so.

Taken together as a symbolic system and a register of communication in public space, New School signs reinforce hierarchy in place. Wordplay and ambiguity function to conceal domination as they help to complicate the idea of context. But for some people, the message is quite clear. One African American informant noted that New School signs often "exoticize" other cultures, but "make no attempt to pull those [other cultures] in. It is either, 'You do not belong here anymore,' or, 'Stick around, but know who is boss.'"

But knowing who is boss and how they assert authority in the landscape is not always clear. In the following chapters we examine some more ethnographic cases where struggles for power and space come at the expense of people already in place, and how these struggles are reflected in and have shaped Brooklyn's linguistic landscape.

At your cervix since 1996

Slogan on a shop sign for Boing Boing,
a Park Slope maternity store

3. Baby/Mama in the Nabe

Gender, Gentrification, Race, and Class

THE TEA LOUNGE in Park Slope was stroller accessible with its double-wide doors. Its signage, though creative, with its artful stained-glass lettering, clearly advertised some of the beverages and its casual "stay a while and relax" feel. Inside, its careworn furniture and wide stroller-friendly pathways signaled its openness to moms and their kids. The Tea Lounge was a place where moms felt welcome to breastfeed, where "kids are treated like high royalty," and where a children's singalong was regularly held.[1] One Brooklyn mom noted that, as of 2015, the Tea Lounge was not the exception in certain neighborhoods in Brooklyn such as Park Slope or Cobble Hill:

> I would breastfeed in restaurants, in lounges, in parks. Any place that I had my child with me. Which made it a very nice place to live, because I never feared leaving the house. I never thought, what if my kid gets hungry? What if he starts crying? I never thought anything like that. I knew that, obviously, my breasts are on me at all times . . . so that I literally could comfort my child anywhere at any time. And that literally gave me a lot of freedom. (interview with authors, April 2015)

We have found that this mother's experience is like that of many gentrifying mothers—many of whom are white, married, and college-educated women—who have been remaking Brooklyn for the past two decades as a hospitable place for themselves and their children. At the same time, we argue, such women are simultaneously helping to change cultural norms of motherhood more broadly.[2] We are reminded of feminist anthropologist Sherry Ortner's (1972) classic observation that men are largely credited for creating culture (art, education, religion, law, systems of governance, economics), while women are thought of as primarily relegated to reproduction and childrearing, contributions that are seen as culturally important but inevitably ephemeral or short-lived in comparison to the "lasting" contributions of men.[3] Thus, Ortner's formulation: because women's primary contributions across cultures are babies, and therefore perishable, women are valued less and subject to being subordinate—that is, lower in rank and under the control of men, whose contributions are long lasting.

But in the case of Brooklyn, Ortner's conceptualization of gender and value is getting turned on its head, because in many ways women are creating the culture there for their families and in turn changing the physical and normative landscapes of Brooklyn streets, parks, and shops. And as we saw earlier, the commercial signage of some stores by women or for women also, of course, reflects and contributes to these changes. Nevertheless, we find that while these women are changing the landscape in sometimes inspiring and transgressive ways for themselves, their efforts are still denigrated by traditional powerbrokers. And though they deal with their own struggles against stereotypes and sexism, they may not necessarily be entirely sensitive or inclusive toward people in other socioeconomic, ethnic, or racial groups, even though they say they intend to be. In fact, we find some signage meant to attract these women's business might even send confusing or seemingly mocking messages about nondominant groups.

For example, during our data collection, we found our own neighborhood's version of Bump, the Park Slope maternity store (from Chapter Two), in Bay Ridge. Baby/Mama sells clothing and accessories for mothers and their newborns, and it offers an array of breastfeeding, baby massaging, and baby-wearing classes (Figure 3.1). Like the Tea Lounge, which beckons to gentrifying moms who do not want to stay at home with their babies all day, the owners of Baby/ Mama suggested on their website that motherhood is now taking new forms in Brooklyn. They say:

The seeds for baby/mama were planted when we were having our first baby, and we couldn't find anything we wanted or needed without having to trek to Park Slope. . . . [And] some local moms [were] saying they were having a hard time

baby/mama

Figure 3.1. baby/mama, an upscale store for new moms. The two words are separated with a safety pin.

finding affordable lactation help. We also wished for more baby and kid classes in the neighborhood. It seemed every email we got advertising great classes were available in Park Slope, Cobble Hill, and everywhere but Bay Ridge! Bay Ridge is getting more and more attention as the great neighborhood it is, and especially as a great place to raise kids.[4]

Interestingly, their description of the store's trajectory suggests not that babies are new to Bay Ridge, but rather that there is a new group of mothers in Bay Ridge, namely, those who are aware of Bay Ridge getting noticed as a great place to raise kids. The owners' description of the store's trajectory is very careful not to sound as if their presence makes Bay Ridge a better place for mothers and babies than it was in the past, even though it seems to be exactly what they are saying. First, by juxtaposing Bay Ridge, a neighborhood that had not, for many reasons, been as high on gentrifiers' radar in the 1990s and early

2000s as Park Slope and Cobble Hill, the text sets up a comparison between "great places to raise kids" (i.e., Park Slope and Cobble Hill) and less than great places like Bay Ridge, which apparently had very little to offer to gentrifier moms and their new babies.[5] Rather than saying Bay Ridge has nothing to offer, they blame their emails that state that other (more desirable) neighborhoods have everything. Then, seemingly very sensitive to the typically offensive gentrifying discourse that tends to call "lower-priced" neighborhoods' "best kept secrets," the website states that Bay Ridge is getting "the attention it deserves" without telling us from whom or exactly why it merits such recognition given that it lacks things that new parents are supposed to need. But clearly the sentence refers to outsiders, either those who have recently moved to Bay Ridge or those who live elsewhere. The suggestion that such attention is especially coming from people who want to raise kids in a "great place" directly indexes mothers and parents looking for new neighborhoods to move to. "New neighborhoods" also means "more affordable housing," as these new moms come to the neighborhood from other places, like Park Slope, that are much further along in the gentrification process. These moms come with resources of time, money, and college degrees, ready to reshape and to remake the landscape.

The store's name, Baby/Mama, has many meanings and is a perfect example of the deep wordplay of much New School signage. First, it harkens back to Old School Brooklyn as it "lists" the customers served: mothers and their babies and anyone wishing to purchase something for mothers and babies. But it also conjures up regional, ethnic, and racial images of motherhood because the term *mama* is often associated with English speakers from the south or with Latino, Italian, and African American norms and ways of speaking (Hymes 1974). Moving away from separate literal readings of the name's components, Baby/Mama's sign points to motherhood at the intersection of race, class, and sexuality. Baby/Mama, when read aloud, sounds like *baby mama*, the African Americanism that refers to an unmarried woman of color with a child. According to Smitherman (2000, 59), *baby mama* emerged as the counterpart to *baby daddy*, which has its origins in Afro-Caribbean and African American communities and signals paternity and maternity of a child whose parents are unmarried (Patrick 1995). When introduced in the black community in the US, Smitherman (2000) points out, *baby daddy* was an insult leveled at black men for fathering children who they were not supporting financially or emotionally. *Baby mama* then became the counterpart for women who were seen as equally irresponsible and thus careless and foolhardy within African American communities. *Urban Dictionary* has a long list of mostly derogatory meanings for the term *baby mama*, many of which also index race, class, youth, and lack of education. For example, one of the entries equates the term with "ho," "gold digger," and "bitch."[6]

Terms like *baby mama* that originate in the African American community may lose their original connotations when moved to other speech communities. For example, in celebrity gossip journalism, the term has been used casually to refer to unmarried celebrity parents of the same child (see Turner 2006). This may even be true for younger African Americans, where, for women, *baby mama* has lost some of its pejorative force as they may use the term unapologetically to refer to themselves. In the same way, these women also use *baby daddy* to refer to the fathers of their children. However, when we have asked several of our African American and Afro-Latin/x John Jay College students what they thought of a shop called Baby/Mama, they had puzzled and largely negative reactions. One person inquired, "What does it sell?" When we asked them to tell us what they thought it might sell, another person said, "Club clothes?" Others guessed, "Alcohol?" These responses suggested that they interpreted the term along the lines of Smitherman's research and most of the *Urban Dictionary* meanings. Our students suggested a baby mama was a young woman who has a child but who also goes out to clubs in search of men to hook up with in a sexual way. Others, upon being asked, would respond only with an expression of disbelief, as they just could not comprehend who would put a sign up on a store in a public place using such a distasteful word for women. When we listened to their reactions, we tried to come up with an equivalent term that might similarly shock the sensibilities of white people: "Wenches and babies"? "Sluts and their kids"? Of course, we thought that these sorts of names would never show up on any storefront (although we recently discovered that they have, which we will discuss later). And certainly, we thought, such names would never appear on a storefront that catered to upper-middle-class white women and their babies. We wondered, why then would it be okay to use the term *baby/mama* on a store that catered largely to this demographic?

Below we explore this sociolinguistic puzzle of lexical polysemy and offense by considering the broader context of women gentrifiers changing the city. We will attempt to provide a wider ethnographic reading from which we can then return to the Baby/Mama sign and consider the implications of all its meanings. These public texts are embedded and entangled in complex relationships of urban life where some things change and others remain stubbornly the same.

A New Home: Neolocality and
New Brooklyn Mothers

As we noted previously, our participant-observation in Brooklyn began seventeen years ago when we moved to the borough. At that time, what had begun as a partnership with an equal division of labor became a more traditional household model. Ed was offered a tenure-track faculty position in New York, and Shonna took a leave from her tenure-track faculty position at Florida State University to join him in New York City. Ed went off to work in Manhattan, and Shonna was left to take care of our six-week-old, first-born child in a new Brooklyn home. We arrived in our new apartment—hunted for by Ed while Shonna was eight months pregnant in Florida—on the corner of Caton Avenue and Stratford Road in Flatbush, Brooklyn, on August 18, 2003. Ed had wanted to rent, but we could see from reading the *New York Times* in our home in Tallahassee, Florida, that housing prices were soaring in Brooklyn. It seemed that if we did not buy a place immediately, we would never be able to do so. So, Ed, never having been to the borough before, bought the Flatbush apartment on his colleagues' recommendations in a matter of only three days during his very first visit to Brooklyn.[7]

Alone in a new city with a six-week old strapped into a stroller, Shonna would head out looking for companionship and diversion. In about two weeks, merely by walking around Prospect Park, she met and became friends with ten other women who, like her, were college educated, over thirty, professionals, and recent arrivals to Brooklyn. Interestingly, the average age of women giving birth to their first child in the US is still 26.4 years (Mathews and Hamilton 2016). Many of the over-thirty set of gentrifying mothers in Brooklyn are what doctors refer to as being of "mature maternal age." Thus, in terms of their resources, many of these women, upon becoming mothers, had a funded maternity leave (either by a partner or an employer). And quite suddenly, because of their maternity leaves, these women found themselves with a lot of extra time on their hands, but very little that they could do with it because those hands were filled with their newborns.

In most cases, their own mothers, mothers-in-law, sisters, sisters-in-law, cousins, aunts, and best friends were not in Brooklyn. Having recently moved into what anthropologists would call a neolocal household, where newlyweds reside in a home that is near neither the husband's nor the wife's family, these women found themselves alone with their infants all day long. Their social networks were now in other places, far away from them and from their experiences and struggles with new babies. So these women would meet each other in the park, go for strolls, and go out for coffee and lunch with their babies in tow. They would develop Yahoo groups through which they would communicate with one another regularly. Some would attend "mommy & baby" events like baby and mommy yoga, baby sign language, or music classes. In the winter, they would host playgroups at each other's homes. Occasionally, they talked about their careers, books, or music. But mostly, they focused on a list of topics that second wave feminist anthropologists like Marjorie Shostak (1981) would call women's issues: their birth stories, the difficulties of breastfeeding, sleep disruptions, evolving libidos, and baby milestones.[8] Being in Brooklyn, they also often talked about what they would regularly read on the electronic mailing list known as Park Slope Parents.

Park Slope Parents was started in 2002 by a mother, Susan Fox, who established a Yahoo Group so local parents could exchange information via email / digital bulletin board about parenting. Though being so far from family and friends was often hard, most of these women loved being in Brooklyn generally and in Park Slope more specifically. Before the arrival of Facebook, Twitter, and other social media, electronic mailing lists like Park Slope Parents connected these newly arrived mothers to each other, creating an early virtual community. This community served as a communication nexus and clearing house through which a wide array of topics were raised and questions answered by largely anonymous, but at the same time, personalized and intimate users. For example, "Janice, mom of Ian" or "Rachel, mom of Conner" would provide advice to one particular poster and to all passive participants (like Shonna), who, sitting with their laptops in the apartment in the evenings, could learn about where to find the best, or most reasonably priced, diapers, pacifiers, baby shoes, and the like.[9]

But during a surge of gentrification in Park Slope in the 1990s and 2000s, many mothers' groups were not formed online, as the Internet was still evolving, but actually "on the street" in a local store called Boing Boing. In our data, Brooklyn residents of all ethnic, racial, and socioeconomic backgrounds often refer to local stores as places where they see their friends and neighbors or just "people from the neighborhood," and they describe these encounters as friendly and pleasant. Boing Boing was that kind of place for new mothers, who could walk in with their babies and talk to the salesclerks, the owner, and other moms. It became a community gathering place. In a *New York Times* article, the store's owner, Karen Paperno,[10] stated that her goal in opening in 1996 was to create "the country's first breastfeeding and baby-wearing boutique" (Bellafante 2014). The store's website read:

Our shops were founded in order to make this challenging time easier and simpler, and with our guidance, it is. We only stock parent-tested and BOING BOING approved products. Our expertise is why moms come from miles away to our Park Slope boutiques. *We know what you need.* From a 34G nursing bra to handmade woolies, we see parenting as a lifelong journey, not some fashionable trend.[11]

Paperno's desire to help women "become" mothers—in a cultural sense—was enacted inside the store, where, alongside baby and nursing products, she offered mothering classes.[12] However, her plan was also inscribed publicly on the storefront itself with the words "Boing Boing: Maternity, Nursing, Infant." But the store's name was cryptic and humorous: what, for example, do the words *boing boing* mean?[13] One might begin to ruminate, they are fun and somehow childlike with their repetition, and perhaps reminiscent of play or amusement as they may seem to represent raucous sounds. The list of words that followed "boing boing" explicitly suggested both the people it serves—mothers and infants—and some of the products (i.e., for nursing) it might sell to them.

While we have examined signs as a marker of gentrification and displacement, we can also consider them as a source for reading some other "meaningful forms, symbols, and artifacts" that Ortner (1972, 72) says are generated and sustained as cultural expressions that not only allow for the reproduction of culture across generations, but that also come to have an impact on the values different people are attributed in culture. The sign for Boing Boing is an example of how signage can not only make and mark the history of changing gender roles for women in an urban context, but can also help to establish and, in the case of gentrification, to change the terms of belonging to that area. As we discussed earlier, language on New School signage can create intimacy through wordplay among an anonymous but presumably like-minded public of gentrifiers that is unthreatened by the possibility of misapprehensions. But this playful and laconic language can also be a gating device that stands in stark contrast to Old School signage, which goes to great lengths to be explicit to minimize misunderstandings.

Between 2000 and 2016, the number of women over the age of twenty-five holding college degrees nearly doubled in Brooklyn, from 180,000 to almost 330,000.[14] With the arrival of such impressive numbers of affluent and highly educated women, unfettered by their working husbands and their far-away extended family, Brooklyn became a neolocal space, not for newlyweds but for new parents with infants and small children. And these new parents, many of whom were previously living in Manhattan or one of the earlier gentrified neighborhoods of Brooklyn, or perhaps somewhere else entirely, are in search of an affordable area that will offer them more space for their growing families. Thus, these women are left to their own devices to create new social networks, in turn transforming traditional middle-class motherhood and redefining the place in which they have taken up residence. For these gentrifying mothers, we argue, "making a home for themselves" begins with staking a claim on public space. As gentrifying women occupy space in public, they also renegotiate the politics that govern normative gender behavior outside the home.

The sign for Boing Boing is a good example of how women stake their claim on place by writing themselves into the linguistic landscape. In terms of our sign types, Boing Boing is one of the few examples of what we would call a hybrid sign—sort of between Old School and New School categories. For instance, it includes both the literal honesty of Old School Brooklyn signs (Maternity, Nursing, Infants) and the cryptic minimalism of New School with the words *boing boing*. The store's website explains the meaning of *boing* as representing incipient motherhood as its own kind of liminal period:

> "Boing!" is the sound of your life changing. That's what Karen Paperno thought when she first gave birth to her daughter in 1995. Yes, life had changed, but the challenges of being a first-time mother proved daunting. . . . Who needs more baby clothes? New mothers need help! . . . with that thought *boing boing* was born.

Here, the New School character of this part of the sign draws on the power of ambiguity, code, and taboo. The meaning of the reduplicated words *boing boing* is not readily recognizable in English. In the *American Heritage Dictionary*, between the guide words where *boing* would alphabetically appear, the word *boink* exists. Phonologically, the difference between the two words is found only in the addition of the voiceless word-final consonant /k/.[15] *Boink* is defined as vulgar slang, meaning "to have sexual intercourse." And so right on the sign there is a written allusion to sex, or the biological process that brings on the onomatopoetic *boing* "of your life changing."

In the 2000s, however, Boing Boing's sign underwent a transformation of its own. In its resurgence from facing tough financial times and the danger of going out of business, the sign for the store's new iteration resulted in playing with even more gender taboos. The new sign still heralded its old name, but instead of the Old School explanatory tag ("Maternity, Nursing, Infant") it included the phrase "At your cervix since 1996," a play on the slogan "at your service" (Figure 3.2). The phonological likeness to this well-known business phrase minimizes the gap between the public and the private, and it both literally and metaphorically brings the inside out into the open. Many levels of taboo are played with in this slogan. First, that a woman-owned-business is providing service to the cervix and talking openly about doing so in public is arresting. Second, the cervix itself is a passage or opening between the uterus and the vagina to an all new life, new experience, and new atmosphere. The location of the cervix in the vagina makes a reference to a "private part," traditionally thought to belong to or for the use of one particular person, namely the woman's husband, and then also in the context of any of her child-birthing experiences. This exclusive character of female body parts is diminished by the public nature of the sign whose words can conjure sexualized meanings and images to anyone and everyone. We see in Boing Boing's sign women themselves bringing customarily private issues of female reproduction to the public streets. The explicit reference to the cervix, a reproductive part found inside the vagina, on a public sign undermines conventions of privacy that privilege patriarchal control of space, commerce, and women's bodies. Additionally, the typography on the sign makes the o's in the words *boing boing* appear as cervical caps or diaphragms, devices women use to have sex without pregnancy.

The wordplay in both the name and the slogan on Paperno's sign is bawdy, engaging, and overtly political. With sex, childbirth, and nursing out on the street for everyone to see, the sign speaks aloud of these personal, secret,

Figure 3.2. This sign for a maternity store that opened in the mid-1990s includes a slogan with wordplay.

WHAT THE SIGNS SAY

and innermost issues formerly undisclosed or occasionally mentioned only in hushed tones. Quite literally, the sign defines both the physical land as well as a cultural space where women themselves can display their innermost biology and transcend cultural norms. This open display of women's sexuality and political power to claim urban space both transforms women's private, individual reproductive roles by making women-as-mothers public at the same time it creates public space for them in Brooklyn.

Following Boing Boing's lead, stores, restaurants, and cafes bustling with breastfeeding women and their babies or mothers with their toddlers in tow (and in mind) on many Brooklyn streets have perhaps become the norm in 2019. What we describe above, however, is very different from what urban geographers, sociologists, and anthropologists have found in urban spaces in the past. Let's take a closer look at what these scholars have previously described and consider how urban place-making and changing gender roles are truly interrelated questions in more ways than one.

Gentrification and Women's Work

Urban street life has been imagined as being primarily male-dominated by groups of ethnic and/or nonwhite men (African American, Latino, Italian, and Irish, for example). These male groups—of all ages—congregate in various sections of the city to hang out, play dominoes, drink alcohol, and talk with one another (Gans 1982; Liebow 1967; Suttles 1968). Italian, Irish, Jewish, and other Euro-American immigrant women have historically been imagined to be absent from street and public culture, their locus of relevance being primarily inside and in front of their own homes, on their own streets and blocks (Patch 2008). Places of worship have provided these women social networking opportunities, but rarely are they traditionally thought of as being "on the street." For example, sociolinguist Gabriella Modan (2007) notes how one of her male informants sees the streets of Washington, DC, as unsafe for his mother and his sister but not necessarily for himself.

Exploring this divergent conceptualization of urban space in her ethnography of Washington's Mount Pleasant neighborhood, Modan sketches how the city, influenced by the rise of industrialization in the nineteenth century, was constructed as a "masculine" public space, constituted by the series of streets acting as thoroughfares for men to access and be productive in their workplaces. By contrast, women were relegated to the home, even with the emergence of the suburb in the mid-twentieth century (Modan 2007, 114). The public roles of white ethnic women who lived in the city remained restricted to what Jane Jacobs called "eyes on the street" (qtd. in Patch 2008): women performed surveillance by monitoring their own and their friends' children, watching for strangers in the neighborhood, and controlling the discourse on vacancies so that "their own kind" could move in and other groups of people could be kept out. These immigrant, European American women, like black women in the city (Naples 2012; White 2011; Springer 1999), also assessed the needs of their communities and petitioned the city for services.[16] To a certain extent, women gentrifiers in Brooklyn today follow in this tradition, especially as they need municipal services such as trash, tree limb, and snow removal on municipal property. But gentrifying women are expanding the scope of the traditional roles that women played in urban space, sometimes to the chagrin of others who see them acting with abandon and having no respect for the norms that had historically circumscribed their movement.

In our interviews, gentrifying women from earlier periods talk sometimes of how they did or did not fear the male-dominated city. In fact, some now suggest that they were naïve not to have been afraid. Many of the second-wave gentrifying women we met when we moved to Brooklyn had already lived in Manhattan or in other cities. But some came directly to Brooklyn from the suburbs and had been raised in households where they were not explicitly taught to fear "the city" and the people of color who lived in it. Perhaps this is why white women are sometimes constructed as either "clueless" or "overly entitled" in urban spaces that presumably are dangerous. For example, in 2010 the Civilians theater company wrote, directed, and performed the play *In the Footprint*, a montage of stories gathered from residents in two Brooklyn neighborhoods affected by the Atlantic Yards redevelopment plan.[17] In one scene, an African American mother-daughter pair discuss neighborhood changes since white people have moved in. They poke fun at the presumed poor judgement of a white "girl . . . jogging down Myrtle Avenue in short shorts" at "11 o'clock at night!" In the play, the white girl had asked the mother, "Um, is Myrtle Avenue that way?" In the scene, the African American mother and daughter are still, years later, laughing at this white woman's naiveté; they suggest that not only did this white girl foolishly have no fear, but she was also too dumb or too privileged to know she should be afraid. They seemed to glean this from what they considered to be her inappropriate dress and the inopportune time of day she approached a part of the neighborhood containing mostly public housing, bordering Fort Greene Park, an area that long-time residents considered to be dangerous.

Our own informants echoed some of these sentiments in the "moving to Brooklyn" narratives they told us. In story after story, early women gentrifiers revealed their perhaps naïve boldness and determination to move into places they could actually afford, or to revamp old houses because of their love of architecture, or to practice their craft and make art or write as a profession. Along with most of these stories, these women also said they tried to build community with people from other cultural backgrounds. As Patch (2008) points out in his study of store owners from the mid-1990s through the 2000s, in Brooklyn's gentrification process, single, educated women, most of whom were white, began to stay in the borough and literally set up shop. In Patch's conceptualization, this phenomenon moves gentrification out of the mostly residential spheres of renovated warehouse lofts of de-industrializing districts studied several decades ago by Zukin (1989), into what he calls street gentrification. Street gentrification "occurs in the realm of daily non-domestic areas which are visible as one walks down a sidewalk" (2008, 110). Patch suggests that women entrepreneurs (like Paperno at Boing Boing) actually become a commercial version of Jacobs's "public characters," who act as resources and sources of information and camaraderie, often through "gendered forms of interaction" that transform neighborhood space and "[open] up new businesses . . . and welcom[e] new people" (2008, 123). These women-owned businesses become destinations for other women, many of whom are (or are becoming) new mothers, and who, like Shonna and her new acquaintances, found themselves in Brooklyn all day long every day.

Our ethnographic research finds that these women also put their expression, their ideas, and their plans into place when they moved to Brooklyn with their children. In some ways, the work they undertake is germane to motherhood and homemaking, but in others, it is nontraditional and even threatening because these women often set out to remake parts of Old School Brooklyn that they find unsuitable for themselves and especially for their children.

Women and Children First: Remaking Storefronts, Schools, and Streets

Gentrifying Brooklyn mothers remain both traditional in their focus but innovative in their practice of motherhood. As these highly skilled, college-educated women with financial resources step out of their full time positions as journalists, lawyers, public relations executives, playwrights, professors, and the like, and step into motherhood, they tend to focus on areas traditionally related to women's work such as food preparation, childcare, providing safety, and shopping.[18] And just as Paperno brought sex, childbirth, and breastfeeding to a Park Slope street in the 1990s, many of the gentrifying mothers we interviewed were not interested in centering their mothering efforts on only the privacy of their own households.

In the next few pages, we take a closer look at how women have also brought their professional skills to more public spheres of Brooklyn to make the borough into the kind of home they want to live in. Obviously, because of their preferred consumption practices and desires, as we have already seen, some of the work that these gentrifying women do reshapes the Brooklyn marketplace by helping to bring to their neighborhoods community-owned food cooperatives, community supported agricultural groups (or CSAs), and, by opening new storefronts, new products and services that cater to their needs. As their children enter educational institutions, these women also take the helm of Parent Teacher Associations (PTAs) and lead new parent groups at their children's schools. In these new leadership positions, they try to steer transformations of New York City public schools in ways they believe necessary. As they imagine their children crossing busy city streets, Brooklyn mothers lead pedestrian safety campaigns that change the direction, flow, and speed of traffic. With our time-flexible academic jobs, we would both participate in and make observations of these women-led efforts to make changes to Brooklyn's social fabric.[19] Our research interviews revealed many reasons that women gave for why they turned their professional attention toward their new neighborhoods. For some women, volunteering at their kids' schools and at the budding food co-ops or joining a pedestrian safety campaign meant meeting other people, making new friends, and creating community. Others said they got involved because they saw a need to make a change or felt that there was some injustice that needed remedying. But in all these cases, it seems their central aim was to make Brooklyn a more pleasant and functional place for them to live.

Storefronts

Historically, traditional women's work has always entailed acquiring food for the household, which in the city has meant shopping on the street. In many other areas of gentrifying Brooklyn we have found new retail establishments gearing themselves toward public mothering. But what this means in terms of the kinds of shops that need to be available, and regarding the attitudes and environments other types of stores offer to create space that is more functional for mothers in public, is a more complicated matter. Gentrifying women suggest that they shop not only for what they need but also for new and unique products that they have never heard of before, but that they discover they can use. For example, about Boing Boing, one informant told us:

> I bought maternity bras there and um, I bought a breast pump and anything you needed to assist with that. It was right there in the neighborhood. And there were things, I bought that . . . I might not have used. The Mayan sling, to carry the baby. The Bjorn is the more traditional carrying device. But they had all these alternative things, so I remember buying that. There were things that I didn't know about that I wouldn't have known because they weren't selling at Babies R Us or Buy, Buy Baby! (interview with authors, March 27, 2015)

As mothers themselves both set up shops that sell the kinds of maternity items and services people like them are looking for, these new businesses and their new customers influence the business practices and shops of other retailers in the area, who alter their business plans to meet these women's needs. For instance, right next to Bump (whose sign we discussed in Chapter Two) is a shop called Babeland, a sex toys / information / bookstore for women interested in enhancing their sex lives. While not expressly (or exclusively) for new mothers, Babeland's website announced that its Park Slope store "boasts a diaper-changing table, and aisles wide enough to fit your baby stroller!"[20]

During our fieldwork we also learned that Bump had gone out of business but another mother/baby store quickly replaced it. This shop, called Wild Was Mama, explained its provocative name in the "About" section of its Facebook page: "Wild Was Mama empowers mom to embrace her authentic and wild self by providing products and education that support her own unique journey through parenting." Wild Was Mama, in addition to cool new products for moms and their babies, offered its clientele an array of events, information sessions, and classes. These services ranged in price from being free of charge to costing upwards of $350. A Facebook post from July 28, 2017, advertised, "Hey Park Slope! Wanna get WILD? Check out our upcoming events! Learn a little, love a little, shop, share, hang, change a diaper, feed a kiddo—WWM is honored to be here for you!" The upcoming sessions included a "Breastfeeding clinic for $45," "Financial planning session for new parents for free," and "Choosing a baby carrier for $15 per family."

Over the last two decades many other types of businesses have opened in Brooklyn that include serving new mothers in various ways as a prominent part of their business. Similar to the Tea Lounge, there are a host of restaurants, pizza shops, and toy and clothing stores as well as coffee shops and bakeries that provide easy access to restrooms, which also include changing tables. These stores have seating areas that accommodate strollers, flexible service providers to assist groups of mothers and their children, and other mom-and-kid friendly features. One example is a butcher shop called Fleishers Craft Butchery, again in Park Slope (Figure 3.3). While its storefront does not explicitly say "mothers are welcome," once inside the shop it becomes clear that they are. Directly opposite the old-fashioned glass and enamel butcher's display case, tucked centrally into the shop's wall, is a child's play space, a cubby with various toys, and a chalkboard with chalk. When we visited in December 2014 looking to purchase ingredients for our own Christmas meal, there were both Christmas and Hanukah toys available (Figure 3.4).

Stores such as Fleishers, the Tea Lounge, and Wild Was Mama demonstrate how gentrifying women not only want businesses where they can go with their children, but that they are actually getting them. On Yelp, for example, there is a page titled "Best baby friendly restaurants near Park Slope, Brooklyn." And if a restaurant is particularly kid friendly, there is a place where the Yelp reviewer can place a check, demonstrating that kid friendliness is a criterion that many consumer moms (and dads) desire.

But not all the more-public spheres of Brooklyn neighborhoods, whether completely gentrified or in the process of gentrifying, are changed so easily as a storefront. And new Brooklyn mothers' experiences in trying to transform other institutions and landscapes have presented more of a challenge.

Schools

In the late summer of 2008, when our son was five years old, his grandmother, a former elementary school teacher visiting from Pennsylvania, walked him to the public elementary school in our neighborhood where he would be starting to attend kindergarten the very next day. She wanted to get him familiar with the building before his first day of school. A security guard met them at the front door and told them they were not allowed to enter. Then a staff member from the main office appeared beside the guard and reiterated, "No children are to be in the building!" We found that our child's very first encounter with his future school epitomized the essence of what many gentrifying parents in our research perceived to be a major problem with New York City's public school system: it seemed to be a thoroughly unwelcoming environment, especially for the children that it aimed to educate.

Throughout our data collection parents accused the city's public schools of being a cold, heartless bureaucracy. Gentrifying parents seem to believe that their kids and kids in general are supposed to like school. If kids do not like school, these parents believe that the school needs to change into something that will please their kids and make them want to attend with a love of learning every day. If the school fails to provide the type of enrichment parents think might motivate a love of learning in their children, they try to take matters into their own hands to transform the composition and mission of their children's schools.[21]

Figure 3.3. The meat counter at Fleishers Craft Butchery in Park Slope.

Figure 3.4. These toys were placed directly across from Fleishers meat counter on the floor of the store. Next to them (outside of the photograph) is a chalkboard-surfaced wall with colored chalk for children to draw or write on.

This ideology led many gentrifying parents, especially mothers who stayed at home or worked part time, to volunteer in their children's schools. These mothers thought they could free up the teachers' time by maybe monitoring the schoolyard during recess or the lunchroom during meals, or by making themselves available in the classroom to assist as needed. But despite a desire to help, many mothers were uncertain how they could help. One mother, for example, told Shonna that fear of the unknown was what motivated her to volunteer at her sons' school:[22]

> To be honest, when I got there, I was scared. I felt worried about my kids. I wanted them to be in a good learning environment, and I didn't suspect that they were. For whatever reason, I just didn't know. It was my prejudices about urban living, rough and tumble, overcrowded and underfunded New York public schools. . . . And so I wanted to get involved, whatever that meant, whatever that looked like. So I said, "Well, what about just being in the classroom and observing the children and helping the teacher?" Um, sort of offloading the burden given to teachers. (interview with authors, March 20, 2015)

But she was met with resistance and discouragement from the school staff:

> And so there was just no room for that. So it was just a slow process of, I felt, of . . . convincing the principal of changing the culture to allow parents to get inside the classroom. (interview with authors, March 20, 2015)

Other gentrifying mothers got involved with the schools because they disagreed with what they believed to be very traditional modes of student discipline and old-fashioned and ineffective punishments. One informant complained:

> Right now, we have solid academics, I mean, for the most part. But there are these little emotional growth things that [. . . schools] really need to work on. I mean, like group punishments . . . my school, . . . they feel that this is something that is legitimate. A form of discipline. It is not. . . . If a bank gets robbed on 86th street, do you round up everyone on 86th street at that time and throw them in jail? I mean, in what societies do they do that? (interview with authors, March 13, 2015)

This mother also believed that her sons became unhappy in school because they were never allowed to run outside and "be free"—a sentiment echoed by other gentrifying mothers convinced that their kids were not getting enough time to play during the six-hour school day.

Additionally, many gentrifying mothers considered their kids' lunchroom to be inadequate. Some elementary school cafeterias were in a school's basement, which were of course, hot, smelly, and loud, and deemed "offensive" and "inhospitable" by parents. At our children's school, there were two lunchrooms in the basement of the school: "the hot lunchroom" for children who wanted to eat a free, hot meal provided by the school, and "the cold lunchroom" for those children who brought something to eat from home. One day Shonna volunteered with the PTA to sell ice cream to the children during the lunch period. She was overwhelmed by the noise and the chaos she perceived there. That day, she was paired up with a friend of hers, an immigrant Arab American woman who was very committed to supporting the PTA and who regularly sold ice cream in the lunchrooms. When Shonna mentioned to her friend she was astounded by the level of commotion in that room, her friend said to her, "You think this is bad? Wait until we get to the hot lunch side. The smells, the noise, the screaming lunch ladies. You will need two Advil!"

One of the gentrifying moms was simply appalled at how school staffers constantly shouted at kids during lunchtime. So this mother, a former BBC journalist who moved from London to Brooklyn where she became a stay-at-home mom, spearheaded an enrichment program to improve the lunchroom. She said:

> [We were] looking for something low cost that would engage all the children, something that would give them a sense of achievement, something kind of, you know, [a] "We did that!" [feeling] . . . something physical, to touch, as it were. And so we approached the principal with the idea of doing a mural. Possibly in the lunchroom. . . . We suggested the lunch room because it felt like a prison and we wondered whether it would change the atmosphere in the lunch room, which was just chaotic and loud . . . and the children . . . [were] not allowed to go in the [school] yard [for recess]! (interview with authors, March 6, 2015)

One gentrifier's strategy to get our local Brooklyn school to change was to connect it with parents and teachers at another school in a more gentrified part of the borough. In 2011, this mother at our children's school organized a visit for its administrators and teachers and a group of parents to one of Brooklyn's most coveted elementary schools, PS 321 in Park Slope. This mother, who owned her own public relations firm, came equipped with information-gathering, writing, communication, and networking skills. Her rationale behind the encounter was, "Why re-invent the wheel? We have a model school just a couple of miles away, why not visit it and see how they do things?" But the group became somewhat dismayed and discouraged when it learned that PS 321's Park Slope–based PTA was able to pay for its costly enrichment programs because it had raised more than $700,000 that year alone.

A PS 321 parent, Gloria Mattera, told us that affluent parent groups were game-changers for public schools. Mattera had suggested to her PTA that they share some of the large sum of funds raised with poorer schools in the area. But she pointed out that no amount of assistance could change certain fixed categories that came with a gentrified, affluent parent population, namely, their flexible work schedules, their knowledge of fundraising, and perhaps most importantly their connections to people with money. She mentioned that PS 321's PTA president was the wife of the chief executive of the prominent corporate developer Forest City Ratner Companies:

> Well, [FCRC executive's wife] was president, incoming president of the PTA, so obviously, there was more prominence there. And then usually you give to the charitable places close to home. If your kids go to a certain school or a church you're involved in or your family is connected to a certain business, there, that's going to be the one that they give to. . . . And there would be a school charity and one of the Nets [a professional basketball team] would come . . . (interview with authors, March 24, 2011)

Mattera, who is not just a parent but also a public figure and an activist in borough and city politics, was a key organizer in fighting large scale corporate development projects in her neighborhood.[23]

Mattera, and most of the mothers we came in contact with during our fieldwork, had social justice at the core of their volunteer work with the schools. For example, though only seven percent of the kids at Mattera's zoned elementary school were poor, she spent considerable amounts of time fighting for the rights of underprivileged students at Park Slope's John Jay High School, who, she said, had been subjected to peeling paint, a lack of technology classes, and toilets that did not flush.[24] Other gentrifying parents echoed this desire to make the schools better for all children, not just their own. When we asked one mom where she had been most effective in her efforts to change Brooklyn, she said:

> [In] my children's grade school. I did start a garden committee. . . . I met with the administrators to try to add more enrichment to the school. We, I wrote grants, I was active in the PTA. I spoke directly to teachers about how to change and enhance the curriculum with all students. So, I don't think that my activism was

specific just to my child. . . . Whenever we did anything it was for the greater good . . . because I can make lemonade at home with my daughter! (interview with authors, March 27, 2015)

These interventions, despite the slow going and initial resistance from the local school bureaucracy, ended up resulting in a lot of changes. For example, the trepidatious mom who did not know where to start with her offer of assistance ended up serving as a classroom "learning leader," a PTA officer, a member of a school leadership team, and a key figure in the development of enrichment programs at her child's school. Throughout other gentrifying Brooklyn neighborhoods, we learned about parent groups who helped create and institutionalize all sorts of extracurricular activities in the schools their children attended, including green cafeterias, robotics programs, coding clubs, creative writing clubs, theater groups, jazz bands, yoga classes, and running/jogging clubs, among many others. These gentrifying PTA programs also sponsor all sorts of evening school-oriented but also community-building events such as Sports Night, Arts Night, Crafts Night, and Movie Night. Even the meeting at the storied PS 321 resulted in what parents in our neighborhood considered to be a significant change in our local elementary school's culture. The principal was sufficiently inspired by the example of PS 321 to initiate a once-a-month event for parents to join in their children's classroom activities. In this event, known as Family Fridays, teachers often created an interactive activity where parents could participate in or watch a lesson for the first forty-five minutes of the day.

One of our interviewees remarked on what she considered to be a snowball effect of her early efforts, and those of other new Brooklyn moms, to change their schools, and more importantly, she theorized what she believed was the real source of the change:

[There is an] influx of college-educated, professional parents who are able to give input. People come from other places. And now more parents are speaking up. They are calling the district office, coming to Community Education Council (CEC) meetings, yelling, voicing their opinions, doing the math. And holding elected officials accountable. . . . There is an absolute professionalization of [the PTA] . . . we hired an accountant . . . anybody that has a budget of over $50,000 gets a third party to come in and do the books. You have a lot of moms who are stay-at-home now who used to run . . . companies! [laughs.] (interview with authors, March 13, 2015)

Moving from working for companies to volunteering (and often doing both), women participating in this style of interventionist public mothering attempted to integrate social justice with their own notions of what they thought the standards of public education should be, and they were not at all shy about expressing their ideas. As we will suggest next, many mothers extended this ideology and approach beyond their kids' schools to try to change the very streets of Brooklyn.

Streets

If elementary schools became the locus of these gentrifying women's lives while their children attended them, it was often from there that other issues of social life needing their attention came to light. For instance, many people, including our realtor, suggested upon our arrival in the neighborhood that we should send our children to Catholic School because, they said, the children in our zoned public school did not speak English. But our concern was not whether our children's schoolmates were nonnative English speakers. In fact, as a linguist and anthropologist parenting team, we were happy to have our kids make friends with kids with other languages and cultures. Our only problem with our zoned elementary school was the dangerous traffic patterns that surrounded it. We noted right away that our kindergartner's school was precariously situated among a very complicated convergence of six different streets—two of which merged highway drivers from the nearby Belt Parkway and the Brooklyn-Queens Expressway through confusing on- and off-ramps. We worried about crossing the street at the school's incredibly busy six-point traffic cluster. Not long into our son's kindergarten year, there was a major accident one morning before school that Shonna witnessed seconds after it happened.[25] Three mothers who had just dropped their children off were pinned to the fence by a car that jumped the curb. The accident was traumatic for onlookers and a tragedy of epic proportions for the women who were hit. Some of the gentrifying parents at the school (ourselves included) had connections to the city's Department of Transportation (DOT), and we managed to get a crew to come to assess how the intersection could be made safer. Along with fellow parents at the school, we attended public meetings where several residents of the surrounding area came to protest any changes to the intersection, and where the DOT eventually presented the findings of their study that ultimately resulted in physical alterations to the street that the DOT called "traffic calming measures."

Shortly thereafter, a good friend of ours, Maureen Landers, who was also one of the women who had worked to make the intersection safer, was hit by a car. She had been traveling on foot, crossing 4th Avenue in Bay Ridge with an empty stroller to pick up her daughter at a local preschool. Landers's outrage and terror led her and another friend, Stefania Vasquenz, to cofound B.R.A.K.E.S., "Bay Ridge Advocates Keeping Everyone Safe," whose purpose it was to begin a data-driven, DOT-supported pedestrian safety campaign. Shonna, along with several other mothers in our neighborhood, collaborated on this campaign because they had also been nearly hit by cars. The statistics of rising fatalities from car accidents suggested that Brooklyn's once infamous "mean streets" were in fact deadly. Perilous traffic patterns, unrestrained speeding drivers, and countless illegal U-turns in the middle of pedestrian crosswalks were all the norm. This grassroots group's efforts to make streets safer managed to get a local New York State senator to vote in favor of speed cameras in the neighborhood. The group also won approval for the creation of pedestrian leads on traffic lights that allowed people to walk at least halfway into a crosswalk before a red light turned to green so they would hopefully be well into drivers' sightlines before the usual Brooklyn traffic started to accelerate through the intersection.

While the DOT was in favor of these measures and had data to support their impact in terms of keeping people safe and reducing fatalities and casualties from car accidents, there was considerable resistance from long-standing neighbors who complained the changes would be inconvenient, would add to traffic jams, and would slow down morning and evening commutes. Some elderly residents worried the response time of ambulances and fire trucks would be compromised if these plans got implemented. Many business owners also worried any changes to traffic policies would affect parking opportunities, making life harder for drivers trying to get to their stores. While there was very little evidence to support any of these fears, elderly residents and business owners managed to sway the local community board, which decided not to implement all the safety measures that the mothers' group proposed.

In fact, as new Brooklyn moms attempted to change how people moved "in the street," many of the women we talked to complained that they perceived some of the opposition to their efforts to be quite belittling, denigrating, and hostile. For example, at a March 2012 community board meeting to hear arguments for and against the DOT's plan to put traffic calming measures into place in a section of the neighborhood's congested 86th Street retail corridor, then city councilmember Vincent Gentile said of the measures implemented near our son's school, "We don't want what happened over by PS 127 to happen here. Now that's a mess!" While Gentile's negative characterization was not explicitly gendered, the mothers thought it dismissive of their largely female-led effort to reduce the real and perceived threat of car accidents near that elementary school. The fact that gentrifying women's volunteer work was characterized by this councilmember as "a mess" in front of a largely older community of long-term resident drivers indicated a doubling down on the status quo and a clear disparagement of these women's value and their efforts to change it.

At a meeting in June later that year, a group of mothers organized to speak publicly in support of the DOT's plans to redesign the Bay Ridge section of Fourth Avenue, a busy thoroughfare running from Boerum Hill to the Verrazano Bridge. After each one of six women spoke carefully and clearly at the podium, with prepared statements and supporting examples, a man who sat on the Community Board attempted to refute their input simply by responding, "Now that we've heard from the cackle . . ." before launching into his opposing remarks. Landers, who organized the other speakers, recalled:

> What I remember most was that he was so wrong and so convinced that he was right about everything. And we all listened to his nonsense all the time, so politely without calling him out on it. . . . But he felt he could diminish [and] dismiss us as women *chattering*. We had data and an institution [the Department of Transportation] behind us and he had nothing but hot air, but yet, [he] commanded the meeting. (interview with authors, March 27, 2015)

Landers interpreted his referring to us as a cackle, "as if to say we were just noise and now the voice of authority could speak." She later sent via a text message the dictionary definition of cackle: "the cry of a hen or a goose, especially laying an egg."

So while this group of Brooklyn moms were effective in making a few important changes to the borough's streets, they often encountered community resistance and, in some cases, overt microaggressions from individual residents. Landers and Vasquenz said they were disheartened that more fathers did not join the pedestrian safety group. They felt that if more men had been involved, the organization would have been taken "more seriously." Landers said she got the impression that the larger community saw the predominately female group as "nervous nellies and hysterical women" rather than a serious group of concerned citizens with a practical mission to make the streets of Brooklyn safer for all its residents.[26]

The power of gentrifying women to do what Ortner (1972) referred to as "transcend the givens" of Brooklyn's former nature was met with backlash and resistance not only in the safer streets campaign but also in many other

Backlash against Public Mothering

We found all kinds of denigrating references toward public mothering while conducting our field research. From national news stories about "stroller Nazis" in Park Slope to snarky local coverage of "breastfeeding caravans" on the subway, the takeaway was always that forms of public mothering were offensive in some way.[27] One *New York Times* journalist reported disdainfully that Park Slope moms take "their comfort with nakedness to a whole new height . . . [because in a restaurant, one mother] wasn't wearing a shirt—or a bra for that matter—just a hoodie sweatshirt unzipped with a baby at each breast" (Storey 2007, RE1). In another example, a poster on the Brooklynian electronic discussion boards protested the overabundance of strollers in Park Slope.[28] And a blogger on *Curbed New York* disparaged the arrival of "valet" stroller parking at the local YMCA with a photo showing dozens of strollers outside the building, impertinently referring to the neighborhood as "notoriously spawno-centric."[29] Even after a decade, the backlash against the presence of strollers continued apace. In April 2014, a *New York Magazine* headline announced that the actor Patrick Stewart, of *Star Trek* fame, also "Wants to Ban Strollers in Park Slope" (Hurowitz 2012). Beneath an online *Daily News* story about women breastfeeding on the subway, a commenter named Gingerd posted: "It's one thing to nurse a baby with a light cover on, but to flash yourself to everyone is just downright nasty. And if some perv got on and said anything to them, they would be screaming at the top of their lungs." Another commenter, Michael Mechanic, added: "If these women were serious about displaying their breastfeeding, they should have exposed both breasts. One breast could be for nursing the baby. The second breast would be to display so that the public would no longer have to peep and use side glances while looking at a naked and bare-breasted female" (Matos and Dillon 2014).[30]

From these several examples, it is evident that the press contributes to and reinforces the mocking and shaming of public mothering, characterizing it as unseemly, menacing, and even polluting. This backlash also manifested in our informants' attempts to improve Brooklyn's public spaces. For example, in their engagement with Brooklyn's schools, while several of their ideas to change school practice, policy, and culture were taken up, a lot of their other ideas were met with mixed or negative feelings on the part of administrators and teachers. When we talked to informants about their attempts to transform public schools, many of them focused more on what they were unable to attain: extended playtime from kindergarten through fourth grade; universal art, music, and theater programs; cleaner, quieter and more dignified lunchrooms; more interesting and engaging class trips; larger spaces; and less time preparing for standardized tests. Often mothers suggested to us that there was extensive backpedaling away from, and even pushback against, many of their initial ideas and proposals to help. For example, the mural that the BBC journalist spoke of was actually painted by students and an Argentine artist who donated her time and talent to the school's endeavor. Although it was not created in the lunchroom, as originally desired by this mother, the mural was unveiled in the school's multipurpose room one spring, with great fanfare in front of students, teachers, and parents. But without notice or warning, it was ultimately and unceremoniously painted over in short time.

Many new Brooklyn mothers believe that parent voices are still not given a forum where they can be fully heard. Educational enrichment remains spotty and often available only to those who can afford to do it, or only in school programs where certain teachers are paid to engage in specialized, officially sanctioned activities with students. Many parents remain very frustrated with the bureaucracy that is New York City's Department of Education. Admittedly, it is a mammoth organization that serves more than a million children under the age of eighteen who hail from dozens of different countries and who speak as many if not more languages outside of the classroom. But the fact that these gentrifying women focused on what they were not able to do, rather than what they did accomplish, might also be a testament to the nature of how these professional women work: they are goal oriented, accustomed to being efficient and effective, and they are frustrated by the fact that big bureaucracies do not always lend themselves to what they believe is progressive change.

While disappointment with bureaucratic resistance is one thing, women also found surprising and discouraging backlash in Brooklyn's commercial spaces. In fact, child/mother friendly spaces like the Tea Lounge or Two Boots, a stroller-friendly Park Slope pizza shop, are not everywhere in Brooklyn. We even found explicit disapproval against public mothering practices appearing on store signage. For example, one Brooklyn candy/cake-decorating store displayed two signs: "If they open it or break it, you will be charged for it," and "Please note: No shopping bags, shopping carts or strollers beyond this point." These signs can be interpreted as reading "people [anyone] accompanied by children should not allow their children to roam freely." Comments on a Facebook post to the neighborhood parents group from January 21, 2015, about the establishment reveal that several mothers felt unwelcome and that they and their children were targeted for derision in the shop. One mother posted:

> I have never felt comfortable (especially with my children) in that establishment. Last year, we had such an awful experience with the owner that we both practically left in tears. It was very clear that we were not welcome. We were trying to pick up Halloween cookies for my daughter's class. I also had my son along, who was in a stroller. It was absolutely awful. Have things changed? Is it kid friendly now?

Another mom confirmed her feelings:

> oh geez. funny reading through the comments. well not funny—but we have had similar experiences in there. I stopped going in with my son because the owner has made some comments here and there over the years. There is also a sign on the door that says that [*this is*] *a shop and not a playground.*

And a third commenter confirmed their assumptions that moms, kids, and candy go together, and thus, the moms' expectations to have a place inside with their kids were reasonable:

> I love the store, I patronize often, but no one will accuse the owner of having the warm fuzzies. Definitely acts as though he's doing YOU a favor and not the other way around. I always feel compelled to loudly remind my children "eyes only, no touching," because I can sense the irritation and scrutiny. It's astounding considering the product offerings i.e. HELLO, CANDY EQUALS KIDS.

Notably, the store has an Old School sign and a picture of a child in a baker's hat on its awning. But of course, as we pointed out earlier, it may not be the case that owners of Old School storefronts are as open as their signs say they are. It also illustrates the extent to which new Brooklyn moms expect to be able to be in public with their children and their assumptions that retailers would, and should, change their practices.

Taking a closer look at this seemingly kid-averse candy shop case, we note that it is not that women themselves are not welcome. It is women *with children* who are not welcomed. This distinction raises the question of whether women shopping with their (very young) children is a new phenomenon in Brooklyn and perhaps elsewhere. Are Brooklyn gentrifiers more apt, for example, to take their children into stores than are women elsewhere or than nongentrifying women were? Interestingly, when we discussed this case with the owner of a New School–style kids clothing store, she seemed to echo some of the candy store owner's frustrations with gentrifying mothers' expectations for service. She complained that some moms would come into her store with their children in order to "learn about what the store sells and what it is like to own a business." For her, it seemed outrageous that she was being asked by these moms to give their kids a lesson in small business operations during her workday. When we shared her complaint with a few gentrifying mothers who were themselves professional women with extensive career experience in graphic design and the entertainment industry, one of them admitted that she, herself, had approached store owners requesting that they talk with her children about their business.

So in the commercial landscape we see both mothers pushing for more service and freedom to mother their way and business owners of all stripes in the community pushing back against some of their demands. Thus, it is important to point out that how people go about changing a landscape may be more important than what in fact is being changed. Take for example the experience of Michael Pintchik, a local developer and owner of several buildings on the Park Slope shopping block inhabited by Bump (later replaced with Wild Was Mama) and the sex shop Babeland. He explained to us how he was able to assuage community concern about adding a sex shop on his New School shopping block in part by having women talk to other women and being creative with a storefront display:

> [My tenant who owned Bump] . . . was in a "Mommy and Me" class, and she met . . . the owner of Babeland—which is the sex toy store. . . . And you know . . . I said to my brother and his wife, I said, "I found a new tenant." You know, "for the block and I'm so excited." And they said, "Well what is it?" And I said, "It's a sex toy store." And they looked at me like I was insane . . . I just knew it. I wasn't looking to do more vanilla, you know. And so um, I exerted my executive privilege and did it and you know, we had one [councilman], who was like, de Blasio, and he was like, "How could you?!" And you know, I wrote into the lease, when you look into that store, you don't *see* dildos [in the storefront]. (interview with authors, August 8, 2011)

Pintchik's solution to manage and temper gentrifying women changing his street in an arguably controversial and confrontational way—by putting "sex" right next to motherhood literally "on the street"—brings us back to the case we started with. From this context of both women changing Brooklyn for themselves and their children and the resulting backlash they encountered, we return to Baby/Mama, the Bay Ridge mother-infant store, to have a look at the reactions people have to this provocative name.

Returning to Baby/Mama: Mitigating Gendered Public Space with Race and Class?

On one level, we can read Baby/Mama as a version of Bump—yet another store providing the services gentrifying mothers need and demand. From a basic, sociolinguistic level, however, we see Baby/Mama operating as a mock-like form of African American English. It is used ironically and perhaps without regard for how people sensitive to racial semiotics might perceive it. The sign thus fits right in with the exclusive character of the New School register. On another level, however, we can consider this shop Bay Ridge's version of Boing Boing: something new on the scene but also a bit taboo and certainly challenging of local norms, where mothering tended to happen in the home and not on the street as it does in Park Slope, Cobble Hill, and Prospect Heights. Read in this way, from an intersectional feminist and critical race theory perspective, the store's name might be operating defensively to mitigate the ways in which such public motherhood is felt by women to offend tradition.

Incorporating this perspective, and digging a bit deeper into Brooklyn's ethnographic context, the name's functions and significance get more complicated. For example, when we asked one of the owners how they came up with the name of the store, we were told that it referred to the 2008 movie *Baby Mama*, starring Tina Fey, because his wife and co-owner loved the actress/comedian. He explained that when they polled friends and family about possible names for their store, Baby/Mama consistently ranked in first or second place. In the film, Tina Fey's character, Kate, is an unmarried, professional white woman who hires an unemployed, poorer white woman (played by Amy Poehler) to be her surrogate so that she can have a baby. Near the beginning of the film, Kate tells Oscar, the African American doorman (played by Romany Malco) that she is waiting for her surrogate to arrive. Oscar then responds, "Oh . . . you got you a baby mama coming. You know I got two baby mamas, right?" And Kate retorts, laughing, "No. This is different. You had relationships with those women." And he says, "No, I ain't have no relationships with those women. I had relations with those women." And Kate says, "No, I'm paying her. This was set up by an agency, there are contracts involved. It's strictly business." And he ends the conversation by saying, "You pay the bills, she has the baby. That's called a baby mama.

You ask any black man in Philadelphia." Interestingly, Fey's character, Kate, is an ambitious gentrifier whose very job is to gentrify more areas of Philadelphia. Viewers are meant to celebrate her desire for and eventual success at motherhood, which she could have paid someone for if, in fact, her career choices had made it so she could no longer have a biological child. Unlike Oscar, who made bad choices by sleeping with women he had no relationship with, Tina Fey's Kate actually made all the right choices, and in the end she has it all: a wonderful, successful man who loves her and is the biological father of her own biological child, her incredible, high-paying job, and some new quirky, quaint poor friends. Fey's character herself becomes the baby's mama.

In Brooklyn, we learned that the term *mama* has been adopted by this class of well-resourced gentrifying women, who use it to refer to themselves and each other.[31] Often written as a vocative, the word can be found daily on any Brooklyn internet group for mothers/parents, with salutations such as, "Hey mamas out there . . ." or, "Breastfeeding mamas: Does anyone have a little bit of extra expressed milk?" When we asked our Brooklyn informants about why they used the term *mama*, their answers were interesting. A Brooklyn postpartum doula and certified lactation consultant said, for her, the word *mama* "is . . . a term of endearment, an equalizer, a transitional name into motherhood. Many women feel more like mamas than mothers—in an 'I'm not my mother' kind of way" (interview with authors, November 12, 2013).

Her choice of the phrase "not my mother" suggests that unlike "traditional motherhood," she and her cohort of new Brooklyn moms were doing "mothering" in a novel, and perhaps improved, way. Another Brooklyn mother and childbirth education teacher told us she did a search on Bloglovin', a blog reader, and found the word *mama* appears in more than ten thousand blog titles such as "Modern Alternative Mama," "Don't Mess with Mama," "Mama Birth," and "Mama and Baby Love." So, along with the shop owners' explicitly stated intentions of choosing the name because of a specific interpretation of Tina Fey's use of the term, *baby mama* is a singular focus on the relationship between a mother and her offspring, with all of the contextual challenges of modern life wrapped up into it. Such a term indicates a new appropriation of the word and a new meaning.

In this way, the sign for Baby/Mama contains literal and direct references to new motherhood practices that challenge more traditional conceptualizations of mothers as primary and private caregivers and nurturers. It also claims space for mothers as highly educated professionals who are engaged in their communities. As we have experienced and shown, however, this social equation for mothers is seen as threatening to the institutions and neighborhoods

WHAT THE SIGNS SAY

they utilize and in which they reside. Sociolinguistically, we argue, the threat of this new female equation can be mitigated precisely by appropriating the African Americanism *baby mama*, which, as Hill (2008, 1998) contends, allows through indexicality these new Brooklyn moms a jovial, relaxed, and of course, hip stance. In this sense, the wordplay of this New School sign uses race pragmatically and, in the spirit of Fey's film, humorously to palliate the transgressive public character of white, professional, urban, public mothering and to downplay the transformative and perhaps intimidating nature of their work.

Hill (2008, 134) provides some examples in her analysis of mock Spanish that serve a similar mitigating function. For instance, in her data she describes a sign on a tip jar, "El tip-o suave," at a coffee shop. The phrase is taken from the Spanish phrase *un tipo suave*, meaning "a cool guy," which was used on billboard advertisements in predominantly Latinx neighborhoods to sell Camel cigarettes. The words appeared under the cartoon icon Joe Camel. The mock usage for the coffee shop tip jar goes beyond the notion of simply indexing "laid-backness" to incorporate simultaneous references to gender, sex appeal, and the issue of labor exploitation. In other words, this particular use of mock Spanish can be interpreted as attempting to mitigate the potentially confrontational demand that "we are working for less than what we actually deserve, please compensate us further!" We have found a Brooklyn business with a similar sociolinguistically mitigated demand that plays on sex and sexism. In one coffee shop, the sign "show us your tips" on a tip jar greets customers at the register. Like New School wordplay such a cheeky text is clearly intended to be witty and may evoke second glances as it conjures the famous New Orleans Mardi Gras chant "Show us your tits!" In this phrase, *tips* takes the place of *tits* and thus could be interpreted as being offensive. Whether one is initially offended or simply amused, the sign demands, with intended wit, and thus presumably politely, that service professionals be compensated.[32]

In our case then, we read the mock-like usage of the African American term *baby mama* for a motherhood shop sign as not simply an act of cultural appropriation, but also as a move to mitigate and minimize the gendered confrontation of public mothering that has been happening in Brooklyn over the past two decades. In this way, the mock-like term could be acting as a type of linguistic cover, meant as an attempt to use humor to conjure not only a jovial and hip attitude, but also a non-threatening stance, not unlike the way Tina Fey might be using the term *baby mama* in her film to subvert the patriarchal order by suggesting that high-powered women executives are not really taking over corporate America.[33]

To cover means to place a protective barrier over or on something or someone. And the study of "women and cover" is well established in the ethnographic record through explorations of *purdah*, or the practice of the seclusion of women found in some Middle Eastern and South Asian Muslim and Hindu cultures (see for example Mookherjee 2006). But "covering women" occurs in all kinds of places throughout the world, and it is primarily achieved through practices that keep men and women separate and/or practices that cover women's hair, for example with scarves, veils, or wigs; parts of their bodies, such as shoulders and knees in churches with certain types of clothing; or their entire bodies, as with a burqa. And thus it is never clear whether women are being covered as a means of protecting them from others who might objectify or sexualize them or if the covering is meant to protect others from women who might cause them impure thoughts if they were to see feminine forms. Covering across cultures amounts to an expression of modesty, and in the US, women are encouraged to be appropriately modest in their appearance, expression, and demeanor as well. Western feminists note that patriarchal discourses about "good mothering" function both to regulate mothers and to coerce a certain kind of modesty from them (Wall 2001): that they be self-sacrificing, nonsexual, relegated to private spaces with their children, appropriately covered if breastfeeding, and absent from public debates (Grant 2016; Mathews 2018). That Brooklyn mothers are transforming and broadening the scope of traditional motherhood, redefining conceptualizations of private and public acts, remaking the area itself, and perhaps even feminizing urban space are political acts in the context of competition over space and its regulation of uses and users. So one reading of this usage of *baby mama* could be its power to ameliorate what otherwise might be perceived as a direct threat to the status quo of the established patriarchal order.

We have seen that in Brooklyn women with privilege attempt to make their "nature" (meaning motherhood) into "culture" (people concerned about school reform, pedestrian safety, commercialism) by shaking off the confines of traditional motherhood and taking possession of public space as mothers with children. Many women have achieved this goal despite the criticism launched against them and the obstacles placed before them. But as public mothering comes under increasing scrutiny in media and institutional settings, some gender work might go undercover. In this case, it could be that the storefront of Baby/Mama has gone under the cover of race and class.

The use of *baby mama* by Fey and by this Brooklyn store is problematic, though, not only because it is a linguistic appropriation but also because people in the African American community find the term offensive for the context. After hearing our John Jay College students' initial reactions to a store called Baby/Mama, we tried to find an equivalent case that would challenge the sensibilities of white people. Interestingly, in the fall of 2018, on a trip to attend a family wedding in Utah, a younger relative encouraged us to try breakfast at a Las Vegas shop called Eggslut, located in a nearby hotel. Surprised by the name, we began googling it. At the same time, Shonna needed to inform her aunt and uncle (both in their midsixties) who had been traveling with us of the proposed location to meet for breakfast. Shonna found herself loath to utter the name of the restaurant to her uncle over the phone, because she knew it would displease and maybe even upset him. When she finally said "Well, it's called Eggslut . . ." and tried to explain why we wanted to go (not only to please our younger relative, but also because it looked like important data for our work on signage), her uncle, dismayed, said, "Ok, here, talk to your aunt," and handed the phone over. We later confirmed that he was offended by the term, which neither he nor Shonna's aunt thought was "cute." When we talked this over with our younger relative, a college-bound high school senior, she said: "Why is it offensive? It's just a name that says, 'Come here if you really love eggs!'" We later learned online that Eggslut first started as a food truck in Los Angeles. Hazel Suazo, the business's co-owner, provided a definition of the store's name: "An egg slut is someone who loves eggs so much, they can eat them all day, all night, wet, hard, coddled, easy and with everything" (Pardess 2012). In addition, at the time of this writing, there are several Eggslut stores in the Los Angeles metro area, one in Las Vegas, an Eggslut counter in Manhattan, and a restaurant in Beirut, Lebanon. And indeed, it turns out that restaurants like Eggslut are newsworthy not only because of the popularity of their product, but also because of their names. Media outlets that have written about such names, have, not surprisingly, concluded that some people find them offensive (Pardess 2012, Myrick n.d.).

Back in Brooklyn, we see that gender is one of the most problematic of culture's organizing principles, in both Old School and New School signs. While Old School signage indexes gender sincerely, as it does the other organizing principles of race, ethnicity, class, etc., references to women on Old School shop signs are still quite traditional, confining women to culture's conservative and conventional roles for them. There is Juanita's Bridal Shop, Casa de Quince (a sweet fifteen dress and accessory shop for Latinas), Islamic Fashion (a place where Muslim women can buy stylish head-coverings), and the like, as well as strip joints such as Playpen and Sunset Den, which have silhouettes of naked women on their signs.

New School signage frequently uses gender ideologies both sincerely and ironically. In some instances, New School signs feel confining and reductive of women to their conventional cultural categories (such as Sweet Melissa for an upscale bakery, and the storefronts of Bird, Habit, Sweet Chick, and the Bad Wife, which we analyzed in Chapter Two). And other times, the signs and their stores feel more revolutionary: Boing Boing, Bump, and Wild Was Mama. But in most cases, the heteropatriarchy is implied and asserted so that women's subordination to men continues to be inscribed on the land and re-inscribed in culture. In other words, while there are some New School signs that seem to suggest that gentrifying women are making strides to control and define place as they see fit, in general both Old School (with their sincere references to conventional gender roles) and New School signs (with their ironic usages of gender) make a fairly conventional place for women, despite their own best efforts to act as full-fledged citizens who are more than mothers, shoppers, objectified sexual beings, and targets of derision.

Returning specifically to Baby/Mama, and to gentrifying mothers transforming the city, an irony remains embedded in these accounts of women changing the urban landscapes to meet their needs and the needs of their families. These educated and professional women are making space in the Brooklyn landscape for mothers like themselves at the same time other populations say they feel as if they are being displaced by the lifestyle, culture, and economy that gentrifiers bring. On the one hand, these women embrace notions of social justice, equality, and opportunity for all. On the other hand, their consumer preferences, high incomes, and advanced educations create a culture where the signs, both literal and metaphorical, say just the opposite to other people. Notably, upon asking the shop owner about the possibility of there being racialized overtones in the name Baby/Mama, he replied to us that people had suggested as much, but that racialization was not their intention. He reiterated that the store name was really "just a reference to Tina Fey" and her movie.[34] The store owner's insistence on the meaning of the name being a reference to Fey's film is an example of Jane Hill's notion of a personalist language ideology at work. As Hill explains:

> Personalism insists that each individual has an invisible interior self which is the site of beliefs and intentions and emotional states such as love and hatred. Personalist ideology permits us to say that when a speaker speaks, he or she "means" something. That is, meaning resides not only in the content of the words . . ., but in what speakers intend by uttering them. (Hill 2008, 89)

Paradoxically, the owner himself admitted that people told him that one of the possible meanings had racialized overtones. Even in the US, where personalism governs interpretations of meanings, speaker intentionality is never the be-all, end-all of meaning-making. One informant told us that if the owners of Baby/Mama "just loved Tina Fey," they could have easily called the store, "Tina Fey's." The fact they did not do so was meaningful to this person. So, while their store's name could refer to Tina Fey and her movie *Baby Mama*, it could also be referring to a form of motherhood stigmatized in the black community (and in dominant culture).

Whether one likes it or not, the sign "baby/mama" carries along with it the full semiotic repertoire of available meanings, including those that are negative, classist, racialized, and racist. It celebrates affluent white women's new norms of mothering in public by indirectly making a reference to Other women with lower socioeconomic status. If the sign helps to disguise the take-over of Brooklyn by economically, socially, and culturally empowered mothers in some circles, in others it makes strident the message that a changing of the guard is well underway.

Of course, every shop has its own story to tell. Boing Boing, for example, closed in 2014. Owner Paperno, in a *Daily News* story about its closing, noted that she had witnessed Park Slope "morph into one of the most expensive, baby-loving neighborhoods in the city." Ironically, she also became frustrated with these wealthy gentrifying moms, who, she said, would purchase expensive strollers online, then ask Paperno for instructions on how to use them. As her business struggled in the years after the downturn of 2008, she decided to head to Haiti, a place, she said, "with few resources" where she might be able to do some good working for a baby sling company (Murphy 2014). Along with Boing Boing, the beloved Tea Lounge, with which we opened this chapter, also closed its doors in 2014 after providing local mothers a place to be with their children and with each other for more than a decade. The disappearance of these stores and others like them points to a larger phenomenon changing Brooklyn. These shops were not victims of a cultural backlash or of patriarchal power, but rather of the accelerating rent gap contractions that brought such transformational storefronts to Brooklyn in the first place.

Rising rents and redevelopment have ushered in new Brooklyn texts of place-making that both signify and signal the arrival of corporate chains and the displacement of both Old and New School storefronts. As much as gentrifying women have found inroads to transform culture, with all the multiplicity of the readings at stake in their texts on the street, these new corporate moves do little to make place unique, let alone culturally transformative. That story, and the conflicts and confusions it entails, is the subject to which we now turn our linguistic and ethnographic lens.

I was about nine years old in South Philly . . . my grandmother and I were walking home and there's this . . . construction site . . . and there's this sign: "Coming soon, Society Hill Towers – Luxury Apartments." And . . . I'm like just so innocent – thinking – you know – some benevolent somebody somewhere knows how we are living. And I said, "Grandma, Look!" Because, also my grandmother was illiterate. And she would always get me to read stuff . . . for her . . . I said, "Grandma, look! Look! They're building new apartments! They're not projects!" . . . My grandmother turned around . . . like she was angry at me. "Let me tell you something Bertha Mae, *them people got plans*, and they don't include you!" I've never forgotten that, *ever*.

Bertha Lewis, interview with authors, July 9, 2013

4. Competing Semiotics
Elusive Authenticity and the Inevitable Arrival of Corporate America

IN THE EPIGRAPH, Bertha Lewis, an affordable housing activist working in New York City, tells how she naively read the message posted by developers about their new construction project as a sign of hope.[1] Her grandmother, however, had no trouble interpreting it as a symbol of exclusions and a harbinger of displacement. And as it turned out, Lewis's grandmother was right.

In South Philly, the luxury high rise Society Hill Towers was part of a late 1950s urban renewal effort to restore Society Hill, one of the city's oldest residential neighborhoods, to its original grandeur. The Philadelphia Redevelopment Authority, along with other city entities, assisted "wealthy" or "upper-middle-class" individual homeowners in renovating the neighborhood's eighteenth-century townhouses. It also cleared other buildings and empty lots to build the Society Hill Towers, which were completed in 1964. Society Hill has become one of Philadelphia's most expensive neighborhoods, displacing the area's original residents, many of whom were African American.[2] Having learned about gentrification, development, and displacement early on, Lewis told us that she now tried to make it her business to ensure that when corporate developers have plans, they include her community. She used the Society Hill story to explain to us why she supported Forest City Ratner Companies' (FCRC) multibillion dollar Atlantic Yards arena and residential and office tower project. Bruce Ratner, FCRC Chief Executive Officer, promised her he would include low-income housing and jobs for local working-class people in the neighborhoods around the project site.

Lewis' story from her youth, and her later support for corporate development, points to how urban landscapes can be complicated things to interpret. We previously looked at how two very different patterns or registers of Brooklyn signage are engaged with conflicting forms of place-making. We also looked at these signs in the context of other forces of change, namely the work of gentrifying women. In Lewis's story, we see how signs might easily be misread until one knows more information about a place.[3] This chapter explores two inter-related stories. First we take a look at Lewis' grandmother's reference to "them people," which refers to private developers frequently working in partnership with public government agencies to reshape landscapes. In Brooklyn, their plans are often strategic, involve areas already inhabited, and are driven by economic forces in tandem with cultural, social, and political ones. These strategic decisions usually result in large-scale and long-term changes in place. Second, alongside these plans are people's differing interpretations of what Brooklyn's densely populated neighborhoods were and are becoming. These interpretations (and misinterpretations) of the semiotic landscape also entail ideas about "authenticity," or the notion that a place has some essential appearance, function, or identity. But ideas about authenticity and plans that shape and exploit urban space are complexly connected, and this complexity has implications for conflicts over place as well. Neighborhood activists might see corporate redevelopment of urban space as serving no one but shareholders. But sociolinguistically, one could also read such development as producing a generic place-less-ness that can (at least potentially) serve everybody. What plans are behind urban change that we might not readily see in the landscape if we do not know how to read it? Put another way, to what degree does corporate capitalism and its creation of placelessness threaten the lifestyles and ideologies that we see represented in both Old School and New School signage? To answer these questions, let's first start with a closer look at the Atlantic Yards redevelopment project that Lewis lent her support to and that a lot of local residents, many of whom were gentrifiers, vigorously tried to stop.

Figure 4.1. A diagram of the footprint introduced in December 2003 for the Atlantic Yards redevelopment project between Atlantic and Pacific Avenues in Prospect Heights, Brooklyn. (Photograph of a page from the personal archive of Patti Hagan)

"A Gang of Towers" in Low-Rise Brooklyn

In 2003, FCRC entered into a partnership with the State of New York through its Empire State Development Corporation (ESDC) to radically transform a twenty-two-acre swath of land at the confluence of four Brooklyn neighborhoods (Figure 4.1). Bruce Ratner's original plan included the arena for the New Jersey (soon to be Brooklyn) Nets, which he purchased in 2004, and sixteen high-rise residential and office towers, designed by architect Frank Gehry. In addition to bringing a professional sports team to a borough that had not had one since the Dodgers left for Los Angeles in the late 1950s, jobs for the local community and affordable housing were key selling points of the project. For example, FCRC promised that some 2,250 units out of 6,860 would be made "affordable," and it was because of this promise that Bertha Lewis decided to throw her support behind the scheme.[4]

The plan gained considerable local attention because residents from the four neighborhoods adjacent to the site launched a spirited opposition to the proposal and their arguments were many. Some people complained that the plan's enormity was incongruent with the local neighborhoods. For example, the popular, Brooklyn-born novelist Jonathan Lethem, in an open Letter to Frank Gehry, complained of a looming "gang of . . . towers" invading

Figure 4.2. A mural on the door of a garage in Prospect Heights protesting the abuse of eminent domain by Forest City Ratner Companies and the State of New York to remove people in the Atlantic Yards project footprint. Photo by Tracy Collins.

low-rise brownstone Brooklyn (Lethem 2006). Others feared that the area would be overly burdened with teeming traffic and that asthma rates in the area, already some of the worst in the nation, would be exacerbated. Residents aired concerns about the city's lack of planning to provide services and infrastructure to an area that would soon become home to more than six thousand new inhabitants. Still other critics of the project were also unsatisfied with FCRC's notion of affordable housing.[5] They claimed that Atlantic Yards would bring instant gentrification, or the incidental and unintentional displacement of low-income residents. One of the most contentious issues was the public-private partnership between the developer and the State of New York, which not only allowed tax dollars to finance a significant part of the project, but included what many residents and activists considered to be an abuse of eminent domain, or the power of the state to seize land, for what they thought was a dubious "public use" (for much more on this issue see Snajdr and Trinch 2018a).[6] At the largest anti-Atlantic Yards rally, in the summer of 2006, some 4,500 residents and several national celebrities who happened to live in Brooklyn protested the development in Brooklyn's Grand Army Plaza. Over the next few years, the actual plans for the project changed substantially. After the economic downturn of 2008, Forest City redesigned the project and brought on SHoP, a new, less well-known, up-and-coming architecture firm. For help with financing, FCRC also later partnered with Russian and Chinese development groups. In 2010, despite scores of protests and dozens of lawsuits, FCRC broke ground and in the fall of 2012 cut the ribbon for the Barclays Center Arena, the Brooklyn Nets' new home.

Long before "Atlantic Yards" became a place, and before Brooklyn Nets logos and paraphernalia began to appear on the actual bodies of Brooklynites in the form of ball caps and T-shirts, hundreds of thousands of words were written either to promote it or to protest it. These texts emerged on websites, blogposts, and print and online news and magazine outlets, as well as pamphlets, promotional fliers, legal documents, plays, books, and two documentary films.[7] The physical landscape itself also became marked with public texts in opposition (predominantly) to the project. For example, "Stop Atlantic Yards" posters appeared on the beveled glass windows of the grand entryways of brownstones in Prospect Heights, Fort Greene, and Park Slope. Murals sprang up on the front gates of local garages or on the sides of warehouses (Figure 4.2). These anti-Atlantic Yards messages competed with official signage around the site that directed the curious to call the Community Liaison Office and mass mailings of promotional brochures sent out by the developer enumerating Atlantic Yards' benefits to the area. These brochures were referred to by activists opposed to the project as "liar fliers."

The first person to sound the alarm about Atlantic Yards and the issue of eminent domain abuse was Patti Hagan, a longtime Prospect Heights resident and community activist. After much of the battle was lost she later complained that the opposition "fought the project from behind their computers!" rather than focusing on more traditional protest tactics of street demonstrations, canvassing, and direct actions (interview with authors, September 3, 2010). To their credit, many activists we spoke with showed us plenty of evidence that they had tried on-the-ground organizing and protest planning. But Hagan was correct that much of the energy of the movement manifested in lawsuits, and proliferated online, in digital form, on sites such as DevelopDontDestroyBrooklyn.net, NoLandGrab.org, and AtlanticYardsReport.com.[8] Interestingly, the developer had an initially rudimentary website, with far fewer graphics and links, and less color and style than those created by opponents. Furthermore, many of Brooklyn's award-winning and nationally recognized authors, artists, actors, and musicians, who lived in the neighborhoods that would be affected, lent their writing skills or their names to raise money for the organizations fighting Atlantic Yards.[9]

As if they had forgotten Lethem's "gang of towers" complaint, media reporting of the controversy often focused on the basketball arena and not the rest of the project plan. The media's conspicuous lack of attention to a critique of the overarching plan sometimes reduced the opposition to mere whiners, concerned only about their backyards. However, we saw in this redevelopment project an explicit urban contest, where conflict over space involved "large amounts of energy . . . invested in producing, maintaining and distributing the idea . . ." of place (Dorst 1989, 3). Ideas do not just circulate in their affirmative; they also are creatively constructed through the erasure of facts and of history and the manipulation of public language and semiotics.[10] But as our opening quote showed, Bertha Lewis's grandmother was aware of "them people" and their "plans," and these discursive battles about place are underpinned by economic forces that are the result of and mobilized by strategic designs and schemes.

"Them People": Development, Plans, and the Rent Gap

While Atlantic Yards has been one of the more visible and high-profile forms of corporate development, there have been many others in the city that anthropologist Julian Brash (2011) has called "Bloomberg's New York." These have included the Hudson Yards, the Freedom Tower, the West Side Stadium, the Highline (all located in Manhattan), Willets Point in Queens, and countless high-rise "luxury" condominiums and office towers in Brooklyn, Queens, and Manhattan. Some of these planned projects have been completed. Others have not. But many of them have involved public-private partnerships of some kind, and the work of a team of analysts, urban planners, marketers, lawyers, and consultants, often scouting out and assessing areas that are "ready" for development.

The processes of gentrification and redevelopment are the result of all sorts of planning, plotting, and policy-making that reaches far back into New York City's past.[11] There is, for example, a large literature on broader policies of planning, investment, and development, beginning with long-serving New York City Parks Commissioner and Triborough Bridge and Tunnel chairman Robert Moses and his efforts to build parkways, bridges, tunnels, and housing projects.[12] Alongside this state level transformation of New York is a story of a burgeoning wave of white flight from urban centers to suburban housing markets in the 1950s, '60s and '70s resulting in widespread disinvestment and neglect in many neighborhoods. Many African Americans moved into these neighborhoods from the rural South during what has been called the Great Migration, in search of jobs and freedom from the oppression of Jim Crow laws. These shifts did not happen overnight, but they collectively and eventually left many immigrant and African American communities "behind" to fend for themselves in the disparaged and decaying "inner city."[13]

There were all kinds of social, cultural, and political forces at work in this transformation, including discrimination, racism, ethnocentrism, and xenophobia, and these shifts also had broad economic foundations such as redlining, urban deindustrialization, and the globalization and financialization of markets (Levitt 1983; Dore 2008). As we have mentioned, both the redevelopment and gentrification following this extensive period of urban decay are fundamentally driven by what cultural geographer Neil Smith (1979) called "the rent gap." Smith, as we noted, defined the rent gap as the gap between an area's "potential ground rent level" and the actual ground rent value in the way land is presently used (545). Smith coined the term in his seminal study of Philadelphia's Society Hill neighborhood, the same neighborhood in which Bertha Lewis witnessed the reality of other people's *plans*.[14] Changes in the rent gap, according to Smith, are certainly not random. They are the result of planning and investment, or disinvestment. In Smith's view gentrification is therefore not just an idiosyncratic process, randomly occurring on the ground in the form of the intrepid urban "pioneer" taking a chance on renovating a building in a so-called downscale neighborhood or slum.[15] It is the result of both the search for economic opportunity by individuals and the collaborative plans of government and private corporations to keep redevelopment and gentrification going and to exploit them further.

For example, once gentrifiers enter an area, one of the ways to keep them there is by drastically lowering property taxes for homeowners in certain neighborhoods. This was Mayor Michael Bloomberg's administration's strategy in the early 2000s, which the de Blasio administration also followed: homeowners pay taxes only on the assessed value and not the market value of their properties. So a million-dollar home in Park Slope may see an annual property tax payment of less than $5000.[16] A parallel strategy is to offer large corporations similar tax relief to coax them into building bigger projects, which in turn attracts more corporate development and even more upscale gentrification. In addition to tax breaks for homeowners and corporate developers, another planned practice fueling both urban redevelopment and gentrification is zoning changes.[17] The rapid transformation of parts of downtown Brooklyn were the result of rezoning primarily commercial retail areas into mixed-use residential space, which ushered in a slew of high-rise condo buildings between Fort Greene and Brooklyn's Navy Yard.[18] These purposeful decisions can transform an area quickly and permanently. So, as Bertha Lewis' grandmother warned her, "them people got plans"; it's not always easy to identify who, exactly, "them" is, but undoubtedly, "them people" in the equation are not just gentrifiers but also big corporate developers. Developers often work with government support to drastically change the urban landscape, and as Lewis' grandmother also warned her, their plans might not necessarily include everybody.

Even corporate developers sometimes misread the signs of opportunity for projects and profit in a transitioning area, though. A former FCRC executive admitted to us in an interview that he and the company's chairman, Bruce Ratner, did not initially see the rent gap near the site they chose to build the Atlantic Yards project: "In the late 1990s . . . Mort Zuckerman, the owner of the *Daily News*, asked [us] to come look at . . . [his] printing . . . and distribution center and he was convinced that there was potential to convert it . . . but we thought the neighborhood was nowhere close to being ready. . . . In fact, I think Bruce and I agree now, in retrospect, *we were wrong, dead wrong. We just didn't see it*" (emphasis added; interview with authors, February 18, 2011). Because profitability is maximized by capitalizing on "where the [rent] gap is greatest" (Smith 1979, 546), this executive's emphatic regret of being "dead wrong" underlines the cost of missing the chance to redevelop the *Daily News* building as a high-end residential property, which over even only a couple of years translates to massive lost profit. By 2003, FCRC not only recognized the rent gap in the area but acted upon it merely two blocks away with its Atlantic Yards plan, letting nothing—not a seven-year struggle with neighborhood activists, several high-profile lawsuits, or a global economic recession—stop them from breaking ground in 2010.

The former FCRC executive and Ratner were not alone in their confusion about the area's potential. Media outlets, which are also important promoters and marketers of place, also did not identify the area as "a place to go." For example, a popular *New York Times* guide to the city's neighborhoods (Leahy 1999), published in the late 1990s and marketed toward professionals moving into Brooklyn, did not list Prospect Heights or the adjacent neighborhood of Fort Greene as recommended locations. The "livable" Brooklyn neighborhoods it did identify were mostly along the western side of the borough, running from Greenpoint in the north, through Williamsburg and Brooklyn Heights, and down to Bay Ridge in the far south. Activists who were fighting FCRC's Atlantic Yards were also confused about the skyrocketing land values in their neighborhoods. They told us that when they heard about the plan, they were shocked by its scale and scope. They had perceived their Prospect Heights neighborhood to be emerging organically, despite the fact that they had paid over $500,000 for their two-bedroom condos in 2002. Interestingly, apartments were fetching these prices only three years after the *Times* neighborhood guide came out. Like the former FCRC executive's initial view of the site, these informants described the area as messy, in need of better schools, better policing, and overall beautification. Some felt their home purchases were still economically precarious.

These feelings of precariousness can be linked to the fact that as neighborhoods transform from poor or working-class to extremely expensive places to live, they may go through long periods where they appear neither rich nor poor, but as if they could go either way. As we have noted, a shifting linguistic landscape is one indicator (along with a host of others) suggesting that parts of the borough could be targeted for this type of redevelopment. The appearance of a New School storefront signals small business owners are willing to risk their capital in a downscale area and people are taking advantage of this opportunity. But calculating the endpoint of an expanding rent gap is not a perfect science. Both FCRC's mistake not to invest in Zuckerman's *Daily News* building and the opposition's concern about their community's future reveal how even neighborhoods that are quickly becoming targets of gentrification—and thus highly sought after by newcomers—are still quite hard to interpret, even by people with a vested financial and social interest in them.

Confusing Distinctions: Misreading the Rent Gap

Individual gentrifiers do not generally view their choices and experiences in the systematic and planned manner that Smith so elegantly laid out in his classic rent gap analysis. Instead, gentrifiers encounter the process occurring in mundane and quotidian ways. While profitability from the rent gap and capitalizing on it requires transition, this condition, as we have shown, is quite literally, though not always clearly, written on the site. The inchoate term between what a neighborhood was and what it might become often entails periods of uncertainty. Transition seems dangerous and exciting because it presents a moment of indefinability and risk. A transforming Brooklyn feels exciting to some people, and so gentrification entices them with its promise of renewal and gain. With many areas of Brooklyn already gentrified, such as

Boerum Hill (Kasinitz 1988), Brooklyn Heights (Lees 2003), and Park Slope (Osman 2012), people sought out neighborhoods further and further away from city centers, areas that Douglass (2012) refers to as "edge places." The name itself implies a lack of place-ness, or a marginal place that has not yet become what it may have the economic potential to be.

Michael Pintchik is a property owner and developer who, we noted in Chapter Three, convinced Babeland, the upscale purveyor of sex-toys, to open a store next to the New School maternity store Bump, and who rents to several New School businesses near his paint store, Pintchik Paints, in Park Slope. Pintchik shared an ambivalent observation about the area's seeming transition into difficult times and hence an edge place in the 1960s:

> It was probably in the sixties that the neighborhood was going. . . . We were still very strong in business, but it . . . was dangerous. We had a big accounting staff and . . . my father had to have a driver pick the women up and bring them here and bring them home, because their husbands wouldn't let them come to work on a bus or on a subway. . . . It was pretty grim. And then my father . . . would make arrangements with the owners of the buildings who were abandoning [them] so that he would have these coverings made for the windows . . . [with images] of someone looking out of the window, painted on them . . . with curtains or maybe a cat or a dog, . . . just . . . to sort of make the neighborhood look less abandoned."
> (interview with authors, August 8, 2011)

Notably, Pintchik tells us this was happening at the same time residents of brownstone Brooklyn were renovating their homes—using Pintchik Paints—and all of Long Island, Staten Island, New Jersey, and Westchester were coming to the store to buy what would have been expensive, $6 to $10 per yard wallpaper at rock bottom $1.90 per yard prices from him.

In an interview with a husband and wife who moved into Prospect Heights merely blocks from Zuckerman's *Daily News* building in the 1970s, the couple told us about their original perceptions of their new neighborhood:

SHONNA: So you guys call this Prospect Heights. And that's what everyone calls it?

WIFE: Actually, it was just beginning to be called Prospect Heights when we moved here. 'Cause it was originally called part of the larger Crown Heights. So, if you talked to older people . . .

HUSBAND: I don't think we called it . . . Prospect Heights for some years.

WIFE: Yeah.

SHONNA: People considered it to be Crown Heights?

HUSBAND: People didn't consider it to be anything.

WIFE: Yeah. You know, like downtown . . .

HUSBAND: It was the wrong side of Flatbush Avenue. You know. That's what it was. (interview with authors, June 12, 2011)

In this context, the "wrong side" to them meant the area seemed empty and dismal:

HUSBAND: When our kids were born in the mid-eighties, you could go out on the street, and look up [east] toward Prospect Park and consistently never see another human being.

WIFE: Like on a day like this. [It was a sunny, warm, beautiful day.]

HUSBAND: You would look up [east] and there would be nothing. You would go into the park [southeast] and there would be nobody, nobody. . . . Desolate. Desolate. . . . It was like a *Twilight Zone* episode and all the people were missing. (interview with authors, June 12, 2011)

This impression of emptiness extended to adjacent neighborhoods, like Fort Greene, and to a nearby commercial area along Vanderbilt Avenue, which the wife described as a type of "wasteland":

So [Fort Greene], you never really looked that way [north]. And even now [in 2011] . . . we're focused . . . this direction [south, toward Park Slope]. We don't even . . . go over to Vanderbilt Avenue [east] that much. I mean . . . we have to purposely think to go that way, because there was never anything over there. (interview with authors, June 12, 2011)

The wife's memory does not seem to match entirely with historical records. A survey of tax photos of block and lot properties from 1980, digitally archived at the New York City Department of Records, reveals that, around the time that this couple moved into the neighborhood, Vanderbilt Avenue was an active commercial and retail area. From the photo archive of properties along the seven-block stretch between Atlantic Avenue and Sterling Place, we found two gas stations, a brake repair shop, a funeral home, two storefront churches, a plumbing supplies store, a heating supplies store, a beauty supplies retailer, four grocers, a supermarket, two bars, two wine and liquor stores, a locksmith shop, a barber shop, a pizzeria, a couple of delis/groceries, (more commonly known in New York City by the Spanish word *bodega*), a fish and chips shop, and an electronics store. The tax photos also show several different people standing or walking on or along the avenue.[19]

Interestingly, the emptiness of place felt by these newcomers was also represented in what they considered to be a meaningful lack of vegetation:

HUSBAND: We were walking down St. Marks [Avenue] talking about . . . [The husband is referring to a walking tour of the neighborhood that he and Ed had taken together.]

ED: . . . and [the Husband] said, "by the way, all these trees, you know, were planted in 1970. Before that there were not trees on this street."

WIFE: Right. Right. If you, if you look at that great book . . . of Park Slope, you can see that there were no trees. . . . Um, so that was one thing that really humanized the neighborhood. (interview with authors, June 12, 2011)

Indeed, trees were conspicuously absent in many commercial areas in the borough in the past. Two historical mural-sized photographs of Bay Ridge in the 1940s, one adorning an interior wall of a restaurant called the South Brooklyn Foundry, the other in a TD Bank building, confirm the couples' account of treelessness on 3rd and 5th Avenues respectively. However, in each photo, there are a lot of people shopping on both sides of the street for several blocks. And the storefronts in both images, as well as in the 1980s tax photos from the Prospect Heights' Vanderbilt Avenue commercial district, clearly follow the Old School Vernacular aesthetic in terms of large, abundant wording and literalness.

For this couple, who was able to buy a relatively low-priced building in what is now known as Prospect Heights, the shifting (and increasing) value of their purchase was obscured by their impression of many features of their surroundings. But the illegibility of the rent gap for them became clearer to us when they recounted an encounter from the past with one of their tenants, a thrift shop owner on the ground floor rental space of their property:

HUSBAND: Now, when we got here, we had a tenant downstairs . . . [a] thrift shop.

SHONNA: What did they sell?

HUSBAND: Clothes . . .

WIFE: And not much rent!

HUSBAND: And not much rent. And when we got here, their rent was $125 [a month], and when they left 6 years ago [in 2005] . . .

WIFE: And you have to understand that the building was now being managed by [my husband] . . . who knew nothing of . . . business . . .

HUSBAND: And *when* they left, they were paying more than $2200! I just have to tell you a little tiny vignette. . . . We were going to get a . . . new sidewalk and, it was delayed and we didn't get our permits . . . and finally there was some warm weather around Christmas time. So, the contractor [is] doing [the sidewalk] and they had to make a wood plank to get into the store. And I stayed home from work . . . to help people in and out and mitigate our liability and so forth. And [the owner], a chain-smoking, tough customer . . .

WIFE: . . . who would have on a *mink stole* with the heads on it every now and then!

HUSBAND: Yeah, somebody would donate it and she would put it on, such a mink! And she would come out and she'd say, ". . . this cost me $20,000." And I said, "[owner's name], if I thought you were making that kind of money, you'd never have the rent you do. And I was so annoyed. And I came upstairs and I wrote to the attorney general. *Nothing* was online in those days, but you could get it. And I saw that they were taking in $200,000 a year on donated merchandise!

WIFE: It's crazy!

HUSBAND: Needless to say, the next rental negotiation was favorable to us! (interview with authors, June 12, 2011)

This story highlights how the husband and wife's impressions of their neighborhood as empty and of their tenant as barely making any money in what they perceived to be an area devoid of patrons and people obfuscates the reality that their tenant's shop was obviously selling to someone as they were apparently pulling in substantial sales. Thus, the neighborhood clearly had enough people around—who our informants claim they rarely saw—to spend almost $20,000 a month on low-priced, donated items. Even the owner's expensive clothing accessories are read as "donations" by our informants, when, in fact, our informants probably have no idea how the tenant acquired the minks, which clearly, she could have very well purchased with some of the money she was earning.

If this couple thought "no one was there," they may have developed this sense from the strikingly dramatic demographic changes the area was undergoing in the decades just prior to and during their arrival. In 1970, the broader area of what was becoming Prospect Heights (including the blocks between Atlantic Avenue, Eastern Parkway, and Roger's Avenue) had a population of 48,000.[20] Between 1970 and 1980, around the time the couple arrived in the area, 11,500 people left the neighborhood. This was the decade of New York City's fiscal crisis, the 1977 blackout, and an accelerating process of white flight from the city. Indeed, out of the total number who departed, 9,400 were white. Some 1,500 African Americans also left the area.

Interestingly, a substantial population of some 37,000 people still remained in the neighborhood. And, as the 1980 tax photos show, people still used the commercial district, and there were still businesses that served them. The decade between 1970 and 1980 shows the sharpest decline in population for this area (and for neighboring Crown Heights, just to the east, as well; around 16,000 left this area too). But far fewer people left western parts of Prospect Heights between 1980 and 1990, and about 2,500 people moved into the eastern part of the neighborhood. That decade witnessed a total net gain of about 1,000 residents. Moving forward in time from decade to decade, additional but less dramatic overall population changes occurred, and in fact, by 2010, only 3,000 people have returned to the area over three decades. Indeed, during the time this couple lived there, not many newcomers arrived relative to the neighborhood's past population levels. Since 1970, the area experienced a net population loss of 8,500.

In terms of *who* was living in the area, however, we see a strikingly different story of change emerge. Between 1980 and 2010, the white population for Prospect Heights increased by 9,700. In contrast, the overall African American population decreased by 12,300. In 1970, the racial composition of the neighborhood was roughly a third white and two-thirds black. In 1980, with a large population drop, the ratio shifts to 20 percent white and 80 percent African American. But in three short decades, even with the so-called process of white flight, the black/white ratio in the same area is now 50/50. These changes are even more dramatic when one analyzes only the census tracts of the western portion of Prospect Heights—placing the eastern border of the neighborhood at Washington Avenue, where the ratio is presently 64 percent white to only 36 percent black.[21] Along with this demographic data, median income levels for the neighborhood have gone up sharply, with increases as high as 100 percent (in census tracts 305 and 161, for example). And note that rent for the thrift shop in Prospect Heights in the building owned by our husband and wife informants increased sixteen-fold, from $125 in the early 1980s to $2,200 in 2005. Likewise, the number of people over twenty-five years old with college degrees or higher has risen from only 15 percent of the neighborhood's population in 1970 to 50 percent in 2000. In less than thirty years, Prospect Heights has become a very different place.[22]

As changes like these proceed, however, such significant transitions of urban space are not necessarily dramatically evident. For example, in a 2014 discussion about our research in the borough with a colleague, we noted that while a host of factors contribute to the making of place, retail signage is often one of the only visible and material indicators of a neighborhood's increasing real estate value. "Right," she answered, and added with all sincerity, "because there are no other signs of poshness in Brooklyn!" Her remark highlighted for us the prevalence of so many other physical features of Brooklyn's landscape that people struggle to interpret in addition to and in conjunction with signage. For example, the vast array of nonmatching architectural features and building designs and materials—often side-by-side—do not read as elegant or stylishly luxurious for a place where housing is more expensive than it is almost anywhere else in the country. In addition to these disparate, seemingly mismatched structures, Brooklyn's cityscape includes constant noise and commotion from construction work and from vehicle and pedestrian traffic, which you might call colloquially "hustle and bustle," if you want to be positive, or "gridlock" or "urban throngs" if you cast it in a negative light.

In other areas of the United States with expensive real estate, "signs of poshness" abound: a lack of crowds, ample parking, manicured lawns, flower gardens, residential garages, and large houses. In addition to these features, we could add level and even sidewalk pavement; freshly painted lane markers on streets and roads; fencing of wrought iron, white pickets, brick, or stone; and flower boxes, shrubs, and potted plants, as well as lots of shade trees. Giorgia Aiello (2011) has examined how the use of certain building materials in the cultural district of Bologna, Italy, Manifattura delle Arti, such as brushed steel, tile, brass, and marble, are visible and tactile codes for affluence that residents recognize as civic or private investments in place.[23] One can find these materials in some areas of New York City's Manhattan, such as the Upper East Side or Midtown, where it is generally understood that residents and businesses in these places "have money." In addition to expensive building materials, these places are often literally awash with building supers maintaining clean public spaces or public-facing private spaces. Walking through Manhattan's Midtown streets for commutes to work, pedestrians frequently must dodge the hose or pressure-washer that cleans the sidewalks and the facades of hotels, condos, office buildings, and storefronts on a daily basis.

In most Brooklyn neighborhoods, one enduring problem is the lack of efficient trash collection, exacerbated by the accidental spillage of liquids from garbage that pools in the streets and on the sidewalks, creating a stench that lingers in the summer heat and can be hard to bear. For example, Figure 4.3 shows the entrance to our children's middle school on parent-teacher conference day. Garbage is swirling around in the vestibule and literally blocking one of the doorways into the building. Sewers often get clogged with trash or

Figure 4.3. Garbage in front of the entrance to a highly selective Brooklyn public middle school. Scaffolding covering a school building is also a common feature due to ongoing exterior renovations, which take place outside of school hours but leave the structure shrouded, sometimes for a year a more, during the day.

Figure 4.4. Flooding at the intersection of two Brooklyn streets after a rain. Storm drains often have to be cleared by residents and business owners.

leaves, causing crosswalks for pedestrians to be nearly impassable (Figure 4.4). "Black orbs," which originated as chewing gum cast out of thousands of shoppers' mouths, mar the commercial sidewalks in every neighborhood.[24] Dog waste and other sorts of refuse such as newspaper, Styrofoam deli containers, straws, candy wrappers, and the like collect easily and rapidly on public walkways in front of buildings or businesses that cannot afford daily cleaning. And many Brooklyn public schools suffer from the burdens of infrastructure decay and repair and are forced to "make do" with the urban spaces available. For instance, one elementary school held a dance show in a Brooklyn residential street because the playground, in sore need of an upgrade, was under construction. Children laid their beach towels directly on pavement that hundreds of cars drive on each day while awaiting each class's performance.

Clearly, one group's cultural references are not always comprehensible to outsiders because cultural systems operate within a set of symbols and semiotics that require knowledge and familiarity. These systems are also often implicit, extensive, and complex. Thus we found that when upper-middle-class culture is conveyed through New School signage, not all upper-middle-class people get the reference, but they still sense a shop's exclusiveness through its other semiotic and material features. The semiotics of upscale poshness are also quite dynamic, and they change along with style and fashion. New symbolic forms of "taste" can easily get misinterpreted by those who may not keep up with contemporary developments in the culture of aesthetics. While observing a demonstration by anti-Atlantic Yards activists in front of the newly opened Barclays Center in 2012, we noticed a bystander who, we learned, lived nearby. He ignored the noisy activists with their bullhorns and performance art and fixed his gaze on the completed arena. When we asked his impressions of the construction, he focused on its appearance rather than on the economic effects of its arrival: "When are they going to finish it?" he replied.

His confusion stemmed from the Barclays Center's weathered steel exterior, which to him looked "rusty," making it appear incomplete, as if the builders needed to place a covering on the oxidizing bones of the building. This ambiguous look was intentional, a result of design and planning. The material was designed by Ellerbe Becket and SHoP, the architecture firm that replaced Frank Gehry. SHoP representatives explained in the press that this "natural" and "authentic" look was germane to the Brooklyn context (Brown 2009). A *New York Times* architecture critic wrote that the material had "a toughness that should fit well into its gritty setting" (Ouroussoff 2009). And Brooklyn borough president Marty Markowitz claimed the rusty exterior was "a luminous, iconic structure that celebrates Brooklyn's industrial heritage" (Bagli 2009). American studies scholar Stuart Schrader (2010) suggests that the arena's rusted exterior "abstracts from the past, with cool, nonspecific evocations of decay" in order to market and celebrate the present development efforts as the only possible pathway to the borough's economic development.[25] But clearly not all residents recognized this aesthetic message in the building's postmodern design.[26]

Like the curious onlooker who puzzled over Barclays Center's unfinished appearance at its grand opening, the persistence and prevalence of Old School signage and businesses in more upscale neighborhoods often confuses people unfamiliar with Brooklyn. As an example of this semiotic confusion, nonresidents who encounter Brooklyn, after visits to Park Slope, Bed Stuy, or Williamsburg, tell us that they "don't get it," meaning they do not understand why landlords in these neighborhoods are able to charge such steep rents or why people want to live there so badly. They complain these areas have inconsistent retail shopping and the presence of Old School storefronts detracts from the neighborhoods' overall appeal. However, these same complainers keep coming to Brooklyn, trying to explore and understand it, and ultimately they seem to enjoy the cachet that goes with their Brooklyn adventure narratives. While they may not be completely disparaging of the Old School contexts, they are definitely perplexed by them, especially considering the seemingly astronomical housing prices in the area.

As an example of this confusing mixture on the landscape, evidence from our ethnographic and photo mapping of two commercial areas of Prospect Heights around the Atlantic Yards redevelopment site in February of 2012 yielded findings that supported the transitional feel of place quite far along in the gentrification process. We counted ninety-seven postal addresses on Prospect Heights' seven-block section of Vanderbilt Avenue, the same street we also systematically mapped using 1980s tax photos. Eighteen of these addresses were residential, and four of the eighteen were under renovation, marked by construction permits and notices. Two storefront addresses had signs up saying "for rent," and eight addresses were on buildings whose façades we could not define. Were they empty storefronts, or perhaps inhabited apartments or co-ops? We could not tell by looking on from the sidewalk. In addition to a storefront church and a funeral home, we counted thirty-six retail businesses with Old School signage. But there were also twenty-six new stores, all with New School signs. Similarly, out of the ninety-five storefronts on Flatbush Avenue, the other major commercial district in Prospect Heights, which runs seven long-blocks from Atlantic Avenue to Prospect Park, we counted thirty-nine New School signs, or more than a third of the storefronts that we mapped for the avenue. Notably, we also photographed eight corporate chain stores on this section of Flatbush Avenue. But in spite of the area's upscale demographics and rapid commercial transformation, there were still forty-eight Old School signs on the street.

Interestingly, some of the Old School signs we find on these commercial streets were put up for brand new businesses. Even in a rapidly gentrifying context, new Old School signs continue to go up all the time. And again, it is important to reiterate that the Old School businesses' spirit of capitalism without distinction does not necessarily mean they offer nondistinctive, low-quality products. Often, urban dwellers "in-the-know" know exactly where great products at great prices can be found in Brooklyn. Our point is only that the signs say you do not have to be distinctive yourself to buy from them. But this type of shopping and very wealthy and well-off people's awareness of quality at an excellent price are other elements of confusion in a transitional or a multicultural landscape.

The staying power of these Old School signs in gentrifying areas can create what we term *semiotic vibrancy*. But some gentrifiers to Brooklyn tend to describe them much more negatively, and they suggest the signs make the neighborhood appear as if it is in a state of flux rather than transition. Some of our informants suggested that Old School signs made an area appear not only unattractive but lawless, and they seemed to read nonstandard linguistic features as an "anything goes" statement. When one upper-middle-class Brooklyn newcomer looked at our text-dense examples, she thought the signs "scream[ed] 'developing world.'" Another woman who moved to Brooklyn in 2002 complained that "the multiple word signs indicate desperation, lack of focus, and a lack of confidence." As we mentioned earlier, this mixture of old and new in transition creates a sense of precarity. And certainly, when people experience these areas for short periods of time, they may have difficulty acquiring the code. What they see on first glance may seem bewildering or uninterpretable.

While some gentrifiers suggest that the landscape, still in many ways dominated by Old School signage, is confusing, lawless, and chaotic, others discuss and describe how these signs provoke internal conflict that is also confusing and difficult to interpret. For example, one gentrifier, a white woman who works in NGOs dedicated to social justice, said that one of the Old School signs "appears to market to community residents who are living paycheck to paycheck . . ." but that "[it] could be any neighborhood in Brooklyn, as there are always either residents or employees in a community living on the margins, even if they make a decent income (due to child support obligations, a failed business, loss of a job, etc.)." And while she discussed the vibrancy of ethnically marked stores, she also noted Old School establishments are "Mom and Pop traditional small business, with sort of a working/middle class vibe," and that "Brooklyn still maintains older, traditional hold outs." But then she asked, parenthetically, "but really—who ever shops at this place?!" Interestingly, she concluded that our survey got her to thinking about the New School signs in a new way. She said,

> I lump these [New School signs] together because they all say the same thing. [They] whisper (because yelling is rude) sophistication, affluence, modernity, but it also looks like a uniform when it is lined up this way, which is really interesting. Though tasteful and clearly attractive to a "hip" clientele, compared to the other signs it feels flat and characterless. (interview with authors, October 29, 2015)

A white male gentrifier said that Old School signs we showed him coded "poor," "shady," "ethnic," and outer-borough, whereas the New School signs had "quality awnings" and were moving away from what he called an "ethnic tilt or appeal" (interview with authors, April 25, 2014).

When we look at these two informants' responses, we see a couple of things. First, they perceive the signs to be in dialogue with each other in somewhat competitive ways. The woman seems conflicted, in that she likes the idea of Old School Brooklyn, feels it is disappearing, but at the same time admits that it does not really attract her patronage, even though she tries hard to align herself (and people like her who might struggle financially due to divorce, injury, loss of a job, etc.) with the working- and middle-class notions that Old School Brooklyn conjure for her. The man, however, has a clearer position about Old School signage: it does not attract him. And quite remarkably, this man refers to New School signage as the new order of things in Brooklyn, but he clearly indicates this through the idea of the new signs moving away from what was once there.

Newcomers may also see remaining Old School signage as being "authentic," "quaint," and "interesting." In fact, some of the same gentrifiers mentioned above are grateful for the laundromats, drycleaners, shoe repair, and fabric stores that dot their neighborhoods, and they say they enjoy the feeling of the personal relationships they get from the store owners inside. So it is important to note that while some people might react negatively to Brooklyn's Old School textual density, they interact in complicated, personal, and neighborly ways with these businesses. Nevertheless, what their words reveal is that this aesthetic is not theirs.

All these various data indicate two things. First, semiotic vibrancy can be hard to interpret depending on one's vantage point. For those not accustomed to operating with an Old School language ideology that uses texts to remove obstacles for communication, commerce, and coexistence, the signs might seem messy, and lacking in clarity. For those not accustomed to it or who feel unaddressed by gentrifying storefronts with minimal text, New School signage appears erudite or incomprehensible at best, and unwelcoming at worst. Second, and as importantly, Old School signage can obscure and disguise a neighborhoods' rising rents. The co-presence of the Old School and New School signs can either reveal or obfuscate rent gap opportunities. This ambiguity appears to be a target of planning, not only within the scope of large-scale developers but also at the more local level of state interventions to govern and shape independent neighborhood retailers into particular types of commercial spaces.

Planning Distinctions

One legal development that has implications for texts on retail signage is the designation of certain buildings and parts of entire neighborhoods (such as Park Slope) as historic landmarks. Landmark zoning, like other sorts of zoning designations, is a tool of urban planning. This tool aims to preserve both individual sites, such as older buildings, and entire areas or "districts" composed of residential, commercial, or industrial structures deemed worthy of preserving. Landmark and Historic District designations began in 1965 in New York City and are the purview of the Landmarks Preservation Commission (LPC). Another tool of planning that can influence what shop owners might put up on their signs is the creation of Business Improvement Districts or BIDs. Self-funded governance collectives of private retailers and landlords, BIDs work to improve public aspects of retail spaces such as sidewalks, garbage disposal, gutters, seasonal lighting, lampposts, public clocks, benches, trees and shrubs, and some adaptations to building facades. BIDs organize public information campaigns, sponsor and manage street fairs, and make resources available to small businesses. But mostly, BIDs take care of trash receptacles and sidewalk cleaning on a daily basis. One can see custodial workers hired by BIDs sweeping up paper and cigarette butts on sidewalks and making sure garbage is placed in city trashcans.[27]

The city encouraged and supported the work of both the LPC and BIDs during Mayor Michael Bloomberg's administration and continued to do so under Mayor Bill de Blasio. The city government, the LPC, and BIDS have all begun to promote a particular retail aesthetic and to discourage certain norms of signage and semiotics.[28] The "official" aesthetic includes recommendations about color, material, and other design features of storefronts and buildings. Interestingly, this officially proposed aesthetic does not specifically include guidance for text or other substantive content of signage. Supposedly, text and graphics are left up to each business, itself. However, we have found materials developed by city agencies that suggest what should be on a sign and how it should look. For instance, in a pamphlet published by the New York City Department of Buildings describing the application process for signage permits for Landmarks Preservation areas, there is a photograph of a hardware store somewhere in the city with what the brochure refers to as "excessive signage." The pamphlet does not say whether this is in violation of the rules, but it suggests that this is an example of an unattractive storefront.

Similar examples can be found in pamphlets that provide recommendations for new storefronts and signage issued by the New York City Department

A very simple awning that announces the business can be very effective and costs less than a retractable awning.

These awnings fit into the architectural elements of the building and are visually effective by restricting text to just the name of the business.

This retractable awning is ideal. It can be kept clean and well-maintained while providing shade from the sun.

GOOD   BAD

Not only are corporate logos illegal, but they also mean that customers won't notice the name of your business – which can severely hamper your ability to be remembered.

Awnings must be maintained. This ripped and shredded awning sends a message that the business does not care about its products.

This awning is illegal. It includes more information than just the business name and address.

Figure 4.5. A page from the city pamphlet *Façade* indicating good and bad forms of signage. Note the use of the thumb up and thumb down emblems.

of Small Business Services and archived on the websites of several BIDs. A recent publication, *Storefront Improvements* (2012), includes ten tips, the first being "Less is more." It states, "too much clutter makes it difficult for shoppers to see your business and take notice" (6). These are not rules, only suggestions. But in *Façade*, another pamphlet published a few years earlier in 2005, other clearly Old School signage practices are explicitly evaluated negatively. These proscriptive and prescriptive assertions are graphically characterized as examples of "bad" signage, with legal arguments to support why they are "not good." Moreover, in the pamphlet, a "thumb down" symbol reinforces this assertion, perhaps, for non-English speaking business owners, while a "thumb up" is meant to suggest approval of a "good" sign (see Figure 4.5). Such symbols are what anthropologists call emblems—hand motions associated with a meaning that can be conjured without accompanying words (LaFrance and Mayo 1978). Of course, emblems are culture-bound, and the ones provided in the pamphlet could mean different things to non-native English speakers. For example, a thumb up may mean "up yours!" in the Middle East, or, if the upward thumb is in motion, it means "up yours!" in Australia and in Greece.

A brochure published by the New York State Small Business Development Center (2004, 7) makes no such aesthetic recommendations but warns against restrictive signage codes: "towns that wish to enhance the look of their community by strictly and unfairly regulating commercial signs might ultimately help in making the town less live-able." The standard this publication suggests for the optimal number of words on a sign are three to five. The pamphlet justifies this suggestion by stating that drivers and passengers in vehicles cannot read but a few words while passing by.

The features that are promoted by the *Façade* pamphlet, such as coloring, lighting, and the city's rule about limited lettering on awnings, are not given much justification or explanation as to why they are good. They are simply evaluatively called "appealing." The sign makers we interviewed suggested that the examples of appropriate signage in the *Façade* pamphlet comport with the aesthetics of "landmarks" status, what they referred to as the "Park Slope look." And they noted that this look harkened back to a very particular time period:

SIGN MAKER 1: It's pretty much based on 1920s technology. Sign, awning!
SIGN MAKER 2: That's what the city loves. 1920s, 1910s, you know.
SIGN MAKER 1: *Especially* landmarked zones! (interview with authors, June 29, 2017)

Sign makers argue that one can see this aesthetic reflected in a lot of the New School signage examples we have included in this book. For instance, a near perfect example of a classic "landmarks" storefront, pointed out to us by our sign maker informants, is the restaurant Al di Lá (Figure 1.22), which does not really have an actual sign, only an awning. The sign makers had strong views about the prescriptivist stipulations about LPC regulations and signage:

SIGN MAKER 1: Landmarks requires you to basically put up a sign from the 1900s. No lights at all. The only lights you are allowed to have are the exterior lighting, like gooseneck lighting. And it's all got to be architecturally approved. Vintage style.

SIGN MAKER 2: Vintage colors! Name only, mostly. Limited text. Roll-out awnings . . .

SIGN MAKER 1: There's not plastic letters, everything has to be wood background, or has to look like wood.

SIGN MAKER 2: Or metal.

SIGN MAKER 1: Or painted to look like wood. Raised letters. Uh, [pauses] they have a bunch of regulations.

ED: But once a place is landmarked, does that mean you have to change?

SIGN MAKER 2: *Have* to change? I think it's if you change, you have to do everything with the new. So they'll landmark a neighborhood today. As soon as this guy moves out, the guy who moves in has to . . .

SHONNA: Revert back to the 1900s style?

SIGN MAKER 2: Yeah. (interview with authors, June 29, 2017)

The question we must ask is just how "historical" is this aesthetic we find promoted on city government pamphlets and Landmarks Preservation Commission. Historians of New York City note the emergence of public writing all over the city by the mid-nineteenth century. Streets and avenues were covered in shops' signs as commercial districts and retail establishments grew with population and immigration (Henkin 1998). Along with storefronts, political bills and print advertisements proliferated as more and more New Yorkers became literate. Pre–Civil War New York City quickly became the capital of print advertisement and print media for mass consumption. Historians Edwin Burrows and Mike Wallace (1998, 680), for example, describe a New York street: "Not only were stores festooned with ever more and ever bigger placards and announcements, but so were warehouses, carriages, buses, fences, lampposts, trees—and people: men walked the streets with sandwich boards on their shoulders. One commentator noted with mock surprise that umbrellas had as yet been left blank." Henkin (1998) identifies this commentator as John F. Watson, who, writing in 1846, went on to note that, in assessing the city signage, "every device and every expense is resorted to, to make them attractive, crowding them upon every story, and even upon the tops of some houses, above. One small house on Beekman Street has twelve lawyer signs. And at 155 Pearl Street, the name of Tilldon and Roberts was painted on the stone steps of the door!" (Henkin 1998, 48).[29] These mid-nineteenth-century retail landscapes were rich,

Figure 4.6. A photograph of signage for Painless Parker, a Brooklyn dentist on Flatbush Avenue, from around 1895. (Byron Company/Museum of the City of New York. 93.1.118393)

bold, and literal in their openness, much like the key features we see in our Old School examples. And signage with large fonts, repetitions, and of course, many, many words are clearly represented in photographic records of the time. These historical testaments are supported by historical images, leaving the preferred and presumed "authentic" aesthetic promoted by the Landmarks Commission signage and awning rules hard to find. Figure 4.6, a photograph of a Brooklyn dentist from 1895, clearly shows the prevalence of Old School signage in Brooklyn. In Figure 4.7, an image of a street in 1950 depicts the historical persistence of Old School, as does Figure 4.8, an image by Brooklyn photographer Anthony Catalano from 1970.[30] From these photographs one might ask of the Landmarks Preservation Commission and its supporters in New York City local government whose history is really being preserved and why.

Figure 4.7. Old School signage is visible in this 1950 image of Livingston Street, Brooklyn. (Photo by Max Hubacher, © Milstein Division of United States History, Local History and Genealogy, The New York Public Library)

Figure 4.8. Old School signage on a Brooklyn street, 1970. (Photograph by Anthony Catalano).

What does happen historically, we have found, is that Old School shop-keepers often keep their signs up for a very long time, and original signs from previous owners are also kept and maintained by new business owners. For example, a deli and newsstand in Park Slope had the same sign on their storefront since 1996. When we asked the pair of brothers from Yemen who owned the store in 2015 if they had ever thought about getting a new sign, they told us, "Our sign works fine! Why change it?" At the same time, clearly not all New School businesses follow fully the prescriptive recommendation in city pamphlets such as *Façade*. For example, a new pizza and craft beer restaurant has a very small, off-center, hand-painted sign with one not-so-easy-to-read or interpret word: "Wheated." No other semiotic or textual features are found on this sign, and its building has no awning.[31] One New York City Small Business Services (2012, 6) brochure recommends not installing "over-sized signs that cover building details" and warns new business owners: "don't put too much information on signs . . . they appear hard to read."

It may very well be that certain architectural features are being preserved in the contemporary and growing historic districts of gentrifying Brooklyn, but how historically authentic this makes the linguistic landscape is an open question. The sociologist Sharon Zukin (2010) makes a similar argument, claiming the presence of a historical bias in assertions of authenticity in New York City by noting that Union Square in Manhattan has been redeveloped to reproduce an imagined 1920s aesthetic, but not an equally authentic 1960s and 1970s activist New York vibe. She also points out that billboards and advertising proliferated in the city between 1920 and 1950.

In our research, we do find signs from the 1910s and 1920s that seem to comport more with the aesthetic on the restaurant sign for Al di Lá—the smaller font size, the few words—but interestingly, they seem to be located in what for the time would have been expensive real estate for elites, such as the Upper East Side or the Wall Street district. This suggests that the preferred historical aesthetic in the present has a similitude of class and not simply chronological authenticity.[32]

Rent Gap Messages from the Storefront

The historical preservation efforts of the LPC seek to preserve the grandeur and character of the architectural craftsmanship of a certain past, and Business Improvement Districts attempt to strengthen local retail areas and make streets safer, cleaner, and more profitable. Both of these endeavors are also undergirded by the plans of government and the private sector, and they compose an important facet of the engine of urban capital reinvestment. They are also accompanied by and contribute to waves of gentrification. And this process has mapped the transformation of Brooklyn real estate over the past several decades.

For example, some of the most gentrified areas of the western part of the borough were designated historic landmark districts in the 1960s and 1970s, including Brooklyn Heights, Park Slope, and Cobble Hill. And the process has steadily moved eastward and southward. The FCRC executive's lament about missing a rent gap opportunity, it turns out, was spot on. A Manhattan-based developer got in on the ground floor of one of the widest rent gap expansions when they bought the *Daily News* Building from Mort Zuckerman in 1999 (Oser 1999). The larger target area of the property that FCRC had turned down, the neighborhood of Prospect Heights, received historic landmark designation in 2009. In fact, several working class and mixed-use Brooklyn neighborhoods, including DUMBO, Bed-Stuy, and Crown Heights, have been landmarked only in the last eight years. Emerging alongside this process of LPC designations is the pace and proliferation of BIDs. While BIDs started in Manhattan and grew steadily to reach twenty-five districts over the course of twenty years, Brooklyn has now caught up with its formerly dominant neighbor, with a present total of twenty-three districts in little over half the time. In comparison, there are only thirteen BIDs in Queens and ten in the Bronx.[33]

Not all shopping blocks are the result of large-scale developers or of individual business owners or landlords. Some development is the work of more small-scale developers who operate on the logic of the rent gap and who interface with and try to anticipate the larger moves of city and corporate partnerships and the less predictable currents of gentrification. For example, from Michael Pintchik, the local real estate developer and paint store owner mentioned earlier, we learned that his ten-store shopping block development on Bergen Street in Park Slope was a purposeful attempt to create a collection of retail shops to appeal specifically to gentrifiers. Pintchik's family opened their long-standing hardware and paint business on what is technically the Park Slope side of Flatbush Avenue in 1940. The business witnessed tremendous expansion during the gentrification of the Prospect Heights neighborhood across the street from his store. But Pintchik's shopping block includes a parade of New School storefronts (Figure 4.9). These consist of upscale restaurants Bark and Sun-in Bloom, a bike rental called Ride Brooklyn, a bookstore, and boutiques (one is named V-curated and has only a shingle sign

WHAT THE SIGNS SAY

with a "V"). Almost all the storefronts on Pintchik's block appear to follow the examples of the model storefronts used in the *Façade* pamphlet, but Pintchik did not mention this brochure in his interviews, nor did he say anything about shop owners following it. On this near thoroughly gentrified shopping block, the ten storefronts together contain a total of fourteen words. And only one storefront on this block, at the time of this writing, still follows in the Old School Vernacular format—not surprisingly, it is Pintchik's Paints. Pintchik's sign (at the original corner location at the end of Bergen Street where it crosses Flatbush Avenue) had at least twenty-five words. Recently the paint store moved onto Bergen a couple of storefronts down the block, but it still has an Old School sign. At the former location on the corner of Bergen and Flatbush Avenue, there is now a branch of TD Bank.

If we look at specific storefronts in our data set, we see the effects of these planned and purposeful processes of Brooklyn's changing landscape and can learn some lessons from specific individuals' experiences that are intertwined with them. Not far from Pintchik's gentrified shopping block and the Barclays Center is James, the New School restaurant we discussed in Chapter One. This storefront came up when we were interviewing James Caldwell, an African American community leader in Crown Heights and Prospect Heights. Caldwell was the president of the 77th Precinct Community Council. In 2004, he established BUILD (Brooklyn United for Innovative Local Development), a group of predominantly African American residents from the neighborhood that, like ACORN, pledged their support to FCRC's Atlantic Yards plan. BUILD's focus was on providing job training to people in the community. Caldwell told us, "[Prospect Heights] means a lot to me because it's the only neighborhood that I have ever really known." This comment is immediately followed by an account of his employment on Vanderbilt as a thirteen-year-old grocery boy who was building a reputation for himself among neighborhood businesses. In recalling how he worked to assist his family financially, he said:

> And then, when I got a little older and I became fourteen or fifteen there was a bodega on the corner of St. Marks and Carlton Avenue. They liked my work so they hired me to be the stock boy there in the store. . . . It's gone. They put a restaurant there. I guess it left about ten years ago now. . . . In fact [the new place has] got my name, I think, "James." (interview with authors, July 15, 2011)

Caldwell, like many old timers, refers to places and people in the old neighborhood as constitutive elements of not only his life, but also his person. Local storefronts provided jobs to residents and their children, and these early work experiences are remembered as noteworthy achievements in a person's growth and maturation. Caldwell worked as a stock boy in the storefront that was once in the James location more than fifty years ago, in 1965. And he goes so far as to mention that the new business, James, has his name on it, as perhaps a metaphor for his own placement in a neighborhood that he realizes is swiftly changing. Caldwell's decision to support Atlantic Yards shows that he decided to become a part of the change in order not to become just a victim of it.

While opponents of Atlantic Yards sometimes painted Caldwell and his community as having been exploited by FCRC's corporate development plans, Caldwell may have been on to something regarding what corporations could provide for young people in his community that many gentrifiers could not: entry-level jobs. He was also aware of the conundrum of development in its many forms, expressing wistfulness about what the physical space of James used to mean to him in its earlier iterations. And while Caldwell seems at once resigned and a bit melancholy, he also seems unwilling to have himself or his community left out of what he realizes is an unstoppable process. He told us he supported FCRC because he saw a better chance of keeping a foothold in the community and a possibility for young African Americans from the area to be employed in the coming corporate retail establishments.

Another ethnographic account of the restaurant James reveals a bit more about the direction of Brooklyn's development and what local residents think of it. Daniel Goldstein, the leading Atlantic Yards opponent and the only resident whose home was seized by the state through eminent domain in order to build the Barclays Center, had this story to tell about James:[34]

> We were eating at [James] nearby for [our daughter's] birthday and it was the night that they were holding Maryland vs. Kentucky college basketball . . . and I told [my wife] right before that I hope it's not too crowded because there's a game [at the Atlantic Yard's arena, the Barclays Center], and I can't imagine that there are people going to this restaurant for this game. So, it WAS crowded . . . people who were going to the game. . . . There was . . . a father and son, and they were wearing Maryland [colors], and I said, "Are you going to the game?" They said, "Yeah." I said, "I'm just curious, have you come up from Maryland or are you from the neighborhood, are you from nearby?" [The dad] said, "Oh yeah, I'm from nearby." I said "Where do you live?" [The dad replied,] "Long Island!" (interview with authors, December 5, 2012)

Goldstein's point, punctuated by a loud clap of his hands as he said the words, "Long Island!," was that the Barclays Center was drawing in people from far outside the neighborhood. In an earlier discussion with us, Goldstein had come to the realization that the Atlantic Yards plan was not necessarily ever meant to serve Brooklyn alone, but that it was a regional development project meant to draw customers from outside of the borough to basketball games and other sporting and music events at the arena. While small businesses of distinction, like James, may profit initially from their proximity to Barclays Center (James is only a few blocks from the arena space), Goldstein predicted that corporate chains would eventually replace the small businesses in serving as the "go-to-places" for visitors coming to the Barclays Center for special events.

Caldwell's and Goldstein's experiences both speak of a looming displacement. Their stories invoke the work of Fullilove (2004), who explores the trauma narratives of displacement resulting from urban renewal projects in Raleigh, North Carolina, and Pittsburgh, Pennsylvania. Fullilove called this trauma "root shock," the result of extracting people from long-standing communities. Around the issue of displacement in Brooklyn swirl notions of authenticity and belonging, which involved gentrifiers and long-term residents in divergent ways. People who had recently moved into the borough and who did not want to see Atlantic Yards built were often socially and discursively constructed as interlopers without the birthright to maintain or change Brooklyn. Conversely, opponents of the project often referred to Bruce Ratner, who was from Cleveland, as an *outsider*, illegitimately acquiring land in Brooklyn for personal gain. Complicating these depictions were different segments of Brooklyn's longstanding African American community, some of whom supported the development, such as James Caldwell and Bertha Lewis, and others who did not. In the film *Brooklyn Matters*, for example, longtime residents are recorded as saying that newcomers had no right to get in the way of FCRC's promise to bring affordable housing and new jobs to an area that had been previously neglected (Hill 2007). And in many of our interviews, we heard from people in the African American community who talked gravely about the "bad old days," when Brooklyn had little public or private investment. But we also heard from long-term white residents, so-called first wave gentrifiers, who moved to the area a decade or two earlier than we did, who agreed with their African American neighbors that Brooklyn was sorely in need of investment. But several long-standing black churches and their parishioners rallied alongside white, gentrifying newcomers to oppose the project whenever they could. "Origin-in-place" was a strategy for people on both sides of the debate to claim rights and "a say" about how the city should get built. As we noted earlier, in such a context a playful New School sign like Brooklyn Bread (discussed in Chapter Two) might certainly appear confrontational because it engages directly with the question of rights to the city in a time of displacement of people through gentrification and redevelopment.

Many old timers and newcomers alike have told us that they were astounded by the types of shops that began opening in their neighborhoods in the first decade of the 2000s. In an interview with an Ecuadoran man with what he referred to as "no more than a fourth-grade education," who has lived on Brooklyn's Dean Street for more than forty-five years in the home he bought, we also heard of the "improvements" to the Vanderbilt Avenue commercial district. Echoing Pintchik and the married couple, this man also stated that the area was *decaída y vacía*, or, in English, decaying and empty. He said there had never been such nice stores as the ones that lined the Avenue now, but that nothing was affordable anymore. And then he shared the following anecdote from a day prior to our discussion when he and his wife helped move their daughter into a nearby apartment:

Afterward, my wife asked me, "Aren't you a gentleman?" And I said, "Of course! Why do you ask?" And she said, "Well, if you are a gentleman than invite me to have a coffee." And we went to Le Gamin. We ordered two coffees and two toasted cheese sandwiches, and the bill came out to $37.00 plus a tip. I told my wife, "This gentleman thing is over!" (interview with authors January 27, 2012, translated from Spanish to English by Shonna Trinch)

Thus we see ambivalence all around. On the one hand, this informant seems grateful and happy that the neighborhood has been made more beautiful and has more to offer, but on the other hand, he seems to think that what is on offer is not for him and his wife, per se, though he does not seem to take this fact personally.

The man in our husband-and-wife interview from earlier in this chapter also told us about the newer storefronts appearing on Vanderbilt Avenue, "Now, every time we go over [to Vanderbilt] there's another store open and we're like, 'Oh my God! Look at this!'" Amazed at the change that began with them and others like them almost four decades ago, they likened the crowds they now see on Flatbush Avenue to those of Greenwich Village in the early 1970s. The wife said, "It's exciting," and her husband added, "And it's energizing!" (interview with authors, June 12, 2011).

But one person's energizing excitement about new creations can be another person's concern about the existing neighborhood coming undone. Long-term Prospect Heights residents with whom we spoke about the changing neighborhood lamented that rising rents were forcing valuable and important long-standing businesses to close. One example Patti Hagan, the first Atlantic Yards protestor in her neighborhood, gave was Peña's Food Market, the grocery in Chapter One in which we found IOUs taped prominently to the register for all customers to see. Saddened by the imminent departure of this local market, she said the neighborhood would lose its attentive service and its "beautiful sign with hand-painted fruit" decorating the street (interview with authors, February 6, 2012). Another resident, a gentrifier who was relatively new to our Bay Ridge neighborhood, described to us how she used her phone to photograph an Old School sign for a local dry-cleaning business, because she also feared such signs would eventually disappear. Another of our informants, another Prospect Heights newcomer from upstate New York, told us, when looking at a photograph of Fertile Crescent, the Muslim grocery (Figure 1.9), "these [Old School businesses] are somewhat popular with new foodie Brooklynites looking for authentic cuisine." Clearly, Old School's features of plain-spoken language, images, and inclusivity are part of what makes up the notion of authenticity that some gentrifiers say attracts them to the neighborhoods of Brooklyn (see also Zukin 2010; Osman 2011).

The inevitable rent gap contraction also helps to explain the remark of another neighborhood activist in the Atlantic Yards struggle, Peter Krashes, who suggested that Ample Hills, the ice cream shop that arrived on Vanderbilt Avenue in the mid-2000s with its playful Walt Whitman reference, "will never be as good as it is today" (interview with authors, June 21, 2013). Krashes, a leader of a block association in Prospect Heights that wrangled with FCRC, did not mean his assertion to refer to a premature nostalgia for a past yet to be, but to an awareness of the loss of the conditions needed for the creation of a product of value based on the convergence of creativity and capital. Like the working- and middle-class immigrant population that has lived in the borough and achieved socioeconomic mobility, even New School shop owners have relied on Brooklyn's rent gap opportunities in order to be able to set up their businesses, often with significant risk and creative investment. The owner of one New School Park Slope children's store told us that she and her business partner used credit cards to begin their business, charging between $20,000 and $40,000. As the rent gap closes with the arrival of large-scale redevelopment such as Atlantic Yards, many of the small-scale boutiques may not be sustainable.

Consumption demographics are in fact not relevant to our linguistic analysis. Even though several shops in our data set have closed after only a couple of years, even their temporary presence is suggestive of gentrification or the anticipation of it. Gentrification is accomplished by people who come and go, and a store's ability to stay in business is not solely a function of gentrification. Other factors, such as a store's financing, business plan, advertising, ability to do business, etc., all play into whether it will be successful. Sadly, even the most successful small businesses are not immune from succumbing to the strife caused by exorbitant rents.

Regina Cahill, president of the North Flatbush Business Improvement District, reported to us in a 2011 interview, just before the nearby Barclays Center was completed, that for the moment, many local businesses had benefited from the Atlantic Yards development plan. She told us that retail traffic increased and that improvements to the area's infrastructure were needed by BID partners. But she also noted that some businesses and landlords were concerned about rising costs of BID programs, plans, and services:

CAHILL: Well, last month . . . and the [landlords] sitting around the table . . . are all saying, "Well, I don't know if my tenant can, can absorb that."

And you know, we are talking only a few hundred dollars more, and if you are really so concerned, and I finally did say across the table, "If you really are so concerned, then why don't you pay it, pick up the extra hundred dollars a year [for something the BID had decided to implement], if it's such a big deal?" So, if you are really that concerned, and they are really that hurting than maybe you should cut them a break . . .

SHONNA: And that is a way for you to suggest "maybe your rent is too high . . ."

CAHILL: Right. (interview with authors, June 12, 2011)

And in fact, some informants pointed out to us that some commercial landlords did leave their storefronts vacant to await national chains. Pintchik told us that McDonald's had approached him five times to rent one of his buildings, each time increasing their offer. He turned them down, he said, because he wants to help create a balance between what he called "artisanal" and corporate storefronts (interview with authors, August 8, 2011). Obviously, Pintchik's story, like those of other long-standing Old School businesses, is complicated. But consonant with Pintchik's reputation of being a "good guy," that is, a considerate and concerned stakeholder in the neighborhood—many informants (business owners, landlords, residents, and tenants) said he would try to help them come up with solutions to their real estate needs—he moved the existing tenants on Bergen Street to his other buildings in the area in order to create the distinctive New School shopping block.[35]

Empty storefronts are commonly read as blight or disinvestment, and ironically, they are occurring with more frequency in high rent districts (Wu 2015). A Carroll Gardens resident told us in 2018 that he counted fifty-two vacant storefronts on Smith Street, a section of gentrified Brooklyn that used to be referred to as New York's new Restaurant Row. Recent media reports confirm his observations and characterize this development as "high-rent blight," a phenomenon affecting both Old School and New School businesses alike.[36] Neighborhood activist Peter Krashes' warning about Ample Hills, along with reports of extremely high rents, signals that a gentrifying neighborhood has reached the height of its distinction.[37] What follows are super-gentrifiers and the ritualistic and predictable moves of corporate investment and development. As big developers and national franchises continue to move forward with projects such as Atlantic Yards, corporate signage conspicuously invades the retail landscape. Global and national chains, such as McDonalds, Fed Ex, Gap, and Walgreens, all have storefronts in Brooklyn.[38] But while these shops mark place with textual brevity, they do little to make place unique. On the

Figure 4.10. Barclays Center (on the left), a central feature of the Atlantic Yards project, which opened on Flatbush Avenue September 21, 2012. Note the building across the street with a sign advertising a "flagship opportunity" for potential corporate retailers.

contrary, it is with the ideology of textual and semiotic simplification that corporate signage—through typography and brand logos—vacates notions of local or diverse identities and specific placed-ness.

Such development continues to move forward, along with a wave of other corporate-sponsored development projects in the borough.[39] Dozens of condo projects line 4th Avenue, one of Brooklyn's main north-south local transportation arteries. Industry City, a sprawling, upscale complex in Sunset Park, boasts high-end retail (including ABC Carpet, the Manhattan-based furniture and design store), artisanal food vendors, and occasional boutique bourbon-tastings. As these projects move forward, opportunities for rent gap profit are quite literally, but maybe not always so clearly to the average passerby, written on the signs of the site. Figure 4.10 shows a large sign on a formerly Old School storefront directly across from the Barclays Center arena. It openly advertises the available space not just "for rent," but specifically for rent by a corporate flagship retailer.

WHAT THE SIGNS SAY

If Brooklyn's diverse neighborhoods are to survive, sustained reinvestment in small business retail sectors may be essential. One thing is certain: in the absence of policy, big business will identify the rent gap and begin to capitalize on it, displacing both Old School and New School small businesses in Brooklyn until there is nothing about "place" that is left to imagine.

And if you don't know, now you know . . .

Christopher Wallace (The Notorious B.I.G.),
"Juicy," 1994

5. Lessons from the Street

Offending Moves and Misplaced Apologies

"**IT IS IMPACT** over intent. She is hanging on to *intent*. 'Oh, I didn't mean to. I am sorry that you were offended.' But the fact of the matter is that you DID it," explained Justine Stephens in an interview with us about her concerns with Becca Brennan, the owner of gentrifying Crown Heights restaurant Summerhill, who had peddled fake bullet holes on one of its interior walls (interview with authors, October 4, 2017). For Stephens, the problem with Brennan was not complicated: Brennan never really admitted fault or apologized appropriately about the bad feelings she stirred up with the way she advertised her new, upscale restaurant in the middle of a community that had suffered a violent past.

Summerhill's press release read:

SUMMER OASIS SUMMERHILL OPENS IN CROWN HEIGHTS

Reformed Corporate Tax Attorney Turns a Vacant Bodega into Surf Club-Style "Boozy Sandwich Shop"

CROWN HEIGHTS – An oasis has appeared on Nostrand Avenue just in time for the stickiest, sweatiest days of New York summer.

Summerhill is Crown Heights' most Instagrammable, "let's just crush some watermelon cocktails" hangout. With a boardwalk vibe and a killer cross-breeze, it's easy to forget you're sitting across the street from a Key Food and not the Rockaway break.

Helmed by Toronto transplant Becca Brennan, Summerhill serves up a high-low beer menu from Tecate to Evil Twin, rosé on tap, and bright cocktails with made-in-house purées, syrups, and herbal touches like celery shrub (featured in the #Vanlife), fresh watermelon juice and ginger syrup (in the Answer), torched rosemary (in the Dated Old Fashioned), and strawberry-basil purée (in the Summer Jam).

Summerhill's food menu focuses on lovingly prepared, refreshingly unpretentious sandwiches like the Chicken Fried (hot chicken, buttermilk ranch, slaw and pickles) and the perfect BLT (applewood-smoked bacon, Bibb lettuce, and beefsteak tomato, heightened by a garlic aioli), plus substantial vegetarian options (Brennan is a lifelong vegetarian) such as the Keep Austin Weird (panko-fried avocado, honey, jalapeno-pickled radish arugula, and red pepper aioli).

Brennan was a corporate tax attorney with daydreams of opening a boozy sandwich shop until she discovered the perfect piece of real estate around the corner from her Crown Heights apartment: a long-vacant corner bodega (with a rumored backroom gun shop to boot). Brennan signed the lease, gave notice, and proceeded to spend over a year painstakingly gut-renovating the space with an uncompromising vision: a surf club vibe with a large concrete horseshoe bar, massive accordion windows, and cheekily wallpapered bathrooms. (Yes, that bullet hole-ridden wall was originally there and, yes, we're keeping it.)

The vision, says Brennan, was "to open a place that I could imagine working from all day; that feeling goes for our staff and our customers."

Summerhill has quickly become a favorite among locals as a day-drinking magnet on sweltering summer afternoons. Come winter, Summerhill will provide a similar escape from the chill. (reproduced from archive of Justine Stephens)[1]

Stephens did not have access to the press release at first, which was issued to media outlets in mid-June of 2017, but she read an article from the online media outlet *Gothamist* that criticized it. The title of the article was: "New Crown Heights Restaurant Proudly Advertises Cocktail Next to Bullet Hole-Ridden Wall" (Whitford 2017a). Another article, published by the online food publication *Eater New York*, had the headline "New 'Instagrammable' Crown Heights Restaurant Brags about Fake Bullet-Holes: Summerhill Checks Off All the

Gentrification Red Flags." Instead of writing about the new restaurant on the scene, *Eater New York* reporters Helen Rosner and Serena Dai brought their analytical eyes to the way the new establishment was marketed. They wrote, for example, "Alongside $12 cocktails, and 'cheekily wall-papered bathrooms,' the restaurant also seems to be selling a generous dose of self-mythologizing: 'Yes that bullet-hole ridden wall was originally there. And yes, we are keeping it!'" The journalists added that in the *Gothamist* story, about which they also reported, Brennan admitted she got this idea to incorporate the notion of bullet holes into the history of her storefront from a website where someone had suggested that people bought guns in the "hidden" backroom of the bodega that was there before her (Rosner and Dai 2017).

Feeling that Brennan's marketing ploy was out of line, Stephens organized community members and tried to do something about it. First, she joined up with social activists Jonathan Villaran and another acquaintance, whom she met through social media. The three then canvassed the neighborhood and spoke with residents and other shopkeepers, then quickly organized an "open forum"—a public event in front of Summerhill's storefront in order to get people talking about their concerns about the restaurant's marketing strategy. And people came. On July 22, 2017, a sunny Saturday, over two hundred people crowded onto the sidewalks of the intersection of Nostrand Avenue and St. Marks Avenue. Police were present but mainly tried to keep those who gathered from stepping into the street. Stephens said of the event:

> [It] was really beautiful. Everyone was silent listening to stories of long-term residents speaking of how it [references to bullet holes and forty-ounce wines in the new restaurant's press release] is not okay. People who have seen or who have names of children that they knew who were lost to gun violence. Who pointed at corners and said, "I know [this child] was gunned down right here." And this woman is selling these [painful experiences] . . . you know, it's not right!" (interview with authors, October 4, 2017)

People were really troubled by the way Summerhill's marketing gimmick employed symbols of the community's strife and pain. At the protest, in addition to people speaking, some attendees also handed out computer-printed fliers that said things like, "We're a community, not your aesthetic." They were also upset by the way the press release had characterized the restaurant as an "oasis." They read this metaphor as making a snide remark about Summerhill's Crown Heights' location, because a common definition of *oasis* is "something that provides refuge, relief, or pleasant contrast."[2] Elaborating on the oasis reference, the press release made further implications about the environment being uninspired: "With a boardwalk vibe and a killer cross-breeze [it would be] easy to forget that you're sitting across the street from a Key Food and not the Rockaway break." All throughout the event, people sounded their concerns about what they perceived to be Summerhill's insulting and hurtful semiotics, and they tried to hold the owner accountable for her marketing choices.

But on the day of the public forum Brennan never came out to speak with anyone. Stephens told us, "She stayed inside the whole time. She looked on. She was making cocktails for the few people that were there. But I looked her in the eyes. I said, 'If you want to come and speak, like PLEASE! I think the community wants to hear you speak'" (interview with authors, October 4, 2017). Instead, Brennan's publicist handed out a written statement intended for the journalists who were attending the event. Stephens told us that she just happened to get a hold of one. It read:

Statement from Becca Brennan, Summerhill

I deeply apologize for any offense that my recent comments might have caused. I did not intend to be insensitive to anyone in the neighborhood, and I am sorry that my words have caused pain. I made light of serious issues and that was wrong.

Summerhill is a neighborhood restaurant where everyone is welcome. The reason we maintained the distressed wall is the aesthetic. We have kept other elements of the original space as well to create a visually engaging experience.

The restaurant décor is not intended to make light of any aspect of Crown Heights or its history. We love Crown Heights and we are very proud to call it home. I respect comments that I have received from the community and I recognize that I have more work to do to continue healing relationships with my neighbors. I intend to do that. (Archive of Justine Stephens)

Stephens pointed out that the text was unsigned and undated. She said the publicist took her contact information and told her that they would set up a meeting with Brennan. Stephens assumed that Brennan was going to elaborate on this written apology.

In linguistics, an apology is another excellent example of what Austin (1962) defined as a speech act: an utterance that when stated in the appropriate way and under appropriate conditions not only says something, but actually does something in the world. And Austin's student John Searle (1969; outlined in Battistella 2014, 39) attempted to define the precise conditions under which an apology would be successful. These conditions included: (1) a propositional act, or a statement referring to an offending moment in the past, (2) a preparatory condition, or an acknowledgment of wrongdoing,(3) the sincerity condition, or a heartfelt statement of regret, and (4) the essential condition, or feeling on the part of both speaker and addressee that an apology has been issued. Since Searle's work, linguists have argued over the form apologies need to take in order to be successful, and most conclude that there is no formal structure that aligns with the function of an apology. In linguist Bonnie McEhlinny's (2016) extensive review of apologies, she favors Lesley Jeffries's (2007, 55) functional definition which states an apology is "defined by its capacity to change the formal relations between the speaker and the hearer in certain ways." For McEhlinny this definition works for apologies in both interpersonal and political settings, that is, whether the apology is issued to address a wrongdoing between people on more or less equal footing or to address historical redress in political settings where politicians acknowledge past wrongdoings to entire groups of people.

We like this functional definition to understand why Becca Brennan's various attempts at apologies, which we describe below in more detail, seemed to fail. The context of this controversy is neither strictly political nor interpersonal, but rather somewhere in between, as Brennan's private business is a public space, and the controversy arises because of the sociostructural and political nature of racism in the US. Brennan's ostensible attempt to capitalize on racism for private profit in front of the very people whose painful history it mocks makes the situation both personal and political. Additionally, rather than doing a typical analysis of how politeness formulas are employed by speakers to protect their face wants and mitigate face threats (Brown and Levinson 1987), we will conduct an analysis showing how Brennan protects her privilege throughout her interactions with the community.[3] We will see that Brennan never changes the formal relationship of her relative race and perhaps class privilege over the community. Each time, she suggests that she is the dominant arbiter of meanings, so even while apologizing, she continues to protect her privilege to say what things mean and how they should be interpreted.

Stephens said that Brennan, through her PR firm at the time, did contact her, as well as Villaran and the third organizer of the open forum. But, she said, Brennan wanted a private meeting only with them, and they all declined because they felt that she needed to address the community. Upon learning that she had not covered up the bullet holes after a few weeks, Stephens and her group held another public gathering on August 20, 2017. The energized crowd that Sunday was smaller than the first, but they were able to speak directly to Brennan, who sat outside her shop at a table doing a crossword puzzle. Press reports confirm Stephens' account: "Talk to us," said one woman. But Brennan, after suggesting a coffee date, then replied that she had already apologized (Whitford 2017b).[4] It was only at a town hall meeting two days later, organized by Community District Leader Geoffrey Davis, whom Brennan had asked to intervene in the conflict, that she finally spoke directly to people about the bullet holes.[5] A video of this event was posted online and we transcribed it in its entirety.[6] At one point, early in the meeting, Brennan, dressed in cut-off shorts, a t-shirt, and clogs, addressed the crowd by saying,

> So, I'm sorry I have a sense of humor. And that I said, uh, in this press release that I said, that I okayed, I was alluding to the fact that people asked if those were bullet holes. And I was more trying to focus on the fact that I kept the integrity of this 100-year old building and trying not to cover up the history of my neighborhood and that corner. And, I, that's, that's what happened. Right? And, so there was no ill intention and there was no malice. (Town hall meeting, August 22, 2017, authors' transcription)

Many people in the audience at the town hall meeting began to groan upon hearing these words. It is clear from the sounds the crowd makes that they were, at the very least, unsatisfied with Brennan's attempt to apologize. And they let her know. One community member, named Mike, focused specifically on her mention of humor:

> I'd like to respond to the "sense of humor thing." I'd like to think that I have a sense of humor. I'd like to think that. And I'm reading here from the original "cheeky" press release. "Yes that bullet-ridden wall was originally there." And from what we have heard tonight, you know, is a lie. "And yes, we are keeping it!" And, what we know now, and what we know now a month and a half later, that's what [you] are planning to do. LET ME TELL YOU about humor. [Brennan starts to smile, some people in the audience laugh out loud]. LET ME TELL YOU ABOUT WHAT'S FUNNY, because this is not some idle little joke by someone who has some quirky sense of humor. This is humor like Butterfly with Queen being laughed at in *Gone with the Wind* [the audience gives verbal cues of agreement. They sound as if they are meant to encourage the speaker in his line of thought]. This is humor like people gathering around trees pointing up at a man hanging there [the audience makes more sounds of agreement] and saying, "Wow. That's funny!" [We can hear someone, maybe Stephens, saying, "Thank you!"] Like *Birth of a Nation* and look-

ing at people in blackface getting run down by horses [someone else in the crowd says, "Thank you!"] and people are laughing at that. A "sense of humor" like Uncle Ben, Aunt Jemima, Reconstruction. This is not humor that came out of your head. [Loud clapping can be heard from the audience.] This is four hundred years of your goddamn, bullshit humor. [People in the audience get even louder with cheering and clapping. The speaker is raising his voice and sounding more passionate against the clapping and affirmative hollering.] And it's gotta stop. 'Cause it ain't funny. (Town hall meeting, August 22, 2017, authors' transcription)

The noise from the audience suggests that Mike's words had given voice to many of the community's concerns, feelings of frustration, and the historical expanse of their sadness and grief.

But they also noted something beyond Brennan's words that was upsetting to many people at the gathering. For example, New York assemblywoman Diana Richardson of the 43rd District told Brennan, "I stand back here and I watch you as you are answering this gentleman's question. And the truth is, your words say one thing and your body language and your attitude say something different to us." Richardson seemed to be referring not only to Brennan's body language as she stood in front of the gathered crowd, but also her appearance, facial expressions, and clothing. Stephens told us that while many people at the meeting wore dress clothes or business attire, Brennan showed up in a very casual t-shirt, cut-off shorts, and a pair of clogs. As she listened to Mike's comments, she had one hand placed on a chair beside her, the other on her hip. She took her clog on and off and exposed the crowd to her bare foot, then casually knocked her left shoeless heel against her right calf over and over again, all the while pursing her lips as she listened, seemingly impatient and annoyed by Mike's statement. Although it is not easy to see from the video of the encounter, Stephens told us that when other community members were speaking, Brennan rolled her eyes and shrugged her shoulders. Villaran told us the audience interpreted Brennan's outward expressions of body language, appearance, and manner not only to be dismissive of the official nature and formality of the occasion, but also arrogant and disrespectful toward the audience present, an indication that she considered the community's concerns to be of little importance to her (interview with authors, November 18, 2017).

Richardson went on, again, directly addressing Brennan:

The truth is that after two protests toward your business, you're still here defending, right? DEFENDING your decision . . . Don't you get it? The holes on the walls are offensive. People have died in this community! There's nothing about the architecture to protect. And so, I'm wondering if you are out of touch? I'm wondering if you are out of touch? Because if you do this, then you are out of touch. (Town hall meeting, August 22, 2017, authors' transcription)

Natherlene Bolden, a founding member of the Crown Heights Tenants Union and resident since 1978, echoed Richardson's sentiment when interviewed by reporters after the meeting: "She's out of touch with black people, she never experienced violence as we have, she never had to experience or hear bullets flying, she never experienced crime we had to go through in our community" (Chan 2017).

Brennan's words and appearance notwithstanding, her lack of action following such a public outcry really frustrated and angered people. The only thing Brennan did after the July 18 *Gothamist* article, reporting on the questionable nature of her "humorous" marketing, was to take the 40 oz. rosé off of the menu.[7] But simply removing the wine from the restaurant was not enough. And it was especially unsatisfactory because community members had proposed what could have been an acceptable move to rectify the situation at the town hall. For example, a woman who introduced herself as a mother of a five-year-old, who had lived in the neighborhood for forty years, suggested that all Brennan really had needed to do to make things right was cover up the holes on the wall, "It's Saturday. You could do this overnight. This is not rocket science. . . . You've had five weeks. You could have done it in five days. You could have come and said, 'This is what I'm gonna do guys, I'm gonna change.'" She added that she did not really care that Brennan's gentrifying business had taken the place of a local corner store.[8] To the contrary, she told Brennan that she would have supported her place, saying,

When I see a new establishment, I like to support it, especially when they are in Brooklyn. And I don't have to go to the city and . . . I don't have to go to Williamsburg. And I don't gotta go to Bushwick, I can go right in Crown Heights. So . . . I would love to support you, but you have to just realize that this is really simple. Let's come up with a simple solution and make things happen, so you can last. . . . Somebody else will be there overnight. . . . Somebody else is waiting for your spot. (Town hall meeting, August 22, 2017, authors' transcription)

The Privilege to Not Listen

As the neighbor pointed out to Brennan that her "humor" did not simply "come out of her head," we know that this was not the first time that someone had tried to capitalize financially or culturally on symbols of violence, dispossession, and poverty. Indeed, there is a host of examples of appropriations and exploitations of drug and gun violence as marketing tools for the purpose of profit-making in the American public, from films, television shows, and books to music, fashion, and the digital gaming world. One example is the video game *Grand Theft Auto*, which includes a virtual parade of caricatures of criminality and deviance. The game is marketed to adolescents, and mostly to young men, many of whom have never stolen a car or fired a weapon (see Polasek 2014). And as we have seen in our previous chapters, the symbolic exploitation of certain aspects of the lives of others deemed by a dominant group to be either unfortunate or quaint is not just focused on race. Additionally, a range of intersections of peoples' identities (Crenshaw 1990) such as class, religion, gender, and ethnicity become targets vis-à-vis dominant culture.

Peggy McIntosh's (1988) classic work on white privilege helps us understand the discursive stance of the dominant.[9] McIntosh defines white privilege as "an invisible knapsack" of "unearned assets that [one] can count on cashing in each day, but about which [one] was 'meant' to remain oblivious" (1). This knapsack contains all sorts of tools of advantage that people do not like to acknowledge or admit to having. Nor do they like to submit this condition to any sort of challenge. Moreover, several layers of denial "protect [privilege] and prevent [our] awareness about [it]." For instance, schools teach people to see themselves as simply individuals who depend on their individual moral will (4).[10] In this framework, racism is seen as only an individual act, while the system of racial domination and our part in it remains invisible to us through silence and denial.

Ultimately, three things happen to white people as a result of privilege, according to McIntosh. First, they are conditioned into oblivion to deny its advantage and benefits in what is a presumably competitive playing field; second, it over-rewards white people; and third, it damages them in the end. She comes up with forty-six ways white people like herself benefit from privilege, written out as a list of "special circumstances and conditions" that are not earned but that people "have been made to feel are [theirs] by birth, by citizenship, and by virtue of being a conscientious law-abiding 'normal' person of good will" (5). These conditions and circumstances range from having no difficulty renting or purchasing housing, moving around the world, shopping, or using different forms of money and credit to seeing your culture represented in media or being concerned about racism without being seen as self-interested or self-seeking. Interestingly, many of these conditions have much to do with communication and language that involves representations of the self, opinions that one may have, one's appearance, and how one behaves toward others. We might call these broader categories the pillars of privilege, which, in many ways, is a system of delusion, or a belief in an altered reality that is persistently held despite evidence to the contrary.

A colleague pointed out that the Summerhill incident reminded her of a long history of similarly privileged moves. For instance, in nineteenth century fin-de-siècle society it was a titillating adventure for the high classes to assert a *nostalgie de la boue* (a "longing to be back in the mud") in art, music, and theater as a way to get closer to the experience and suffering of the poor or the minority group.[11] Such mocking reinforces the social hierarchy and has long been used to emphasize the distinctions between the urban working class and wealthier segments of society. Like today's *Grand Theft Auto*, the dime store reading market witnessed countless references to depravity and immorality in the works of Lovecraft and other early twentieth century pulp fiction writers. To "slum it" was also an expression of middle-class Americans in the late twentieth century, meaning to go out to eat at a relatively inexpensive establishment or visit a juke joint or jazz bar to hear "authentic" music. It is not always clear whether the sentiment is one of appropriating elements of "low" or marginalized culture or appreciating them through emulation of or participation in them. What is typically objectionable is the way nonmembers attempt to experience other cultures indirectly, in presumed "safe spaces" where nonmembers use or take elements of social life and reality from the marginalized group's experiences that dominant culture usually disparages and worse, vilifies, criminalizes, or pathologizes. The "bullet holes" in the walls of Summerhill, lending its customers the safe yet thrilling experience of the neighborhood's violent past, adorned a room in which patrons could eat a $16 hamburger and drink an equally expensive cocktail in air conditioning.

Within the context of this history of upscale or upper-middle-class exploitative emulation of poverty or ethnicity (whether in music, entertainment, or an indulgent visit to a "hole-in-the-wall" restaurant), the explicit selling of the semiotics or aesthetic of the pain and suffering of an actual place with an actual history of suffering by an outsider was poignant, disturbing, and even heartbreaking to local Crown Heights residents, Stephens said. Crown Heights has been no stranger to drugs, gangs, and violence. In fact, the corner on which Summerhill sits, Nostrand Avenue and St. Marks Avenue, has been named in memory of two local community heroes: James E. Davis and Damon Allen, both of whom were killed by gun violence (see Cooper 2003 and Santora 2006). And the neighborhood has suffered other conflicts in its history, including the three-day Crown Heights demonstrations of 1991, which erupted after two children of Guyanese immigrant parents from the neighborhood were struck by a car belonging to the motorcade of a renowned Jewish religious leader (see Daughtry 1997).[12] In this context it is perhaps an understandably disturbing irony that a white newcomer would capitalize on this history for her business.

Brennan is of course not the first gentrifying retailer in Brooklyn to use this potentially offensive irony publicly for profit in the very neighborhoods for which it is a reference. In 2013, *Brokelyn* published a story by David Colon, a Brooklyn writer and journalist, about forty- ounce alcoholic beverages that were sold in paper bags at Beast of Bourbon, a bar in nearby Bed-Stuy. Colon, like Stephens and others who protested Summerhill, also tried to articulate what was so wrong with Beast of Bourbon's ploy:

> If you want to sell 40s at your bar, fine, go right ahead. . . . But why put it in a paper bag? A 40 in a paper bag signifies urban poverty, the kind that's been swept off the far corners of the city these days. You aren't reclaiming anything doing it, you're not removing a stigma. It feels more like laughing at poor people from a position of privilege . . . (Colon 2013b).[13]

And as we have shown earlier, this position of privilege can be read in the larger semiotic system of retail signage itself. Take for example the name *Beast of Bourbon*. Like many other New School storefronts we have described and discussed, its polysemy holds clues to the systemic nature of the privilege that it signals. It could be a reference to the Rolling Stones song "Beast of Burden"; to actual animals often referred to as beasts of burden, such as donkeys or oxen; or in this case, it could refer to the negative way someone becomes—bestial—when drinking alcohol. It could also be an attempt to refer to alcoholism and addiction in a light-hearted or fun way.

Other examples of what could be read as exploitative profiting include using the word *crack* to name food items for sale. Ample Hills, the New School ice cream shop on Vanderbilt Avenue in Prospect Heights we have mentioned earlier sold a flavor of ice cream called Salted Crack Carmel. And Milk Bar, a New School bakery and coffee shop across the street in the same neighborhood offered a dessert that was named Crack Pie. No one organized a demonstration or protest against these shops, but both establishments changed the names of these items in 2018, after the events surrounding Summerhill occurred. Milk Bar now calls their signature pie Milk Bar Pie, which sells for $48. And Ample Hills altered the word *Crack* to *Crack'd*.[14]

Summerhill's sign is cast in the New School register. It does not say "restaurant" but instead is named after another place, perhaps personally significant to Brennan herself, as it refers to a tony neighborhood in Toronto, the city from which Brennan came. It is at once an homage to her former home and an expression of the license which she has—like The Farm on Adderley (discussed in Chapter Two)—to claim a space on the street and give it a name that honors her origins. But unlike Nio's West Indian Restaurant, which we discussed in Chapter Two and which also personally and nostalgically employs a reference to the owner's origin of place, Summerhill is expressed in a register that is cryptic and insiderish. Interestingly, Stephens, as a Crown Heights gentrifier of Afro-Caribbean heritage who grew up in Connecticut and worked in Manhattan, immediately noticed from Summerhill's sign that it was an upscale, gentrifying restaurant.[15] But before Stephens could patronize it, she discovered the offending information online. And like the New School register in which Summerhill's sign and its irreverent semiotics are created, the crass marketing of the restaurant also suggested a gaming nonchalance toward the function of ambiguity as well as an indifference toward the community's perspective on it. In what follows we will try to explicate how white privilege, as well as other dominant cultural privileges (education and class, for example), get in Brennan's way of repairing her relationship with the community.

To begin with, a close reading of the press release and Brennan's first subsequent statement about the controversy reveals a bet made on the attractiveness of playful ambiguity for people who do not have to care about the impacts of such playfulness on others. On a deeper level, another reading of Brennan's utterance, "And yes, we are keeping it" appears not simply to refer to only the holes in the wall, but to the ambiguity of the aesthetic a patron suggested was represented by the holes. So the assertion that "And yes, we're keeping *it*" could also mean "Yes, we're keeping the ambiguity. We are not covering up the holes, and they are real holes, not made-up holes, and we are not going to change the holes by covering them up. By being ambiguous about the holes in the larger context of a neighborhood that has been notorious for gun violence, customers can pretend they are bullet holes."

Not to have to be clear, not to have had to articulate or anticipate any and every possible miscommunication from the beginning—the complete opposite of the essence of what we find in meaning-making of the Old School register—was central to Brennan's ability to defend herself when she was challenged. Also in her defense, Brennan then drew on historical preservationist ideology to justify the maintenance of what she called the "architectural integrity" of the 1905 building. Along with using ambiguity, Brennan seems to assume a presumably more palatable or sensitive stance of exercising a unique opportunity to save the community's (architectural) history. In this way she defended her inaction—that is, not covering up the holes—as a form of paying "homage" to the authenticity of place. Brennan's conflation of historical preservation and architectural integrity with her inaction and refusal to cover up the holes that her press release opportunistically suggested originated with gunfire, actually backfired. It was as if she was arguing that she knew that they were not bullet holes, so she did not need to cover them up. She seemed to have the desire to let others wonder and imagine where the holes came from. This case drives home how a semiotics of polysemy and ambiguity are assumed by some as their prerogative in place and place-making processes.

But as Brennan's arguments for ambiguity failed, she resorted to the claim that her intention was to be humorous. Suggesting a humorous intention makes it possible to accuse others of being "unable to take a joke." From there, a speaker can claim those who say they are offended are either forcing the speaker to be "politically correct" or worse, censoring his or her "free speech." As we mentioned previously, Hill (2008) has suggested that this sort of sociolinguistic logic-making—of intent crafted through the stance of a personalist language ideology—is a common discursive tactic that serves to uphold dominant cultural hierarchies.

One might also, at first glance, connect Summerhill to other women-owned Brooklyn businesses. Framed in this manner, its owner seems bold and courageous and sounds outspoken and opinionated. She certainly takes over a Brooklyn corner and remakes it in her image in many ways. A reporter for online magazine the *Outline*, Jeff Ihaza (2017), captured Brennan talking about herself as a woman restaurateur in a man's world in an audio-recorded interview. But Brennan uses the idea of her being a woman trying to do things in a man's town to ask for a pass for her own lack of understanding and consequent semiotic mishaps. Here is how Ihaza reports that Brennan uses her identity as a woman defensively:

> Brennan's combative nature was immediately confounding to me. Perhaps, because I'm black, she sensed that I wouldn't be entirely sympathetic to her cause.

More than once before we began our interview, she cited the fact that she was a woman opening a restaurant as a point of difficulty in her life. It's true, the majority of restaurants in New York are owned by men, and it is no small marvel that this woman, who only moved to Crown Heights two years ago, had gotten her business off the ground. (Ihaza 2017)

The woman-entrepreneur narrative pushes the pioneering feminist trope among the many other gentrifier stories, and it pulls from the vulnerable parts of the owner's intersectional identities as a woman, who has bravely done what so few other women have been able to do. And while Ihaza commends her for this remarkable feat, he also writes immediately afterwards that Brennan "remained defiantly oblivious to the difficulties faced by others." "When I asked whether or not the fact that Crown Heights was a black neighborhood occurred to her as she opened and promoted the space, she seemed puzzled. 'Did I notice that black people live in the neighborhood? Yes, I noticed,' she said." Ihaza writes the story in a way that frames the controversy as if the racist semiotics would be a problem for Brennan only in a black community that saw it. Put differently, this framing suggests that it might be okay for Brennan to invoke this trope of romanticizing gun violence in black communities in any non-black community in the US. The research from critical race theorists (Matsuda et al. 1993), from linguists on the nature of public and private discourse (Hill 2008; Pagliai 2011; Gal 2005), and sociologists (Eliasoph 1999) certainly suggests that white people tolerate racist talk and semiotics, but that, while black people expect it, they report feeling actual physical pain when confronted with it.

Returning briefly to the case of Baby/Mama, in Bay Ridge, several of our African American informants—both older and younger residents of other Brooklyn neighborhoods—were offended by the use of the name, particularly when they learned that the store was mostly patronized by married, white women gentrifiers. As a young, single woman, Stephens herself had not heard of Baby/Mama, as it was located in a neighborhood fairly far from the one she lived in. When we told her about the store's name, she grimaced, as if responding physically to pain.

In various conversations with white people about the store's use of the term *baby/mama*, we found only two white men who said there was a problem with it. One of them, a college professor, told us,

Honestly, given race and class implications, I would have chosen another name. . . . I know it serves as a support base for new moms and [I] see posts about it all the time—classes, groups, etc., but I can't help wondering if they were purposely using [the] name as a marketing mechanism given its current social usage? . . . I guess I'm uncomfortable because the term is used to perpetuate culture of poverty myth: black/poor people are poor because of intergenerational dysfunction, poor choices, single parenthood, spending over saving and other so-called habits . . . (interview with authors, November 13, 2013)

Most other white people we spoke to who live in the neighborhood suggested there was probably no ill will or racist intention in the usage, because they felt the owners were not racists. They therefore concluded that the sign was not racist either.

In what follows, we will examine more closely how the Crown Heights community, both white and black people living there, attempted to make Brennan see why they thought that language and semiotics mattered so much. The community seemed to want her to apologize, change the wall, and acknowledge their feelings. Current criticisms of white people's (in)actions when it comes to incidents with overt implications for race and racism often elicit allegations of "cluelessness," "tone deafness," "being out of touch," and "not being woke." Our analysis of Brennan's discourse and stance in her various attempts to apologize concludes that hers are defensive gestures that, at every turn, seemed aimed at protecting and guarding her privilege to the detriment of herself, her reputation, and even her business.

Ihaza, the *Outline* reporter, pushed Brennan further to think about her privilege, which she contextualized in a particular hierarchy of power in yet another defensive move, one that placed her in a subordinate position vis-à-vis corporate America. But notice how in this placement, she seemed to maintain her belief that she should be able to limit and control how others perceived and treated her:

I told her what I thought a lot of people wanted to hear from her, which is that she understands white privilege, that she on some level recognizes the systemic advantages she has that make opening a restaurant in Crown Heights possible in the first place. "I understand and I want to help, but there's bigger fish to fry," she said. "I'm not part of a huge conglomerate and *I'm not a corporation*. I'll help you if you ask me to help. Just don't yell at me. *That's not going to go anywhere ever.*" (emphasis added)

There are two key assertions in Brennan's response here. The first is a suggestion that she should get a pass because she was not "corporate" but rather just a little fish in a big Brooklyn pond trying to make a place for herself and for others who are either opposed to or in need of options from what can feel like a corporate takeover. This argument links directly to the larger processes of neighborhood change at play, where, as we showed earlier in Chapter Four, the arrival of corporate chains alongside larger-scale redevelopment projects rapidly and significantly alter the urban landscape. And, as we have also noted, there is actually a very strong anticorporate stance amongst most gentrified and gentrifying Brooklyn neighborhoods. A random probability survey we conducted in 2011 of residents of Fort Greene and Prospect Heights showed that, out of 259 respondents, 80 percent (207) did not want chain restaurants and 70 percent (182) did not want big-box retail stores. A strong majority (171) answered that they needed small retail stores such as groceries and dry cleaners, and slightly more than half (139) indicated that they desired more specialty retail stores. Opposition to the corporate is a feature of many New School businesses that try to be unique, different from the homogenizing nature of corporate, cookie-cutter businesses and their mass-produced products.[16] And certainly, an anticorporate stance is another function of the distinctive, irreverent, and anti-establishment spirit of New School signage's wordplay feature. But while the borough is notorious for resisting big chain stores such as Walmart, many other chains have moved in anyway: Rite Aid, Costco, Fairway, Trader Joes, and Best Buy, to name only a few. So both Brennan's assertion of her anticorporate-ness and her assumption that it might appeal to some people were probably quite valid in both Old School and in New School Brooklyn retail communities.

Her second assertion, however, that there is an appropriate way to approach her, is a remarkable stance for several reasons. First, she complains about the very complaint that her place-making semiotics were hurtful and insensitive to a group who has suffered the repercussions of gun violence. Sociolinguist Greg Matoesian (1993) argues that complaining about complaints is a classic move of the powerful who defend themselves in public forums, such as courtrooms and tribunals, by alluding to the deficient communicative norms of their accusers. As if a parent correcting a child, Brennan asserts that there is a "preferred way of speaking" that everybody agrees upon, which was violated by the protesters. It also suggests that Brennan herself has the right to dictate to others how they should address her.

In the audio version of Ihaza's *Outline* story, Brennan explains that, at the town hall meeting on August 22, she might have appeared flippant in front of that crowd by saying:

I've sat in my restaurant and at the protests, people yell "white supremacist" or "racist" and "colonizer" and that, those are definitely misconceptions about me or any of my friends or staff or family. . . . You have to understand that I've been dealing with this for almost seven weeks. Those people who acted all calm and collected at the town hall meeting would come on weekends outside my restaurant and yell racial slurs to me and my staff. (Ihaza 2017)

Stephens told us that people did not show up to accuse Brennan of being a racist or a white supremacist at the initial open forum that she and her like-minded activists had organized in front of Summerhill on July 22, 2017. They gathered to raise awareness and bring the entire community—white gentrifiers, black gentrifiers, Latinx gentrifiers, and long-term African American, Afro-Latino, and Afro-Caribbean neighbors—together to learn about the issues, air their concerns, and give Brennan a chance to talk (interview with Authors, March 24, 2019).[17]

But on August 20, a full month after the first open forum, Stephens and others held what Stephens referred to as a "protest," and at that event people in the crowd were calling Brennan a "racist," and a "white supremacist." Stephens sent us the audio for this event, and we transcribed statements that were yelled out by what sounds like a man's voice: "Shut this plantation down." "White supremacist out of Brooklyn!" "Come out Becky!"[18] "You're lucky Trump isn't deporting you white racists back to Canada!" "No white supremacists in Brooklyn! Get the fuck out!" Others are heard saying: "That's the owner over there laughing and joking? Because she thinks this is joke!" "Shame, shame, shame, shame . . ." At some point someone chants, "Close down Summerhill," but we can hear Stephens and others saying, "Boycott Summerhill." Also, someone is chanting, "You are the problem."

In the context of a community controversy where Brennan was perceived to have made a wrong move as a newcomer in a place that she had just moved to, her suggesting that the community should have known how to treat her, when she was seemingly clueless about how to treat them, comes off as condescending. Stephens and her friends found Brennan's response to be patronizingly snobbish toward and scornful of them.

From the beginning, Brennan's stance and stature suggest that, in the US context, she is free to have the humor she desires and to be the person she wants to be. She seems to believe she can express herself however she likes, irrespective of the effect on others. Emphasizing her own prerogatives assumes that her behavior is somehow more proper in social interaction and raises the hierarchical assertion that her actions are not accountable to others.

Put differently, if she says her intention was not to harm, then she is not responsible for the feelings and welfare of others.

Building on Stephens' paradigm in which she interpreted the Summerhill case as one in which Brennan pushed for intent over impact, we find another feature of a privileged stance: the ability to avoid responsibility for the impact of one's actions. Brennan does this by refusing to explain fully her intent. She invokes her individual rights to her own personal intentions, regardless of other possible interpretations. Upon hearing of the negative impact of her actions, she then attempts to hide behind the notion of equality. After the hurt to others is revealed, Brennan shirks responsibility by suggesting she is just a cog in the meaning-making wheel, on equal footing with those aggrieved, and not at all powerful or threatening. In other words, not only does Brennan seem to have the right to her intention, but she seems to believe she has the right not to be judged for the unintended consequences of her own actions by claiming that she is nobody special, just struggling to make her way in the world, like anybody else.

From what was said in the town hall and from talking to Stephens and Villaran, one could glean that people seemed willing to forgive Brennan's ignorance. In other words, people seemed to suggest that it was okay that Brennan did not understand what the big deal was, but once told, she needed to do the right thing. People struggled with the fact that, even once she was made aware of the impact her actions had, Brennan appeared unrepentant, insincere about her apology, and still unconcerned about their feelings. While the community portrayed a willingness to forgive her, they were not willing to relent if Brennan continued to disrespect their history, their pain, and their humanity. Community members seemed to want her to acknowledge sincerely her thoughtlessness at the open forum. However, she declined at this initial opportunity to act in a way that would "change the formal relations" (Jeffries 2007) between herself and the community.

Brennan finally did cover up the bullet holes one night in September, almost a month after the town hall meeting and right before a formal Community Board hearing that she attended because she had applied for an extended-hours license (Whitford 2017c). Stephens was surprised to learn how much of an impact her own efforts to alert the community made. She said:

> So, in this meeting on Monday there was a lot of backlash from the community. I mean people that we hadn't even met through this whole process who were standing up against Summerhill. And voicing their concerns about—you know— "If you're a steward of this community." "You're a forward face, and you need to

uphold the values of this community in order to receive, be rewarded with extra hours to be open." (interview with authors, October 4, 2017)

The Community Board denied Brennan's request for those extra operating hours. For Stephens, Villaran, and other people in the community, her lack of speedy action, her refusal to respond adequately to the concerns that were raised at the open forum, and her resistance to alter the original apology only issued in writing were all unsatisfactory. Furthermore, Brennan's actions subsequent to the original press release about the "bullet holes" exacerbated the negative impact felt by her neighbors. For example, Brennan complained at the town hall meeting that even if she changed the wall, the community would remain dissatisfied, and then they would just, in her words, "move the goal posts" on her. With this comment it seems Brennan suggests that she was in fact conceding something in her interactions with the community. For the community, however, after the gravity of her initial misstep, her attempts at repair never succeeded in being interpreted as a successful act of apologizing. Following McIntosh, we contend that Brennan does give up little bits of her white privilege with each interaction with the community, but that an apology for her initial racist act of glorifying and romanticizing the bullet holes is never successful because it never has the "capacity to change the formal relations between" herself and the community. By pretending the holes in the wall came from bullets, Brennan acted without thinking about the people whose community has been ravaged by gun violence. This acting without thought could stem from those examples of white privilege as being allowed to "remain oblivious of the language and customs [and history] of persons of color . . . without feeling . . . any penalty for such oblivion" (McIntosh 1988, 7). The posters that went up anonymously boldly challenged this privilege by stating that Summerhill was racist, and the open forum served also to counter this privilege by reminding Brennan that her "aesthetic" stemmed from real people's real lived experience.

With her written but unsigned apology, delivered by a third party, Brennan concedes this privilege of being able to act without thinking about black people, but still does not acknowledge the ramifications or impact of her having done so. Instead, she writes about her own intentions and never makes a convincing overture to try to understand the people's experience from their perspective by coming out to hear what people had to say. Her not doing so suggests another of McIntosh's (1988, 7) examples of white privilege which Brennan did not concede, namely white people's ability to be "casual about whether or not to listen to . . . [people of another] . . . race."

A full month went by after the open forum and Brennan still had not recti-
fied the wrong by covering up the holes to show the community she would not
profit from pretending with her gentrifying customers that they were vicar-
iously experiencing the cool, stereotypical thrill of a violent black neighborhood while they ate and drank in her establishment. Once again, this inaction
rings of yet another of McIntosh's (1988, 7) examples, namely one that states,
"My culture gives me little fear about ignoring the perspectives and powers of
people of other races." The fact that the bullet holes remained even after the
open forum and Brennan's inadequate apology led people to form in protest
outside of Summerhill. And this time, as if to say, in the words of Biggie Smalls,
"And if you don't know, now you know . . . ," they did so to accuse her of being
"the problem" and called for a boycott. As if the community could no longer
excuse Brennan for being merely ignorant of the issues black people deal with,
it seemed some of the protesters concluded that Brennan was indeed a "racist"
and a "white supremacist."

Two days later, at the town hall meeting, Brennan had to face the community, conceding parts of her white privilege but maintaining and guarding
other parts of it to listen to what they had to say. Her casual, messy appearance was not lost on the community as Stephens hastened to tell us about it,
and thus, again, Brennan demonstrated quite predictable instances of white
privilege metaphorically akin to several points described by McIntosh ("I can
talk with my mouth full and not have people put this down to my color"; "I
can swear, or dress in second hand clothes, or not answer letters, without
having people attribute these choices to the bad morals, the poverty, or the
illiteracy of my race" [6–7]).

Her literal stance as well as the linguistic stance she took with her
responses suggest that she was there not to concede any more, but to defend
her privilege. Beginning with the line, "Sorry if I have a sense of humor,"
Brennan asserts herself in a manner akin to what McIntosh refers to as the
privilege white people think they have in deciding whether "there is a racial
issue at hand, or there isn't a racial issue at hand" (8). Throughout the interaction, Brennan never really looks nervous or uncomfortable, but she does
seem annoyed and put off suggesting that what is being called into question
is her ability to "arrange . . . activities so that [she] will never have to experience feelings of rejection" (McIntosh 1988, 9). Ultimately, it seems Brennan
thought she had the right to establish the position of the goalposts, first with
her actions and then with her inaction.

After Brennan finally covered over the holes, *Gothamist* reported that Stephens and the other organizers of the open forum issued a statement:

"The act of covering a wall which was originally marketed as displaying 'real bullet holes' is purely performative and does not merit any level of praise," they said, citing her "continued dismissiveness at meetings. . . . She may be able to cover up the holes, but she cannot undo the harm she has already caused," they added. "In light of this action, the organizers against Summerhill emphasize the boycott against this establishment." (Whitford 2017b)

Stephens told us the protestors ultimately considered her move to cover up the holes to be insincere, indicating that Brennan did not want to listen to others or try to repair the harm she caused. Instead, Stephens argued, Brennan decided to maintain her rights to expression and her privileged status and to defend them by denying that she ever had any privilege in the first place. The last our informants on the Summerhill case heard of Brennan, she was threatening to bring a defamation lawsuit against them.

Listening to the Street the Old School Way

We have found that when shop owners make changes to their Old School signage, it is usually to make their signs even more inclusive. For example, Frank Santo, the owner of Aunt Butchie's Desserts, a Dyker Heights dessert and cake shop, added Chinese characters to his storefront on 13th Avenue. When we asked him why, he put it very succinctly:

I put the Chinese signs up about ten years ago because my neighborhood used to be all Italian. It's not Italian anymore. It's all Asian. And one in every four customers is Asian now, because of that. . . . They come in and they buy the cheesecakes, and they buy our tiramisu. . . . [They didn't come in before]. They didn't know what it was. (interview with authors, December 8, 2017)

Santo added that he was careful to make sure that the translations were correct, because he did not want to offend anybody with the wrong message:

I asked ten people. Maybe fifteen people. So, I didn't want anybody giving me the wrong message. And being, you know, negative, or I didn't want to be in the papers for [having the wrong message on the sign]. And then, the doctor who delivered my kids was Chinese. Dr. Lee. I went to his office, and I asked him and showed him [the characters], and he said, "That's it." It means, "sweet things." . . .

He delivered my kid, I'm gonna trust him with my sign! (interview with authors, December 8, 2017)

Santo's story shows not only responsiveness toward people who live in his changing neighborhood, but a thoughtfulness and a thoroughness in considering that his sign carries an appropriate message. Not only did he incorporate a language that he does not speak onto his storefront, he also vetted the characters, first by seeking the expertise of a dozen or so people, but reassuring himself of the correct meaning only after a confirmation from the most trustworthy expert on Chinese he could find: the obstetrician who delivered his children. His remark that he did not want to "be in the papers" indicated his awareness that incorrect translations of Chinese in public might be so offensive as to be notoriously newsworthy.

Santo's signage makes his storefront into an interesting hybrid form as its purpose is to attract specific customers as opposed to advertising varieties of food from different parts of the world (Figure 5.1). It reaches out to newcomers (Chinese immigrants) while still trying to serve those who had been in the area (Italian Americans) as well as anyone who likes Italian desserts. In this sense, Santo's ancillary Chinese signage is not a modest move, but it is not a privileged move either. In Dyker Heights, a traditional Italian American

Figure 5.1. The Old School sign for Aunt Butchie's Desserts in Dyker Heights, above which two additional signs with Chinese characters hang.

neighborhood, not all residents are so welcoming to the Asian population that has moved into the community. So adding Chinese to a long-standing English-language sign such as the ones for Aunt Butchie's Desserts makes a particular statement of acceptance about the changing nature of a place and the people in it.

Santo's sign is not ambivalent about communities in place; it is clear he wishes to attract them with an unambiguous message free of wordplay. The addition of the Chinese text to his sign highlights another characteristic of the Old School place register: its ability to change in novel ways. We call this quality of Old School *generative inclusivity*, which refers to the register's capacity to add information in order to adapt to a changing environment while maintaining all its other functions and keeping its paradigmatic integrity. This adaptability also helps to explain the persistence and endurance of the Old School style as a place register in Brooklyn.

Since Old School is sensitive to what is happening in the area, it changes as the neighborhoods around it change. Its "all-eyes-and-ears-on-the-street" approach then makes it not surprising to find that it also incorporates, and thus welcomes, gentrifiers as well. For instance, on the side of a sign for a deli in Bay Ridge with the words "Deli Beer Flower Juice" is the name of the company, Ridge Organic Inc. On another Old School grocery in Prospect Heights is an ancillary sign announcing "Stop 11 Organic Deli and Grocery" (Figure 5.2). *Organic* is a common term appearing on the signage of other delis and markets throughout our data. The word *organic* calls to newly arriving residents from Manhattan or from other more gentrified areas of Brooklyn who presumably have upscale needs and tastes. Before we first moved to Brooklyn, a realtor driving Ed around the neighborhood (now known as Kensington) to show him properties for sale noted, on more than one occasion, that local stores had "organic produce," or some other organic merchandise. He knew this because the information was displayed on the shops' signs. However, sometimes it does not seem to matter in Old School businesses just how gentrifiers get coded onto their storefronts. In Figure 5.3 there is a sign advertising that a shop sells "organic candy." When one of us popped in to the store to ask the clerk where the organic candy was located, he replied, with a wink, "We ran out. Maybe soon we'll get more."

Along with *organic*, other upscale words in Old School signs seem to target newer residents in many gentrifying neighborhoods. For example, a storefront on 3rd Avenue in Bay Ridge displays the words "Gourmet Grocery" with large white lettering on a dark green background. Aside from this name, however, the shop has all the other Old School features. And there

are often handmade ancillary signs, usually taped onto the glass of either a store's door or window, such as "Credit Cards accepted here." While many Old School businesses operated on a cash-only basis in a lot of Brooklyn neighborhoods in the early years of the twenty-first century, the move to accepting credit cards is accelerating, and of course, now depicted on Old School signage.[19]

Figure 5.4. In front of this New School clothing store a sandwich board sidewalk sign has been added, providing more information for passersby.

If anticorporateness was one of Brennan's defenses in her conflict with Crown Heights residents over Summerhill's semiotics, we see other New School establishments trying to explicitly assert their uniqueness from the corporate, or perhaps simply stay in business, through Old School techniques. For example, the Bookmark Shoppe, a small Bay Ridge bookstore, often puts a sandwich board out in front on the sidewalk that states, "Friends don't let friends shop chain stores!" The quip plays on the law enforcement public service message "Friends don't let friends drive drunk." Still other New School stores have taken to placing sandwich boards on sidewalks or posting smaller signs in their windows to advertise job openings, highlight sale information, provide the hours of operation, and once in a while, identify brand names that they carry (Figure 5.4).

Perhaps in response to the meaning of exclusivity that people read into New School signage, we do see some New School businesses that attempt to make a claim for openness to all. The Flatbush Food Co-op provides one such interesting example. Located on Cortelyou Road, not far from Picket Fence and the Farm on Adderley, the Flatbush Food Co-op's new sign includes an explicit expression of inclusivity: "EVERYONE IS WELCOME," written in all capital letters and repeated five times on its awning (Figure 5.5).[20]

Figure 5.5. A new sign for the Flatbush Food Co-op includes the slogan EVERYONE IS WELCOME. Although not visible in the photograph, the slogan is repeated across the front of the building. Note the text on the right with the name of the shop and the images of fresh produce.

If aspects of Old School's functionality are being taken up by gentrifying businesses, it is also important to point out that Old School's inclusivity also extends to its adoption of the corporate world. When it is perceived to be beneficial, as in the case of ARENA Bagels with which we opened this study, Old School signage tries to appropriate the corporate and exploit it. Some Old School businesses, then, incorporate the emblems and logos of corporate branding into their signage, because people often can easily recognize corporate logos and feel invited in by them. Figure 5.6 shows a symbol on an Old School sign that closely approximates the logo of Brooklyn Brewery (Figure 5.7), the local brewery we mentioned in Chapter Two whose business has grown significantly, nationally and internationally. Sign makers told us that placing corporate logos on signage is illegal. And the brochure *Façade*, published by New York City's Department of Small Business (discussed in Chapter Four), reiterates this idea by stating, "Not only are corporate logos illegal, but they also mean that customers won't notice the name of your business—which can severely hamper your ability to be remembered." Arguably, the idea that Old School announces and encourages the practice of capitalism without distinction applies to its engagement with the corporate as well.[21]

In Brooklyn's dynamic urban context, Summerhill's owner is, as we have shown, not the only one capitalizing on the semiotics of place. And the line between honor and homage versus mocking and appropriation are not always

Figure 5.6. (above) This Old School shop sign includes an image the seems to mimic the logo for Brooklyn Brewery.

Figure 5.7. (above right) The actual logo of Brooklyn Brewery found on a bottle of the brewery's Brooklyn Lager.

clear. But given this lack of clarity, the wisdom of Old School's abundance of caution stands out. What Old School businesses such as Aunt Butchie's suggest is that these establishments are interested in doing open business, without racism and without aggression or harm toward anyone.

Stealing from the Bodega

While Summerhill replaced a long-standing bodega, or corner store, and became a place for "getting away from" all the "authenticity" of the neighborhood, a startup company landed in hot water by appropriating the term *bodega* itself. In 2017, around the same time as the Summerhill protests in Crown Heights, a new retail business venture in San Francisco created a vending machine that looked like a bookshelf. It could be stocked with an array of items depending on the publics it served in different places. The strategy was to "disrupt" the ways people convenience shop for the things they need rather immediately by introducing a new delivery method. By housing the vending machine on the premises of dormitories, libraries, gyms, and condos, the company would create a business that did not pay high rental fees. They planned to tailor inventory through artificial intelligence as part of the vending machine's program, which could "learn" the shifting demands of its particular public. Inventory on the shelf could vary and even be altered from building to building within the same dorm complex, for example, at major universities. The start-up named their idea Bodega.

Bodega as a business plan was meant both to emulate and capitalize on the function of actual corner stores or bodegas.[22] The word *bodega* originates in Spanish and is a general and widely used term in New York City to refer to these multifunctional corner stores that seem to sell everything that anyone might need from deodorant and dog food to potatoes and fresh flowers. Because of New York City's cachet as a meaning-making and taste-making cultural center whose particularities are known to and experienced by literally millions of residents and visitors a day, it stands to reason that New York's ideas, concepts, and idiosyncrasies would be mined by profit-seeking entrepreneurs. The company founders said their intention in naming the venture *Bodega* was to pay homage to actual bodegas that have served customers for decades. But within a day of their announcement, the internet magazine *Fast Company* posted a story about the venture:

> The major downside to this concept—should it take off—is that it would put a lot of mom-and-pop stores out of business. In fact, replacing that beloved institution seems explicit in the very name of [the] venture, a Spanish term synonymous with the tiny stores that dot urban landscapes and are commonly run by people originally from Latin America or Asia. Some might bristle at the idea of a Silicon Valley executive appropriating the term "bodega" for a project that could well put lots of immigrants out of work. (One of my coworkers even referred to it as "Bro-dega" to illustrate the disconnect.) (Segran 2017)

And indeed, this choice made people bristle. A sample of tweets about the story reveals the negative public response. One poster said, "I smell white privilege with this #bodega startup BS" (@stylefeen, September 14, 2017). Others argued, "The new startup that goes up against the beloved community" (@walrusnyc, September 14, 2017) and "I think we've hit peak white gentrifying hipster" (@mindhue, September 14, 2017). The acrimony and extent of such responses were completely unexpected by the company founders who claimed that they had vetted the name.[23]

Still others on Twitter noted that this case seemed to ignore larger issues of corporate appropriations. They wrote: "How does a #startup like #bodega get criticized for replacing small biz, but #amazon is hailed? #ImJustAsking #hypocrites #VentureCapital" (@ImJustAsking, September 13, 2017). Amazon, the hugely successful online bookseller-turned-department store / media streamer / major Internet retailer, is named after the largest river in the world. The reference could be to the river's network quality, connecting everyone to everywhere and to everything.[24] And this online corporation has not only usurped and disrupted countless local retailers, the mom-and-pops that make up vibrant urban spaces across the US and elsewhere, but it has also put many other corporate retailers out of business as well (Taylor, Hanbury, and Green 2018).

It is not just language, then, that is the issue, but how language is tied to place and context. One business writer suggested that Bodega went after the wrong entity to disrupt, the corner store. The writer argued that had Bodega positioned itself as an improvement upon bad vending machines, it would not have met with the same resistance, because in addition to the name appropriation, the company seemed to be thumbing its nose at, and perhaps threatening the very establishments that inspired it (Grossman 2017). Local bodega owners in New York City argued that such a venture could never put them out of business. In support of this idea, someone else posted a comment to Segran's *Fast Company* story: "we doubt that the new #BODEGA startup can make us a baconeggancheese or give us advice about our relationships." As the responses and tweets suggest, the New York bodega—famous for lots of reasons—is, in addition to an Old School establishment that sells anything and everything to everyone and anyone at any time, more than just a store.

This "more-than-a-store" idea was the foundation of the Chairman of the NYS Coalition of Hispanic Chambers of Commerce's criticism, confirming that for him, the startup was culturally insensitive and disrespectful of these Old School businesses. Segran's (2017) article quoted him as saying, "To me, it is offensive for people who are not Hispanic to use the name 'bodega,' to make a quick buck. . . . It's disrespecting all the mom-and-pop bodega owners that started these businesses in the '60s and '70s. . . . Real bodegas are all about human relationships within a community, having someone you know greet you and make the sandwich you like." People saw the name as an appropriation of real place-based institutions that rely on local connections, familiarity, and openness for successful business operations. Bodegas are a place where people convene, watch television together when big news is breaking, talk to one another, get advice about the neighborhood, see a friendly face, and even break bread. And gentrifiers also seem to appreciate the multifunctionality, individuality, and ubiquity of the Old School bodega. As one business writer says, "At a time when New Yorkers are getting increasingly frustrated at their streets becoming copy-and-paste clones of each other, filled with big brands that lack any connection to the community, the bodega represents one of the last entities that captures a unique sense of place, the one non-corporate corner of the neighborhood with real character" (Grossman 2017).

The experience of Bodega shows us not only another example of how language makes place, but also how certain people, who define themselves by place and whose imaginary of place is well entrenched, resist the displacements and re-emplacements of those who attempt to profit from it. These forces are subtle and not always completely comprehensible, and sometimes the arguments are difficult to grasp in their entirety. While a corner store may be a staple of the neighborhood, its function may not serve forty-five-year-old women in the same ways it serves men and high school students, for example.[25] But as we mentioned in Chapter One, most bodegas and corner groceries are highly receptive to individual customer requests, as demonstrated by Peña's Market's IOU system of "paying" for goods without any cash, or the move toward acceptance of credit cards in transactions for credit-card-carrying gentrifiers.

The idea and the experience of a bodega is thus essentially tied to context, and therefore it has a *place credibility*. In other words, the bodega, as a concept, is dependent on location, setting, and the people in place in order to be credible. The start-up Bodega proposed to take the concept out of its place, and this act immediately resonated negatively on social media where many people weighed in with their opinions.

To understand the depth of this context of the placed-ness of local Brooklyn mom-and-pop bodegas, we take a closer look at an actual bodega that we learned about from our field research. In 1986, on the corner of St. Marks and Carlton Avenue (not far from the Atlantic Yards project site and about a mile down the same street from Summerhill's location on St. Marks and Nostrand), the Peralta family bought a local bodega in Prospect Heights. They put up a new, hand-painted Old School sign that had "Peralta Supermarket" in large lettering framed on the left by an image of an apple and a watermelon, and on the right with renderings of a ham and bologna. In style, the shop resembled Peña's Food Market, not far away on Vanderbilt Avenue and also adorned with a hand-painted sign and similar images. Peralta Supermarket was the place where Patti Hagan, the Prospect Heights neighborhood organizer and activist, first alerted many residents about the looming Atlantic Yards arena plan in 2003. At the time, people had heard rumors about a "stadium," but it was Hagan who confirmed this gossip through her close reading of local newspapers. It was during Hagan's visits to Peralta's bodega that a lot of people first learned that eminent domain would be used to seize local properties for the development.

In December of 2004, eighteen years after opening and about a year after Forest City Ratner announced plans to develop the railyard and build an arena

Figure 5.8. A watercolor of Peralta Supermarket. (Scan of an image by artist Robbin Gourley from the personal archive of Patti Hagan)

and towers in the area, a small sign appeared on the front door of the shop with the following words, written as if a poem:

Thank You
Your unending support through the years has
Been greatly appreciated
We've gained wonderful neighbors and felt welcome into this
community. We've experienced a sense of family with many of
you like no other.
However, due to circumstances beyond our control
Peralta Grocery will be closing its doors.
The past eighteen years has been an
Honor and a Pleasure!
May the holidays and the New Year bring
Much joy and happiness to all.
Once again, thank you from the bottom of our hearts! (Archive, Patti Hagan)

Hagan recounted for us how dismayed she was upon reading these words. She quickly got more than thirty people from the block to sign a large fare-well card, which included a beautiful watercolor rendering of the storefront painted by Robbin Gourley, a local artist and neighbor (Figure 5.8).

A brief sample of the short but heartfelt notes that customers in the community covered Hagan's card with are vivid examples of the ways this corner shop touched the lives of people in the neighborhood:

"The hood will really miss the Peralta bodega Community Center!"
"Thanks for teaching our son all [those] bad Spanish words!!"
"Thank you for making my neighborhood better and safer."[26]
"You will be missed on the morning walk to work and the evening walk home."
"Your store was the first place our daughter walked to by herself when she was six.
She is 22 and she still loves your store."
"I miss sitting in the store and joking with you all!"[27]
"We love you like family . . . you were always there for us!"
"You have always been a part of my landscape."
"The block will never be the same again." (Hagan archive, 2004)

And the block never was the same. In place of the Old School corner bodega, a new establishment moved in, took down the colorful, handcrafted sign-age, and put up a new, almost unadorned brown awning. In contrast to

Peralta Supermarket's bright, wordy storefront, the new lettering on the awning was barely legible. There were only five letters. All in lower case, they spelled the word *james*, the New School restaurant we first pointed out in Chapter One.

Un-credible Places

A vending machine is efficient and convenient, and all about a person getting what they want, when they want it. You do not have to be part of it to be able to use it. In this sense, the bodega as vending machine was care-less and thought-less, with no human touch. The vending machine is impersonal, coldly turning interaction into the pure transaction of goods. Used by corporate disruptors, it appropriates real bodegas, displacing them from real places where people come together. In the eyes of many, the company was appropriating the bodega and using it inappropriately, insincerely, and in an un-credible way. In contrast, real bodegas give people meaning and belonging in place and make people feel a part of it. Hagan's homemade card for the Peralta Supermarket owners is at once a love letter, a statement of loss, and a heartfelt farewell.

The case of Bodega typifies the worst of what people feel not only about gentrification but about gentrification fueled by white privilege, where newcomers come to take but not to partake in the "credibility" and imagining of the community in place before them. The start-up Bodega tried to take the "cred" of actual bodegas out of their place, but in doing so, the venture was immediately accused of having no credibility because people saw this move as an insincere and crass marketing ploy.

In these cases, and in the presence of New School signs replacing Old School ones, we see a contest for credibility in place-making. As populations in place shift and change, so do local notions of what makes place credible. The semiotics of credibility shift as people move in and out, and in this contest for space the locus of credibility-making changes. In fact, powerful newcomers appropriating place, claiming it as their own, and establishing a new credibility of place is an old New York story. It is also an American one. Fueled by the ideology of Manifest Destiny and the origin myths of Manhattan's purchase by the Dutch from Native Americans for a handful of trinkets, the frontier remains a signature feature of the American historical imagination. Neil Smith (1996) pointed out that this spirit lived on through frontier language—the pioneer, the settler, the colonizer, the squatter—as it was used by Manhattan real estate agents to sell the Lower East Side, transforming it from poor tenements turned counter cultural havens to upscale hipster enclaves in the course of a couple of decades (see also Mele 2000). More recently, Richard Ocejo (2011) has gathered the nostalgic stories of those earlier inhabitants who, despite their own role in the process of gentrification, pass judgement on wealthier LES newcomers. Most of Manhattan is considered to be unaffordable as a place to live, but in 2012, *New York Magazine* declared on its cover, "Brooklyn is finished." In an issue featuring the weathered-steel rusted finish of Forest City Ratner's Barclay's Center Arena captured against a bright blue sky, the magazine's cover story suggested that everything Brooklyn had been imagined to be becoming was complete. But the significance of being finished also has the negative connotation of "having no more use, value, or potential" or "to be doomed to death or destruction."[28] Entailed in this simple sentence is the idea that Brooklyn is no longer being created, no longer interesting, no longer a promising place to offer anything to imagine. It's as if everyone knows what is coming next: Manhattanization of the outer borough, including still higher prices, cookie-cutter everything, and rich people.

But regardless of housing prices and what media and real estate brokers may say about a place, the fact remains that people living in Brooklyn neighborhoods are still trying to remain engaged in the process of place-making. In 2013, not far from James, A.R.E.A. Bagels, the new Barclays Center, and a growing crowd of nearby high-rise offices and condos, Leroy McCarthy, a local resident, started a movement seeking to name the corner of St. James Place and Fulton Street after the late Christopher Wallace, also known as the rapper Notorious B.I.G. or Biggie Smalls. This award-winning, internationally acclaimed rapper grew up in a building near the Clinton Hill corner where McCarthy sought the honor. Murdered in Los Angeles in 1997, Biggie Smalls has since become a Brooklyn icon. A signature line in his song "Juicy," "Spread love, it's the Brooklyn way," has become an unofficial motto of the borough (Remnick 2017). In his formal application to Community Board 2, which represents neighborhoods near Downtown Brooklyn including the super-gentrified Clinton Hill area, McCarthy presented supporting letters from the neighborhood block association, from two area churches and a local mosque. He also submitted a petition with more than three thousand signatures. At the meeting, however, community board members argued that Wallace was not an appropriate role model for youth because of his lifestyle, criminal record, and the way he represented women in his music. Opponents remarked that even his heavyset appearance made for a bad role model (Upadhye 2013).[29] The board ultimately denied the request to memorialize Christopher Wallace on the street sign.

Many local residents were perplexed and angered. They asked why it was possible to market and profit from depictions of black culture, without being a part of that culture, when, at the same time, attempts to publicly honor and pay homage to individuals who contributed directly to that culture are discouraged or downright thwarted. When we discussed this case with John Jay College students, they hastened to point out that lots of streets, plazas, and squares all over New York City are named after people with imperfect and sometimes even murderous histories, such as, they suggested, Columbus Circle near Central Park. Why, they asked, does a famous black man have to have an unblemished past to be memorialized in a place? If the Bodega startup was disembodied from place, then Wallace's name on a street sign was all about marking and preserving the actual place from which the rapper emerged and in which he became famous.

In order to circumvent the opposition of the Community Board 2, residents relied on the more traditional and grassroots forms of memorializing: the mural. Since Wallace's death, several murals of the artist have appeared throughout this area of Brooklyn and on a wide variety of local businesses.[30] Murals of course are painted on private property (most often with the owner's permission) and are a long-standing form of public place-making in working-poor communities (Sieber, Cordeiro, and Ferro 2012). Artists are often commissioned to paint murals, but murals do not enjoy the status of official public texts the way street signs do. Murals are informal, homemade, handmade, and temporary. If murals are not put on public surfaces, they are vulnerable to the whims of property owners. In fact, one mural in which Biggie Smalls appears was in jeopardy of being taken down by the building's landlord (Walker 2017).

The community finally achieved success in securing official, municipal public recognition of the neighborhood's famous son in 2017, when the New York City Parks Department agreed to designate basketball courts at a park between Bed-Stuy and Clinton Hill the "Christopher 'Biggie' Wallace Courts." The official naming was part of the city's renovation plan for the Crispus Attucks Playground, which received new fencing, recreational equipment, landscaping, and other improvements. From what Remnick (2017) reports, this effort was also met with resistance from some community board members, many of whom were white, who launched the same arguments suggesting that Wallace was unworthy of the honor. Recognizing the recent and accelerating influx of largely white gentrifiers to the area, Robert Cornegy Jr., the City Council member who helped spearhead the basketball court dedication campaign and who had been raised in the same building on St. James Place as Wallace, stated, "Now, no matter how much this community changes, there will always be a record of the culture that lived there" (Remnick 2017). It was a victory against a small but vocal and very powerful group.

If our case study of Summerhill we see how certain people—both gentrifiers and more long-term residents—negotiate the meanings of semiotic symbols that offend some members of their seeing publics. The case of Biggie Smalls reveals the politics of credibility of belonging and how this needs to be constantly negotiated and fought for in the face of newer residents rejecting certain semiotics in the places they are trying to make. How people choose to capitalize on and/or memorialize the past in public places, as well as how they decide to preserve private architecture, are clearly subjected to how those with privilege in place wish to position and thus create the space.

With Summerhill, it was not just the manner in which Brennan claimed space on the land that was ultimately so offensive to Stephens and others. As Stephen's co-organizer Villaran put it, "There are white people that recognize their privilege, and it's not just white people who are gentrifying. There are white people interested in learning about the community that they are gentrifying. And then there are other white people . . . who basically just see [gentrification] as kind of a financial issue" (interview with authors, November 18, 2017). As Stephens also explained, "I am a gentrifier myself. And I am not sitting here attacking her as a gentrifier . . . the woman is, you know, NOT apologetic. And her answer was 'I am sorry that you were offended.' Which, I mean, *personally* I don't think that's an apology. An apology is 'I am sorry for what I did'" (interview with authors, October 4, 2017). Brennan's various different responses fell flat, never quite rising to the level of sincere apology for the community. Each failed apology just made matters worse. In the end, Brennan's efforts looked as if she were more interested in protecting her white privilege than in protecting her business. With each interaction, there came an even more unsympathetic, insincere statement with no credibility in her pursuit of becoming part of the community.

In a recent article, African Americanist writer Michael Harriot wrote, "I was once asked, by a white person, what was the difference between a gentrifier and someone who simply relocates into a minority neighborhood. 'It's simple,' I explained. 'Gentrifiers put their feet on the couch.' The difference between colonizing a space and simply being a user of said space is the privileged mindset of assuming ownership" (Harriot 2018).[31] Many might argue, as Brennan did when she cast herself as a small fish in comparison to corporate redevelopment, that Harriot goes too far by conflating the merely privileged with the truly powerful. While privilege is clearly a stance and a perspective anchored in a system of power, it deceivingly seems to operate separately from that system as it gets enacted on the level of individual beliefs and behaviors, many of which are simply normative ways of being, that go without saying or reflection. In McIntosh's metaphor of the invisible knapsack, privilege is carried around by those who possess it almost imperceptibly and unwittingly. People who carry the knapsack exercise and benefit from privilege that those who do not have privilege can feel quite threatened by and with good reason. But those who have privilege do not necessarily have significant access to influencing sources of power.

Brennan seems to suggest she feels powerless in a system of corporate power that is much larger than she is. In her complaint about the community's complaint, she appears to wonder why people are angry with her or why they might feel threatened by her when there are bigger, more threatening "fish to fry."

Returning once again to the case of ARENA Bagels, a different dynamic between privilege and its relationship to power is evident. Antidevelopment, mostly white gentrifiers complained about an immigrant man's use of the development's anchoring feature, the arena, to sell bagels. The signage offended people, not because it erased or mocked their past, but because they believed they should have some decision-making power about the future of the place in which they live, and they had organized against FCRC's planned arena. They saw themselves as place-makers, and they exerted both power and privilege in that endeavor. Many anti-Atlantic Yards activists were, after all, affluent consumers with substantial economic resources, advanced education, and access to media outlets.

If local residents could take on and potentially stop a powerful developer with substantial state support, there was nothing stopping them from insisting a bagel shop owner change his store's name. These empowered individuals certainly felt they had the right to say something. And as it turned out, the shop owner, stating that he wanted to fit in with the neighborhood, heeded their concerns. And though Daniel Goldstein and DDDB remained focused on FCRC's cooperative agreement with the State of New York to use eminent domain to clear the area for an arena, local media outlets such as the *Brooklyn Paper* and the *New York Times* were happy to exploit the story of how these entitled residents "bullied" the "little guy" into changing his name, as if language on the sign were trivial.

In the end, like the Summerhill demonstrators who never felt they got a sincere apology from Rebecca Brennan for her racist semiotics, the Atlantic Yards protestors did not achieve their primary goal either. They won their battle against a bagel seller, managed to call some attention to the redevelopment process, and perhaps succeeded in stalling the coming arena with lawsuits. But, ultimately, Atlantic Yards protestors were defeated by the developer and the State of New York. Just as those who supported a city street named for Biggie Smalls and settled for murals, Atlantic Yards protesters resorted to putting up murals on the street. These could be readily seen by residents out walking their dogs or commuters going to and from work. These informal public murals have vanished now, and with them several public streets and dozens of residential and commercial buildings have also disappeared. But the opposition movement against Atlantic Yards did succeed in the creation of an archive. Their twelve-year battle against Atlantic Yards is documented on websites and blogs and in thousands of news stories, in addition to a host of other sorts of artifacts—brochures, posters, flyers, fundraising materials, news blasts, and the like—many of which we tracked down in our ethnographic research. The Atlantic Yards protestors had been building this archive since 2003, the year that FCRC announced the Atlantic Yards project, and also the year we moved to Flatbush, Brooklyn.[32]

FCRC named the project Atlantic Yards, a term that takes *Atlantic* from Atlantic Avenue, one of Brooklyn's main commercial thoroughfares, and *Yards* from the Vanderbilt Rail Yards, the patch of recessed land nestled in between the neighborhoods of Fort Greene and Prospect Heights and upon which much of the development would be built. But in July of 2014, FCRC renamed the project Pacific Park. This name makes a reference to Pacific Street, which runs parallel to Atlantic Avenue just a block away, bordering the southern side of the project site. After years of community protest, court battles, and hundreds of thousands of words printed about this battle for Brooklyn to create and halt the creation of a place called Atlantic Yards, FCRC erased the history of the controversy with the stroke of a pen.

Those of us who enjoy wordplay cannot help but notice the Manifest Destiny implied in this linguistic turn that began at Atlantic and, at least for the time being, seems to have ended at Pacific. The entire archive of the struggle against what many saw to be a corporate land grab and a threat to the essence of Brooklyn as a place, the voices of conflict and contest from the streets and the local neighborhoods are now buried under a new name, especially for those who are yet to come. For anyone interested in how Brooklyn got built at the beginning of the twenty-first century, some linguistic archeology will be needed to expose the struggle that the powers-that-be have unapologetically obscured. As a built environment, the new Brooklyn itself contains no record what-so-ever of the conflict. Only the outcome remains.

Conclusion: Public Language Matters

JUST AS WE were putting final touches on this book, the *New Yorker*'s April 1, 2019, issue arrived in our mailbox. The cover cartoon shows the Brooklyn Bridge coming from Manhattan, but instead of connecting as a pathway to Brooklyn, the famous 150-year old bridge is shaped in a U-turn, so that cars coming from Manhattan can be rerouted right back into Manhattan.[1] A big overhead sign on the bridge's east tower informs drivers, "No Vacancy, KEEP MOVING," but the caption of the cartoon, always found at the very bottom of the table of contents page, reads "Brooklyn or Bust." There are two smaller signs in the drawing by cartoonist Bruce McCall as well. One is an overhead federal highway sign, green with white lettering, on what looks like the Brooklyn-Queens Expressway that says "No Exits," reinforcing the idea that Brooklyn is now closed to newcomers. As the word *exit* comes after *no* a viewer of this cartoon might think of French existentialist John Paul Sartre's 1944 play *No Exit*. Or, as Brooklyn and the word *exit* are textually brought together, one might also conjure the 1964 book *Last Exit to Brooklyn*, by Hubert Selby Jr., a collection of short stories about the struggles of poor and working-class residents of Sunset Park, later made into the movie (1989) by the same name. We leave readers to ponder those possible meanings in the context of this book and the *New Yorker*'s cover.

The other sign in the picture is a storefront sign, tucked right under the bridge on the Brooklyn side. It says "Kayak Korner," announcing a business that rents kayaks to those who would like to row on the East River. While this may be just an eerie coincidence, we would be remiss not to point out the replacement of the letter *C* with the letter *K* in the word *Corner*, which for us brings to mind the work of Candacy Taylor (2016a, 2016b) on textual codes of segregation found on storefront signs along Route 66 that we highlighted in the Introduction.

John Austin (1962) showed quite some time ago that language is action in speech. Language is never just words, referring to things in the world; language is a powerful tool of social action. Like all actions, language "does things" through the force it has on people and the meaning it lends to context. In this book, we have tried to show that shop signs and the semiotics of storefronts in urban space are also doing much more than we might at first think. Storefront signs inform us, but they can also attract our attention by pointing to aspects of our own or others' identities. They can inspire emotions, from intrigue to nostalgia. They can also generate frustration and anger. More importantly, in the very heterogeneous urban space of Brooklyn, storefront signs suggest who belongs in the landscape and who does not, who is at the top of the social hierarchy and who is not, who is coming and who is going. More than just a symbol of commerce, signs operate as a technology of place, lending meaning to the land, and subsequently, to the people who inhabit it and move within it.

With this exercise of sociolinguistically reading storefronts to see what the signs "say," we suggest how signage works as a communicative tool that collaborates with other mechanisms in making space into place. The linguistic and semiotic contrast between Old School and New School signage shows how each of these place registers defines and creates space for different types of users. The very different meanings and messages of these two sign-types become apparent when one is compared to the other and when considered diachronically within a dynamic context.

Old School signs, taken together as a system that creates a message on the street, suggest that all groups of people can participate and even belong in the local economy and community. Thus, Old School signs reinforce the notion that any group possesses a similar status to that of their comembers, irrespective of their obvious differences. Ostensibly, the signs say no one group should consider itself dominant over any other. The vast array of difference itself as well as the way difference is explicitly and thus sincerely referred to suggests that, in Brooklyn, there is a place for everyone. At the same time, each sincere reference to an identity protects and holds a place for every other possible identity. One's right to be different is on par with everyone else's right to be so, as an ideal equation, is what the signs, at the very least, seem to say.

In contrast, the New School signage suggests the opposite of egalitarianism in place. Gentrifying signage comes from either lettered knowledge, cryptic meanings, ironic puns that suggest insider intimacy, or jokes about others. Both erudition and othering have the potential to become alienating and/or offensive in the linguistic landscape. In concert with one another, New School signs assert a sociocultural hierarchy through the language ideology of concision in writing, erudition in thought, and catchy polysemy that acts as cover for jibes about people not at the pinnacle of a socially stratified system of valued identities.

Our analysis of signage is not about individuals in place. Old School signage does not create a utopia where each person exists harmoniously with each other person. Nor does our analysis suggest that New School signage indicates all gentrifiers see themselves as superior to others in their new urban homes. Rather, the data we present show us how the two sign types form two different meaning-making systems that sociocultural significance are attached to. As systems, the signs contribute to the creation of culture in place. Put another way, where any one sign is an attempt at "say," signs that share characteristics and features when displayed collectively across space become a particular register or a patterning of language use that occurs predictably and locates people in context. Each register with its regularity creates an intelligible form that produces and reproduces the condition and opportunity for a certain type of "say."

From this systemic perspective, public storefront signs then do not just statically represent Brooklyn's reality. They also contribute to the borough's socioeconomic transformation by, yes, physically marking, but also by actually making that change. McCall's recent *New Yorker* cover showing "No Vacancy" in front of Brooklyn suggests, as does our data on storefronts, that Brooklyn is now a center unto itself. Where New Yorkers thirty years ago might have thought it impossible that Brooklyn could rival Manhattan in any way about anything concerning distinction, today it seems like a no-brainer. Brooklyn was, after all, a land mass separated from Manhattan topographically by just a river. Through sociolinguistics and anthropology, we hope to have shown that the barrier to thinking about Brooklyn as a distinctive place unto itself was not however, "just" a slender river; it was instead divergent socioeconomic systems overlaid with contrasting systems of meaning-making. Today, Brooklyn's shift from a marginal space to a central place is now vividly represented through language, literally and legibly right in front of us in and on public spaces: from the *New Yorker*'s cover and New School storefronts that originated in Brooklyn that now exist in Manhattan (such as Ample Hills Creamery and the Clay Pot), and storefronts and merchandise in Manhattan and elsewhere around the world that incorporate the word *Brooklyn* into their names.

Of course, every storefront sign, taken by itself, has its own story and ambit. A brief update of some of the shop signs we featured in this book can show how the dynamics of place affect individual storefronts and reveal a more complicated trajectory for any one storefront in place. For instance, Hipsqueak, the Bay Ridge New School sign for a kids' clothing store that opened in 2006, is gone. The shop physically closed in 2013 but transformed to an online subscription box retailer with a website and Facebook page. In its place, an Old School travel agency, Empress Travel, opened in 2014. But after three years it moved its location twenty blocks to the north on the same avenue. The present storefront has a sign that reads "R hair studio," which looks like a New School sign. While some of our Old School examples in previous chapters got makeovers, they persist in the Old School register. For example, Fertile Crescent Grocery on Atlantic Avenue replaced the hand-painted sign with a new red awning with just as many words as the old one. Garden Tortills, with its nonstandard Spanish *tortills* for *tortillas*, replaced its old awning with a new one, this time with the word *tortillas* spelled correctly. But yet again all its important information repeats on each side of the shop as well as on an additional awning at the store's entrance. Some stores continue to carry on with their Old School signs, such as Little Lords and Little Ladies (open since the mid-1990s), with no change at all.

But other dynamics clearly indicate the broader transition of Brooklyn's gentrification process. Peña's Food Market in Prospect Heights is now The Little Cupcake Shop—a business that first originated in Bay Ridge, opened a second store in Manhattan, and then opened its third store in Prospect Heights, Brooklyn, in Peña's place. The Law Offices that provided "Free Consultations" [fig 2.18] is now Sofreh, described on Google Maps as an "ingredient-driven" Persian restaurant in a "white-washed space." Notably, Sofreh, according to the *New York Times*, gets the serious distinction of being one of the ten best New York City restaurants (Wells 2018). And often where New School shops have closed, they are frequently replaced with more New School shops. The upscale maternity store on Bergen Street, Bump, shut its doors in 2015 and was replaced by Wild Was Mama, which then relocated to the less gentrified neighborhood of Greenpoint. In its place appeared a new shop, Lash Eyecon. The upscale bar Cornelius on Vanderbilt Avenue in Prospect Heights closed in 2014. It was replaced almost immediately by an upscale ramen noodle shop named Chuko. Likewise, Brooklyn Urban Monster, not able to stay in business, gave way to an upscale upholstery and design store called Indigo 2 Ash. Some storefronts provided us with very clear stories of Brooklyn's change, as in the case of James, but only after learning of its previous iterations through ethnographic interviews with key research participants, who themselves related quite differently to the same site and its individual trajectory in space and time. Three of our informants' experiences (Caldwell, Hagan, and Goldstein) were all linked to the site upon which James sits today. Finally, AREA Bagels and Bialys [fig 1.2], the Old School shop near the Barclays Center that had changed its name to appease angry neighborhood activists fighting redevelopment, closed its doors in 2015. Another bagel store suddenly appeared in its place in March of 2016. Its name: Brooklyn Bagels.[2] And interestingly, its location on 5th Avenue near St. Marks Avenue starts at a point that dramatically follows the borough's changing demographic data, marking its relentless gentrification and redevelopment from west to east on one Brooklyn street. Only a few blocks from AREA Bagels and Bialys is James, and, a few blocks further, Summerhill.

The language and other semiotic features on storefront signs matter in the making of Brooklyn: how it was before, how it is now, and in terms of what it will be in the future. *To matter*, as a verb, means to be of importance, and except for the occasional protest, it seems that most people take signage for granted, as it seems just a common and ordinary part of human life, perhaps because of its very ubiquity in most places. The job of the linguist and the anthropologist is to show how "ordinary" or everyday practices create culture, or that tacit system of implicit meaning that guides a people in thought, action, or beliefs. As Clifford Geertz (1973) pointed out, culture exists in the realm of common sense, those things that "go without saying," that people generally do not explicitly question or explain or remark on. In other words, culture is a set of rules and norms that regulate social interaction and that get acquired by its members as a system of meaning-making that, for the most part, goes unanalyzed by people.

We have seen that the written law which formalizes the rules for the creation of signs is violated more than it is followed in Brooklyn in both Old School and New School texts. It seems that people go against the law because of their "feeling" that there are better ways to communicate their messages of either openness or distinction than what is permitted by law. The signs suggest that shop owners are loath to resist their cultural inclinations and ideologies just to follow the law. These cultural actors might not be able to explain how texts operate on public space and on their users, but the data reveal their unequivocal opposition to the written law and suggest they are in fact, being governed by cultural forces, meanings, and norms rather than by the official rule of law.

Culturally, the signage on storefronts does more than mark a business in place. Signage is one of the social mechanisms that helps organize communal life, by setting the tone and tenor for the neighborhood. In other words, signs create, through their texts, as Michael Warner (2002, 51) notes, an "idea of a public." In Brooklyn two very different types of signs put forward two very different conceptions of that public. We have seen how a multiethnic, multi-classed, multiracial, and multireligious space reflected in Old School signage takes very little, if anything, for granted in designing and erecting texts that create an atmosphere of coexistence and openness to others. Conversely, with New School signage, it appears that people with privilege, generally those in the dominant and affluent class, use language and othering however they like without concern for the way such usage impacts others.

The language ideology of concision deployed in New School signage makes the wordiness, repetition, reiteration, translation, pictures, and drawings of Old School signs look chaotic, messy, even dirty or cheap, by some accounts. As New School signage comes to mean demure and clean, then the word-rich Old School signage, along with the rest of its features, signifies old-fashioned or in the wrong time. In the new context, Old School signage comes to look, in the words of anthropologist Mary Douglas (1966), like "matter out of place." Along these lines, perhaps because ethnonyms have often been so frequently used as ethnic slurs in the United States, any mention of a person's or a people's race, ethnicity, or national origin seems racist outside of Brooklyn or to outsiders who visit.[3] National forces of assimilation, shifts from languages other than English to English monolingualism, and the secularization of religious groups all foster and create a culture that not only homogenizes people, but also suggests that any labels sound anachronistic and misplaced. Today, in many places in the United States, it sounds politically incorrect to mention ethnic or racial backgrounds. But Old School signage shows how mentions of race, ethnicity, and national origin are not, in fact, matter out of place in Brooklyn. Just the opposite seems true. These mentions not only matter in place, but the words themselves create a place in which people can exist holding a space for themselves and for each other, out loud and in open public space.

WHAT THE SIGNS SAY

Alongside both sign types, of course, the corporate hyperdominant appropriation of space has emerged, threatening to make Brooklyn no place special, just like any other place. Our survey data suggest that Brooklyn residents, whether newcomers or old timers, in some ways resist trying to become a place full of consumers with the same placeless or ubiquitously placed retail and commercial operations as every other American city and suburb. Urban development guru Richard Florida (2012) has put forward the notion of the creative class as both an engine of the socioeconomic transformation of North American cities over the past three decades and as resistance to their impending corporate takeover. Florida defines the creative class as "people paid to use their minds—the full scope of their cognitive and social skills" and who are in a quest for "rich and multi-dimensional experiences" (9). But anthropologist Arlene Dávila (2012, 189) cautions us about the limited scope of this class identity, which leans "toward middle-class and upwardly mobile sectors," and how its neoliberal, exclusionary boundaries "do not account for the racial politics involved in creative economies" and leave out so many other groups of less affluent and more culturally diverse creative producers. Our ethnographic and linguistic investigation indicates the growing prominence of Florida's creative class in Brooklyn's linguistic landscape. It also indicates that, while its members may not earn the same income as Wall Streeters, they bring enormous amounts of cultural capital through higher education and the privilege of sometimes working for very little pay for long periods of time on their way to higher earnings, and significantly, a central engagement with texts in moving within, defining, and propagating this new economy.

Moreover, this new economy continues to sustain social systems built on long-standing but complex hierarchies that make for places where most nondominant identities are fair game for mockery. We saw in Chapter Three that merely being nondominant does not exclude people from manipulating and employing the social identities of others to create a more palatable or fun-loving version of themselves. And certainly women of any stripe, but definitely white women, who think they have the right to say out loud what is wrong with a place as well as the gall to attempt to change it, will come under scrutiny. Notions of white womanhood loom large in the construction of race and masculinity in the United States, and so white women tend to attract a particular type of criticism and disparagement, partially because they enjoy unearned privilege as white people, so their insistence on being taken seriously can meet with a caustic backlash meant to remind them that they are nothing more than women, that is, second class citizens who are supposed to be, like the children they care for, seen and not heard. And so as many gentrifying mothers suffer backlash for their feminist urban innovations, it seems that some have attempted to take cover under racialized and classist linguistic and semiotic devices.[4]

By looking at storefronts both systemically and systematically, we have also tried to engage with the problem of intention and impact. It seems that some people do not always understand how and why some language uses and some specific semiotic devices offend. It also seems "not knowing" why something is offensive is forgivable. But the offender's inaction of not changing course once an awareness has been raised seems unpardonable. Our analysis of specific instances of the gulf between intentions and impacts reveals how the cultural organizing principles of social stratification are not only deeply embedded in everyday discourse but seamlessly become part of the construction of systems of racism, classism, ethnocentrism, and sexism that remain obscure to language users, who, McIntosh (1988) says, are brought up to deny their privilege and to be oblivious to the ways it gets supported. As Warner (2002, 88) puts it "dominant publics are by definition those that can take their discourse pragmatics and their lifeworlds for granted." But Old School signage suggests that there are many shop owners who appear to be fully aware of the threat of offense—so much so that they work hard to stay "out of the papers."

Different signs of course matter to different people in different places for different reasons. But our study attempts to locate how privilege is exercised through public texts as forms and models of communication. Through shop signs we see who can and cannot say certain kinds of things in public, as well as who is more concerned about what they say and to whom. Old School signs, as a system that "says" egalitarianism, may be somewhat rebellious in Brooklyn. In the US context they may, in fact, be subversive, as they seem to resist conformity and the national orthodoxy of assimilation. The presence and ostensible acceptance of nonstandard, nonprescriptive language on Old School storefronts disrupts notions of standard language ideologies that support elite culture that presumes and attempts to convince people that they cannot communicate adequately without a particular set of imposed, formally taught rules. The functional use of languages other than English flies in the face of conventional mantras that suggest that success depends on English-only or English-preferred business practices. The explicit references to ethnicity, race, and national origin go against homogenization and assert that it is okay to be different in Brooklyn. The multiple words and textual styles are meant not to offend bourgeois sensibilities of decorum, rather they seem meant to communicate with as many people in the market place as possible.

And these features, along with the generative nature of Old School is both indicative and performative of openness, vividly espousing a work ethic of capitalism that makes no distinction among consumers.

Brooklyn's shop signs also tell us that privilege and power appear to be bound together but are quite separate in the building of cities. As elements of social structure, privilege and power are hard to disentangle analytically. Occasionally, people may protest cultural appropriation or mockery of nondominant cultural groups. But for the most part, those who have been offended by signage do not seem to say so outside of the cyberworld of Twitter or the comments sections of other social media. When controversies do arise, where one group of people suggests that public language, symbols, or monuments are offensive, the various sentiments expressed often get conflated as the same thing (the threats to boycott a bagel shop depicting acquiescence to corporate development versus the threats to boycott a restaurant because of its owner's nonchalance toward what the community suggested was racist imagery). Arguably, in the face of opposition, speakers are free to carry on: free to think about the possible consequences of their speech actions and free to ignore those consequences. Their speech actions or inactions after protest may or may not be what affects their business. Some store owners worry about their business and negative press, and some seem concerned about their privilege to say what they want.

We identify storefront signs as registers of place-making because they are highly functional in creating context, or place. But we could also theorize storefront signs as a speech genre (Bakhtin 1986, 60) with its own "thematic content, style and compositional structure." Linguistic anthropologist Richard Bauman (2001, 79) defines genre as "one order of speech style, a constellation of systematically related, co-occurrent formal features and structures that serves as a conventionalized orienting framework for the production and reception of discourse." Though they do not have to be, genres are often associated with writing and written texts, and storefront signs engender reading and reading practices. Thus, one could categorize shop signs as a particular type of public text, which would imply that a particular set of norms of reading signage would be associated with or grow out of this genre. Signs are usually thought of as quite basic and simple literary artifacts. Indeed, they are short texts—though some have more words on them than others—but shop signs with fewer words are not necessarily "easier" to read. Certainly genres are mediated by ideologies that link to social groups, human endeavors, historical moments, political practices, genders, and professions (Briggs and Bauman 1992, 145). Through these associations, social value is conferred on genres of writing (and speaking).

As a genre of writing that is notably public, material, and long-lasting, shop signs are unique texts for a sociolinguistic analysis of power and privilege. They endure in the landscape as if uttered anonymously, in contrast to spoken utterances that can be negotiated among the interlocutors who hear them.[5] The nature of a spoken utterance, having disappeared into thin air as quickly as it came into it, benefits the speaker who can always deny that he or she said the offending words or claim that the hearer misheard them. Spoken language offenses can also be chalked up to the rapid nature of talk and a speaker's inattention to the details of what they say. An offending speaker can always say "I am sorry. I misspoke," and then give excuses for the mishap. Signage, in contrast to the short-lived, spontaneous, and impermanent nature of rapid speech, includes language and semiotic devices that require planning and deliberation and generally a discussion with others who fabricate the signs. The people who decide to put words and images up on a sign have to think about and perhaps even ponder with others what their sign should say. Once the deliberations are done and the sign is constructed and hung, the written utterance is meant to remain in place in a fixed and stable way. The costly nature of sign making and sign hanging make frequent changes impossible. And the fact that the sign is placed in commercial spaces—out in the open, on the public street—makes it perpetually visible to all. And at this point the intentions of the person who is responsible for the sign and the words on it are irrelevant, because most onlookers will not be able to inquire about them. As a genre, signs, once made, quickly belong to and become part of the public.

We could compare the issues we have raised about language and the place-making power of storefronts to recent conflicts about the function and meaning of another set of public and enduring texts: US Confederate Civil War monuments and the names of buildings that memorialize individuals who fought for the Confederacy, or the Southern states in the mid-nineteenth century that broke away from the Northern states in order to maintain slavery as an economic and cultural system.[6] In some cases, these Confederate statues and the names of individuals who fought for Confederate ideals have been removed. The likeness of Nathan Bedford Forrest, a North Carolina planter who enlisted as a private and then rose to the rank of general, adorned a public space in Memphis, Tennessee, but was recently removed by the city because local government said it did not reflect the community's contemporary values (Hale 2017). A statue of Robert E. Lee, the leader of the Confederate's military effort, in Charlottesville, Virginia, was recently shrouded in 2017 after a vote by the Charlottesville City Council. However, a state court ordered the statue to be uncovered, citing a law protecting memorials and monuments.[7]

In this most recent case, this conflict has opened a wider national conversation about the multiple meanings of these public symbols and about the intentionality of those who defend them. Also entailed in this conversation is the effect these memorials have on members of the public. People on both sides of this argument seem very emotionally invested in this issue. Those who oppose the monuments' and memorials' existence in public space today argue that these icons may have the power to intimidate people whose descendants were oppressed by this system, as well as all people not part of a white supremacist hierarchy. And many white people also oppose such monuments, because they too, denounce white supremacy. Supporters of such monuments, however, say their history and their identities (as Southerners whose families were supporters of the Confederacy or as Southerners whose family members died in the war) are being attacked through demonstrations demanding these symbols be removed, arguing that these monuments function as a remembrance of the past and of a region's and a people's history.

But within this conflict there are embedded the subtler geosemiotics of these monuments, that is, their power to symbolically shape our imaginary about place. By virtue of having been selected to be remembered, one could argue that likenesses of Forrest and Lee are seen not as mere remembrance but as people from the past who are supposed to be exalted and esteemed in the present. And in fact, monuments and memorials function in both of these ways. Additionally, Confederate civil war generals (like Joseph Johnston and John Bell Hood) or statesmen (such as Alexander Stephens, vice president of the Confederate States of America) may be barely known by many contemporary users of space, yet their names hold and define place in meaningful ways. For instance, their monuments occupy positions and spaces on land where the names and statues of others could be instead. As space is being held by obscure historical figures, the contributions of others go ignored and even become erased from history. Public space, then, for the contributions, the history, and the humanity of others becomes limited or nonexistent. Recently, Yale University, arguably one of the most elite linguistic landscapes in the country, has sought to correct the imbalance of representations by renaming Calhoun College, formerly named after Yale alumnus, slaveholder, and proponent of secession John C. Calhoun, Grace Hopper College, after a pioneering computer programmer who was a woman (see Malinowski 2017 on how the controversy unfolded). No matter the proponents' stated intentions, the opponents' claim that these monuments represent historical figures who fought to maintain white supremacy cannot be fully denied. Also undeniable is the argument that these monuments continue to create white supremacy by giving it revered meaning in public life and by taking up space that could be inhabited by memorials for others. Still, removing these monuments altogether, some claim, is tantamount to concealing a troubled history and thus possibly condemning us to repeat it. Interestingly, Old School signs show us that inclusion is not necessarily about removing difference. In this Old School spirit, just as we were finishing this book, the Brooklyn city council finally approved and erected a street sign at the corner of Fulton and St. James Place in honor of Christopher "Notorious B.I.G." Wallace, but only after a six-year-long, diligent campaign by members of the community. When space is considered a limited good, we see how it, like other resources, gets accumulated by elites who possess it by either marking it with their own representational resources or regulating the process of representation.

Any attempt to review and control storefront signage would be repressive in a society that prides itself on its freedom of speech. Freedom of speech is enshrined in the First Amendment of the US Constitution, and for many Americans it is a fiercely held right. Even complaints about someone's utterances are themselves seen by Americans as attempts to thwart someone's right to free speech. At one level this sentiment is understandable. People want to be able to say whatever they want without consequences to themselves and their livelihood. Linguists Penelope Brown and Stephen Levinson's (1987) analysis of face and politeness predicts that this desire would be universal: all people everywhere want to move about the world without having their actions intruded or impeded upon. But Old School signage suggests that not all people think they have the right to speak without consequences. So, at another level, the idea that there should be no response to one's articulation not only contradicts the very right of free speech, it also actually professes one's sole privilege to speak over others' rights to say what they want. Speakers who resist being told that their speech is offensive seem to believe that they are entitled to say whatever they want about others, but that those others are not supposed to talk back.

It is understandable that a response that suggests someone's utterance or signage is sexist, racist, or religiously insensitive might make the originator of the utterance or the promoter of the sign uncomfortable, especially if such ideas were not their intention or if they did not know what made their utterance insulting. It seems many people in privileged positions are genuinely, and all too often unaware of why or how the employment or adoption of some semiotic and linguistic features feel oppressive to people.

From these case studies we see place and privilege in place are two important dimensions to the impact language use has on different groups of people.

For Brooklyn, while Smith's (1979) rent gap may explain how investment and capital move into place to revalue the price of the land, linguistic register on shop signs is a communicative workhorse that culturally redefines the land as "the place to be." The wordplay of New School Brooklyn signs looks like fun and games, but it also does the work of establishing on the signs a social and linguistic hierarchy in a place where the signs previously said there was none. The jokes, the historical references, and other features of signs that draw on certain forms and realms of linguistic capital traditions are not used only to elevate whiteness (Hill 2008), but as we have shown, they are used in the gentrification process to reshape public space where an ostensibly nonethnic, nonreligious dominant group of more affluent people can set the tone, price, and culture of the neighborhood.

People often continue to insist that language is "just words." They argue it is innocuous or that all users should have equal access to linguistic resources and to claiming them however they want. This latter view persists even when history, statistics, individual testimonies, and social science have shown us that for a variety of reasons, men and women are not treated equally. People of color do not receive the same consideration as white people, and not all religions get viewed and respected on par. The cultural beliefs and practices of certain groups are more highly valued than those of others. Thus, not everyone is allowed to say or do the same things. And when dominant culture is challenged, often it responds in ways that preserve its hegemony or its dominant status. We thus see how language can subtly (and not so subtly) maintain dominant culture's privilege to use others' cultural capital in the service of its creation of dominance and in its experience of domination.

Our findings indicate that what constitutes being mindful in the design of public signs varies from people to people. Indeed, there are social and linguistic reasons why some textual choices are catchy and others are not. While the power of language to have a negative impact on others seems to be sometimes lost on people with privilege, it also seems that the power of language to define the world is never really lost on people with power.

Linguists have done a lot of work describing and understanding how words do harm, and how language, in many cases, really matters. In her writing on racialization in American culture, sociolinguist Bonnie Urciuoli (2011) asserts that explaining how hierarchy works and how discourses of covert racialization function are among the few ways to start combatting common-sense notions and normalizations of these practices. No doubt, some New School signs operate in covertly racializing ways through polysemy, cover, humor, and the like (see also Dick and Wirtz 2011; Pagliai 2011; Blanton 2011; Wortham et al. 2011).

As we have shown, they operate in covertly sexist, misogynist, ethnocentric, and classist ways. In concert with critically reading New School signs, we might also take the time to read Old School signs more critically. The linguistic features of Old School signage provide a model of text-making to counter discrimination, racialization, and other forms of cultural domination. Old School's many linguistic and semiotic features are tools that have created a space for everyone in Brooklyn. Thus, they are the resources that could be used against discursive domination, discrimination, and racism. If Old School's representational resources produce a site of cultural pluralism, what other models of parity may be out there to provide strategies of cultural inclusion?

Returning to the April 1, 2019, issue of the *New Yorker*, we wonder who has decided that Brooklyn has "no vacancy," or no more room for newcomers. It is strange to ponder that someone now has the "right" to suggest that Brooklyn is closed for new business, since Brooklyn Old School signage has been open to everyone. As Poe's protodetective Dupin pointed out in "The Purloined Letter," often the solution to a problem can be found in the most obvious of places. We believe the answer is in the signs, right there in front of us on the street.

Appendix: Demographic Information about Informant Sample for Sign Type Survey

Informant	Age (Years)	Gender	Ethnicity	Education (Degree)	Years in Borough
1	40–59	M	CubanAm	PhD	16–20
2	40–59	F	Wh	MA	16–20
3	40–59	F	IrishAm	BA	16–20
4	25–39	F	IrishAm	MA	16–20
5	40–59	M	Wh	MA	6–15
6	>60	M	AfAm	HS	>30
7	40–59	F	CubanAm	MA	16–20
8	<25	M	AfAm/Lat	BA	21–29
9	<25	F	AfAm	BA	21–29
10	<25	F	Lat	BA	21–29
11	>60	M	AfAm	BA	>30
12	<25	F	AfAm/Lat	BA	21–29
13	40–59	M	Wh	MA	16–20
14	40–59	F	Wh	BA	16–20
15	40–59	F	Wh	BA	16–20
16	40–59	M	Wh	MA	16–20
17	40–59	M	IrishAm	BA	>30
18	40–59	M	IrishAm	MA	16–20
19	25–39	F	Wh	BA	6–15
20	25–39	F	AfAm	HS	>30
21	<25	M	Lat	BA	21–29
22	40–59	F	Wh	BA	N/A
23	>60	F	AfAm	BA	>30
24	<25	F	AfAm	BA	21–29
25	<25	F	AfAm	BA	<5

Key: Age is given in ranges: under 25 years old (<25), 25–39 years old, 40–59 years old, and 60 and over (>60). Gender: Female (F) or Male (M) Ethnicity includes White (Wh), African American (AfAm), Latino/a (Lat), Cuban American (CubanAm), Irish American (IrishAm). Irish American is a culturally recognized ethnic category by many New Yorkers, but also could be considered White. Education: High school diploma only (HS), BA (4-year college degree), MA (Master's degree), PhD. Years in Borough are provided as ranges: less than 5 years (<5), 6–15 years, 16–20 years, 21–29 years, and more than 30 years (>30). N/A indicates a nonresident.

Notes

Introduction

1. We use the terms *informant* and *research participant* interchangeably throughout this book.
2. This format followed a 1980s federal regulation setting the standard for all US street signs. Prior to this, borough street signage varied: Manhattan was yellow with black lettering, Queens and the Bronx were blue on white and white on blue respectively. And Brooklyn had black lettering on a white background.
3. Stewart shows how local tradition can persist in naming even after takeovers, as in the case of the state of Mississippi—its name was originally proposed to be Washington, after the first US president, but the older name won twenty-three votes to seventeen at the new state's constitutional convention (Stewart 1982, 228).
4. Literary theorist Vicente Lecuna's (2017) research on Parque Central, a massive redevelopment project in Caracas, Venezuela, from the 1970s, shows that the place, Parque Central itself, became a character in Venezuelan artistic and literary work from the time it was built.
5. We thank anthropologist Elizabeth Chin for the particular wording of this assertion.
6. Scholars of ancient Greece and Rome find texts throughout landscapes of antiquity, and classicists call these inscriptions epigraphs (Pavlenko and Mullen 2015).

7. In Las Vegas, for example, one can visit the Neon Boneyard, a collection of Las Vegas's retired neon signs housed at the Neon Sign Museum (See also Nowak 2017).

8. Forms of signage can also mark the dominance of emerging socioeconomic identities. For example, one early form of graffiti marked and made a claim for space in the Spanish city of Salamanca in the late 1500s, when recently minted "doctors of philosophy" wrote their names and titles on the sides of important buildings throughout the city center as part of the ritual that celebrated their new status but also served to expand the reach and importance of the university (Rodríguez-San Pedro Bezares and Weruaga Prieto 2011).

9. An extensive archive of photographs of Jim Crow signage is housed at Ferris State University's Jim Crown Museum of Racist Memorabilia.

10. Route 66, an older road spanning half the country on which Americans would enjoy the freedom of automobility and travel, was also a route upon which African American drivers needed to proceed with caution. Disney depicts Route 66 as getting put out of business by the federal interstate highway system in the 2006 movie *Cars*. American studies scholar Cotten Seiler, in his 2008 book on automobility, suggests that *The Negro Motorist Green Book*, a New York City publication by Victor Hugo Green that advertised businesses (gas, food and lodging) that could be safely patronized by African Americans (and which was referred to in the 2018 Hollywood film *Green Book*), was also put out of business by the federal highway system. Seiler points out that the federal interstate system was constructed with major exits at which most motorists came to stop and national fast food chains and gas stations began to dominate the market. According to Seiler, national chains were less likely to deny services to African American travelers than were mom-and-pop stores, not necessarily because they were "enlightened" or "non-racist" but because they were vulnerable to national boycotts. For a more detailed history of sundown towns in America see Loewen (2018).

11. Warner's innovation in conceptualizing "a public" is the recognition of its fundamental discursive and relational character. He defines "a public" as self-organized, oriented to strangers, whose membership is achieved through "mere attention" and which is at once personal and impersonal, and critically, it comes into being as "a social space created by the reflexive circulation of discourse" (Warner 2002, 62). See also linguist Allan Bell's (1984) earlier work on speech style and audience context.

12. The data on neighborhood in-migration are from a random probability survey we conducted in these neighborhoods during our research on the Atlantic Yards conflict (which we explain in more detail later in this chapter).

13. Census data, including household income, are from 2010 (www.census.gov, accessed July 12, 2014).

14. Lees defines super-gentrification as "the transformation of already gentrified, prosperous and solidly upper-middle-class [neighborhoods] into much more exclusive and expensive enclaves" (Lees 2003, 2487).

15. For an overview of neoliberalism see Harvey (2005) and Smith (2002).

16. In this book we use the names of those informants we interviewed who were public figures in Brooklyn provided they consented and the names of other individuals where

they appear in the press. We do not disclose the names of the rest of our informants.

17. Most of John Jay College's more than thirteen thousand undergraduates are from underrepresented groups; as of 2019-2020, the student body is 46 percent Hispanic, 20 percent African American, and 13 percent Asian. (www.jjay.cuny.edu/fast-facts).

18. Though we did not set out to write an autoethnography about our experiences in Brooklyn, this work will at times feel inevitably autoethnographic to the reader, because autoethnography, as Waterston (2013) writes, incorporates "the self-conscious voice of the researcher in the course of producing and representing ethnographic fieldwork and writing." Much of what we write about is personal to us, because it relates to a place we call home. However, while we in no way are trying to obscure our own "emotional, intellectual, and social positionality" as ethnographers (Waterston 2013, 36), we do not see ourselves as using those facts systematically to shed light on the larger social phenomenon. And finally, we refrain from over-defining our work as autoethnographic because we do not wish to dilute the meaning and power of that genre, given that we can imagine an autoethnographic book about Brooklyn that would be very different than this one. For excellent examples of autoethnography see Ruth Behar's *Translated Woman* (1993), Carolyn Ellis' *Final Negotiations* (1995), and for what has been coined by Waterston and Rylko-Bauer (2006) as *intimate ethnography* see Alisse Waterson's *My Father's Wars* (2014) and Christine Walley's *Exit Zero* (2013).

Chapter 1

1. We thank our colleague Avi Bornstein for assisting us with translating these Arabic words and the Hebrew and Yiddish in some of our figure captions as well.

2. Though out of business now, when we first moved to Bay Ridge there was a shop called The Catholic Store.

3. Note how this sign also contains nonstandard linguistic elements.

4. Aficionados of Italian culture might know the song "Al Di Lá," written by Carlo Donida and lyricist Mogol, or the later versions by Italian American singer Connie Francis or Emilio Pericoli.

5. Signage materials include varieties of wood, metals, and plastics (corrugated, vinyl, or acrylic).

6. This information was compiled from interviews with sign makers, New York State and New York City government guides and webpages, and *CityLand*, a newsletter published by New York Law School (Thompson 2012) for small businesses.

7. The rules governing commercial signage and permits for signs are located in the New York City Zoning Resolution (Article 1; Chapter 2, Section 12-10 defines terms, but regulations are dispersed in other chapters as well). The number of sign permit applications average around a few hundred a month and vary significantly from borough to borough. Buildings must make separate applications for each sign. Manhattan gets the most applications, followed by Brooklyn, then Queens, Staten Island, and the Bronx. Applications are archived on the Department of Buildings website (nyc.gov/buildings).

8. They also note that signs are different from advertisements, which, they say, "refer to goods and services sold at another location."

9. New York State proposes standards for signage and is responsible for ensuring that state law is followed (New York State Division of Local Government Services 2015).

10. "In *National Advertising Co. v. Town of Babylon,* the Second Circuit Court of Appeals declared unconstitutional the Town of Islip sign ordinance which only permitted signs on [businesses] . . . to display information concerning the name of the business or the goods and services offered. The Court invalidated the Islip ordinance because it was content-based" (New York State Division of Local Government Services 2015, 7).

11. If a building is landmarked, meaning it has a designation of historical significance, there are additional rules and regulations that need to be followed regarding signage. We discuss this in more detail in Chapter Four.

12. Other crackdowns included one in 1999 (Topousis 1999) in Queens, and in 2017 in both Queens and East New York, Brooklyn (Acosta 2017).

13. The sign makers we interviewed were licensed professionals who maintained their credentials for hanging and installing signs and who closely followed city rules.

14. Most of these respondents had in some way provided data or assistance on our Atlantic Yards research.

15. The signs included in the survey were Cleve A. Brown—a sign for tax services; Fertile Crescent (Figure 1.9); Little Lords, Little Ladies—a sign for children's formal and christening wear; james (Figure 1.19); bird (Figure 1.20); and Cornelius (Figure 1.28). Additionally, we asked, "Why do you think the first three signs have so many words on them and the last three have so few?"

16. One might argue that explicit expressions of identity are intended only for like-identified customers. One observer, for example, insisted to us that seeing Greek and English on a sign for a travel agency was only calling out to Greeks and that the accompanying English text (which simply repeated the information that was in Greek) was also targeting Greeks who do not speak or read Greek. As regular shoppers in these types of places, we argue that there is nothing stopping non-Greek English speakers from reading the sign.

17. The source of the written error is not always clear. It could be a result of the store owner's or the sign maker's nonnative English, nonstandard dialects, typos, or misspellings.

18. Linguistics is a descriptive science—one in which experts attempt to describe what speakers say and explain why they generate such forms—as opposed to a prescriptive science, which attempts to dictate what is and is not correct.

19. "Gargiulo's Restaurant," on Coney Island Fun Guide website (2017), coneyislandfunguide.com/?food-drinks=vendor-name-4.

20. Though not in Brooklyn, Bailey (2000) and Barrett (2006) have observed interethnic and/or interracial conflict in small-scale businesses in Los Angeles and Texas, respectively. In Bailey's (2000) research among African American customers in a Korean-owned liquor store, the African American informants complained that Korean shop owners did not treat them with respect. One forty-six-year-old woman

said, "They wouldn't acknowledge you in any way . . . you were nobody" (Bailey 2000, 91). Conversely, Korean owners thought African American customers were loud and disrespectful, "self-centered and inconsiderate of others" (Bailey 2000, 93). Bailey attributes their communicative difficulties not only to different cultural norms and ways of speaking, but also to long-standing histories of oppression of African Americans in the United States. In Barrett's (2006) study of language use in an Anglo-owned Mexican restaurant that primarily served white patrons, he noted how monolingual English-speaking employees exerted dominance over their monolingual Spanish-speaking co-workers through higher status positions (Anglo employees were bartenders, waiters, and hosts, and Latino employees were busboys, dishwashers, and prep cooks) and language ideologies regarding Spanish and English that they deployed in interaction. Barrett found that in addition to making fun of their Spanish-speaking co-workers, Anglo monolinguals also held them accountable for any incident of miscommunication.

21. Smith and Eisenstein (2013) reported the importance of such backgrounds to their participants by noting that they often derailed conversations and narrative trajectories to first remember whether the person about whom they spoke was Greek, Italian, or Lebanese.

22. Though our academic speech communities tended not to make mention of people's ethnic and racial backgrounds in references to them, Shonna remembers hearing such talk a lot while growing up in western Pennsylvania. So, on the one hand, these Brooklyn residents' usage of ethnic labels sounded strange and on the other hand, they sounded very familiar to her.

23. For an example of recent research on typeface and lettering as social artifacts, see Rahman and Mehta 2017.

24. The quote comes from Shakespeare's *Hamlet*. The oft-cited line is used to reinforce the value of being short and sweet and full of meaning in communication. However, Shakespeare himself juxtaposes the line and its meaning to the contradictory reality of his character Polonius, who then ironically launches into a very lengthy monologue.

25. When our daughter was in the sixth grade, her school-sponsored vocabulary-building program, gave the word *diffuse* in one of its vocabulary lists with a definition akin to "being at once verbose and ill-organized." Because the program takes the student through a five-part study of the word that includes categorizations of a words' peculiarities, possible confusions with other words, and five clues that are meant to help the student internalize the word in their lexicon, the exercise made it clear that being verbose and ill-organized went hand in hand. So, even as our daughter was building her vocabulary, she was also learning the time-honored language ideology that values writing that uses as few words as possible.

26. See also literature scholar Aimée Boutin's (2015) *City of Noise*, which examines the social construction of noise in nineteenth-century Paris, where bourgeois culture demanded the removal of certain city sounds, such as street criers and peddlers.

27. An open letter has everyone in mind as an audience. The genre has origins in Pauline New Testament writing, with modern examples including Émile Zola's involve-

ment in the Dreyfus Affair, Martin Luther King Jr.'s "Letter from Birmingham Jail," and Vaclav Havel's "Open Letter to Gustav Husák," following the communist government's repression after Czechoslovakia's Prague Spring.

28. Two Boots offers food from Italy and New Orleans. Calexico serves Californian and Mexican food and Naruto Ramen and Blue Ribbon are Japanese-inspired.

29. This public broadcasting of a narrow message is quite different from the recent trend of narrowcasting in political campaign advertising and cable television programming, which discretely targets specific demographic groups (Goodman and Dretzin 2003).

Chapter 2

1. Pipa is a restaurant serving Spanish cuisine. In Spanish, *pipa* means sunflower seed.

2. To add to an outsider's confusion, for example, Manhattan, Brooklyn, and Queens all have a 59th Street. And in both Manhattan and Brooklyn, 59th Street is the location of major subway stops.

3. See Sagalyn (2003) and Reichl (1999) for more on how iconic Times Square has changed.

4. For other approaches to analyzing wordplay on signage in a linguistic landscape see Lamarre (2014) and Curtin (2014).

5. As fifty-plus-year-olds, we also remember "the bump" as a dance introduced in the 1970s where partners would bump their hips and their buttocks together on the dance floor.

6. See for example *Nose, Legs, Body!*, a book on the art of wine, whose title employs wordplay in a similarly sexually provocative way (Napolitano 2013).

7. For an in-depth look at the experience of artisanal labor in New York City, see Ocejo (2017).

8. 2010 US Census. See factfinder.census.gov.

9. Both the affluent, probably white child and the taxi seem "new" to Brooklyn for this time period. When we moved to Flatbush in 2003, taxi drivers from Manhattan and JFK, La Guardia, and Newark airports were reluctant to drive into Brooklyn at all. Some would ask aloud why we, as white people, would live in such a neighborhood. And many gentrifiers often talk about the days when yellow cab drivers refused to drive people into Brooklyn.

10. Lexico.com of Oxford University Press also defines "monster" as "often humorous, a person, typically a child, who is rude or badly behaved" (lexico.com/en/definition/monster).

11. "Urban Male Initiative," John Jay College of Criminal Justice, jjay.smartcatalogiq.com/en/2018-2019/Undergraduate-Bulletin/Student-Affairs/Urban-Male-Initiative.

12. The *American Heritage Dictionary* defines "catchy" as an adjective, meaning "attractive or appealing" and "easily remembered." *American Heritage Dictionary*, 5th edition (2011), s.v. "catchy."

13. The *American Heritage Dictionary* lists at least fifteen meanings for the word *dig*, including verbs such as "to break up or move earth," "to excavate," "to hollow out," "to investigate," and "to poke or prod." Among its noun forms are "an archeological excavation," "a forceful, snarky remark," "a snide joke," and "a gibe/jeer." And then, in what the dictionary calls "informal slang" there are the meanings "to like," "to appreciate," and "to understand." *American Heritage Dictionary*, 5th Edition (2011), s.v. "dig."

14. These are what are termed "slang" references by the *American Heritage Dictionary*, which notes that the origins of these meanings in African American Vernacular English were first recorded in 1930s jazz circles. *American Heritage Dictionary*, 5th Edition (2011), s.v. "dig."

15. See Rotenberg (1993, 28) on garden areas in urban space and their link to cultural conceptions of health, "salubrity," and "enclaves of the well-to-do and powerful."

16. In her work, Hill includes many examples of mock Spanish. For instance, the line, "Hasta la vista, baby!" from the movie *Terminator* functions as a humorous stance, but the phrase is not at all representative of Spanish as it is actually used by native speakers. Other examples include Spanish morphological additions to English like "No problemo," pejorative use of Spanish loan words such as "Adios," and hyperanglicization of Spanish as in "mucho grassy ass" (for *gracias*) (Hill 2008).

17. Octavio Paz (2002, 22) in his famous essay "The Sons of La Malinche," writes the following about the word *chingón*: "The magic power of the word is intensified by the fact that it is prohibited. No one uses it casually in public. Only an excess of anger or a delirious enthusiasm justifies it. It is a word that can only be heard among men or during the big fiestas." A Mexican slang dictionary from 1996 defines *chingón*: "A tougher, more masculine, street connotation, it could describe a car, a motorcycle, or a person, and it might be thought of as meaning 'stud.' Not polite, but highly visible on t-shirts and caps" (Robinson 1996, 42). And there are various websites for Spanish slang words that consider it vulgar, but common. *Urban Dictionary* gives some of the following meanings: "*Chingón* is a Mexican word used for multiple purposes. It comes from the verb *chingar*, meaning *to fuck*, and *chingón* means 'fucking cool or a person that is the best,'" "A real bad-ass," "A vulgar way of saying cool," or "Kick ass." (www.urbandictionary.com/define.php?term=Chingon, accessed March 29, 2019)

18. In Barret's (2006) ethnography of Spanish in an Anglo-owned Mexican restaurant, he reports that Anglo waitstaff would harass their native Spanish-speaking kitchen staff coworkers by running up to them and shouting scatological words such as *caca* or taboo terms such as *cojones* in Spanish.

19. To their point, in 2014, there was a rash of armed robberies among businesses along Cortelyou Road, quite near Picket Fence and The Farm on Adderley.

20. The Holiday song is based on the poem "Strange Fruit," written by Abel Meerpol in 1937.

21. For more on blackface, minstrelsy, and American culture see Mahar (1999) and Rodriquez (2006).

22. Akeya Dickson (2014), in an article for the Afro-centric publication *The Root* titled "Thug Kitchen, A Recipe in Blackface" about this cookbook said: "[Thug Kitchen] just

doesn't work as well when you discover that it isn't other black people who are the creators. When that's the case, it can feel as if they're not sharing in the joke but laughing at you instead of laughing with you. In effect, their actions are all thug in the way that they completely pilfered black culture and capitalized off of it. . . . Stop trying to repackage black cool or trends as if it's some sort of brand-new idea."

23. We thank our undergraduate research assistant Loakeisha London for noticing this business.

24. Stewart's work is full of examples of explicit linguistic marking of place. For instance, New York used to be called New Amsterdam, when it was controlled by the Dutch before the British.

25. For more on intentionality, see Duranti 2015.

26. In this regard we invite the reader to think about the name Picket Fence for a restaurant and how catchy it would be in an upper-middle-class or wealthy white neighborhood and then in a poor, underserved African American neighborhood.

27. See the blog Life+Real Estate+New York, October 22, 2013, grecobs.wordpress.com/tag/gentrification/page/11.

Chapter 3

1. nymag.com/listings/restaurant/tea-lounge02. Accessed November 28, 2017.

2. The literature on gentrification and women's roles in changing urban space is sparse, but see Bondi (1999); Warde (1991); Patch (2008).

3. Ortner (1972, 72) says the creators of culture "[engage] in the process of generating and sustaining systems of meaningful forms (systems, artifacts, [institutions], etc.) by means of which humanity transcends the givens of natural existence, bends them to its purposes, [and] controls them in its interests."

4. Baby/mama's website is no longer active but it can be accessed at web.archive.org/web/20140413101216/http://www.babymamabk.com:80/about-us. Archived on April 13, 2014.

5. In the first decade of the 2000s, people posting in online forums would occasionally ask about Bay Ridge as a possible site to look for more affordable housing. We remember one response referring to it as "just a place with a lot of red sauce joints": a stereotype of the neighborhood being conservative Italian-American with nothing of interest to newcomers. Bay Ridge was once considered to be geographically too far from Manhattan. Also, rents in Bay Ridge never really declined during New York City's period of disinvestment (see Bonanos 2004).

6. *Urban Dictionary*, s.v., "baby mama," accessed March 29, 2019. www.urbandictionary.com/define.php?term=baby%20mama. Mark Anthony Neal (2002), scholar of African American popular culture, shows how once popular television comedies such as *Good Times* and *What's Happening* have served to concretize what Patricia Hill Collins (1991) called "controlling images" of black women, such as "mammies," "matriarchs," "welfare queens," and "baby mamas," in the dominant cultural imagination to align with dominant cultural interests.

7. We were introduced to the phenomenon of co-op apartments only upon moving to New York, as we had never heard of them before. In short, rather than buying the unit or the rooms that we inhabited, we essentially purchased shares in the building. We found when we talked to non-New Yorkers about "our apartment," they were confused as to whether we owned or rented it, because typically in American English and throughout the US, one rents an apartment and owns a condo.

8. Shostak's classic ethnographic life history, *Nisa, The Life and Words of a !Kung Woman*, covers these mothering issues from the perspective of a member of a traditional foraging society in South Central Africa.

9. The sheer volume of information exchanged between mothers on Park Slope Parents prompted the moderators to organize questions and responses ("threads") into subcategories, like nursing, clothes, pediatricians, etc.

10. Paperno was a "child of leftist parentage, she had spent her early years in the Grand Street co-ops, the Lower East Side housing complex developed by trade unions in the middle of the last century. She went to college in Austin, Tex., and worked variously as a waitress, a roofer, a bartender, a substitute teacher, a phone sex operator, a saleswoman" (Belefante 2014, MB1).

11. www.boingboingbk.com. Boing Boing has closed for good and its website is no longer active, though some of its pages are archived on webarchive.org. Unfortunately, the pages from which we quote are not available.

12. The classes cost about $30 each and lasted six weeks.

13. We do not have a high-quality image of Boing Boing's original storefront, but photographs of it are available on other websites, such as ny.racked.com. Examples of the community of mothering that the shop fostered are archived at www.dailypronews.com/boing-boing-park-slope-hours.html.

14. In 2016, there were 88,465 more women, aged twenty-five or older, living in Brooklyn than there were in 2000. Also in 2016, of Brooklyn's nearly one million women over the age of twenty-five, about 326,400 hold at least a college degree compared to just 179,805 in 2000. In other words, today there are at least 80 percent more women with college degrees than in 2000. The raw census data from which we calculated these figures are available at factfinder.census.gov.

15. Note the sound differences between "boing" [bɔlŋ] and "boink" [bɔlŋk].

16. Historian Rhae Lynne Barnes told journalist Amy Goodman (2019) on *Democracy Now!* about her study of the campaign by black mothers during the civil rights movement to eradicate the inclusion of rampant blackface and minstrelsy in American schools and military institutions in the 1950s and 1960s. Often at odds with activists who wanted to focus the movement on voting rights, these mothers maintained that their children were discriminated against and even lynched because of the grotesquely dehumanizing images and ideologies of blackface entrenched in the American educational system.

17. *In the Footprint*, 2010, written and directed by Steven Cosson, performed by the Civilians, Irondale Center, Brooklyn, November 12–December 11. The Civilians' dramatic method involves interviewing real-world stakeholders and bringing their exact words to life.

18. Other professions among our informants included graduate student, IT specialist, real estate agent, pharmacist, teacher, graphic artist, designer, birthing specialist, and therapist, among many others.

19. There were a few other dads like Ed who worked both from the office and from home and thus could often participate in these women-led efforts to change neighborhood institutions. But in our research, most of the leaders of these local efforts of change, as well as their primary participants, were women.

20. www.babeland.com. Babeland's first location was in Soho. Its Park Slope branch is an indication of the migration of Manhattanites to Brooklyn neighborhoods. For more on how Brooklyn has accommodated mothers and their sexuality as public discourse see Trinch and Snajdr 2018.

21. Interestingly, these moves on the part of gentrifiers also coincided with a period in the city's public school system where teachers were feeling pressure from the state and the city to improve students' performance on standardized exams. These tests were also the foundation of and the key to the city's "choice model" for public education, which purported to allow parents and students to "choose" the "right" middle and high school for their children. The emphasis placed on such testing caused a variety of responses from parents. Some parents did not object to testing but did not want tests to be used punitively against teachers and schools. Others thought the copious test preparation did not allow for enough educational creativity in the school day. Some parents encouraged their kids to achieve the highest possible test scores to ensure spots in the highest performing middle schools. And there were immigrant parents who often saw their very bright children do well in the classroom but poorly on the state tests. Poor scores could lead to a "promotion in doubt letter" from the Department of Education warning parents that their children might not pass to the next grade. Our ethnographic observations found all this created anxiety and stress for all Brooklyn families irrespective of their origins or status.

22. Characteristic of gentrifying Brooklyn motherhood, this woman arrived at our house for an interview with her younger son, who was home sick that day from school. She did not call to cancel or even to let Shonna know that she would be bringing her son along. Shonna was accustomed to doing business with her own kids and other people's kids around. Interspersed throughout the interview/conversation are the little boy's questions about how to spell and read words.

23. Mattera ran for borough president on the Green Party ticket in 2005. She is also an example of a person who is both native and gentrifier but also doggedly invested in making Brooklyn better for everyone. The daughter of Italian immigrants, she went on from CUNY's Hunter College to get an advanced degree at Columbia's Teacher's College. At the time of our interview, she was the director of the Child Life and Development Services at Bellevue Hospital. Critical of inequality, she pointed out the glaring differences between the concerns of parents at PS 321 and those at far less affluent schools nearby. Mattera was a key participant in the anti-Atlantic Yards movement.

24. John Jay High School (no affiliation with John Jay College) shares its building with

two other high schools, a situation that creates another dimension of inequity and conflict over space in gentrification.

25. The story was reported on Brooklyn News 12: "Elderly Driver Jumps Curb; 5 Injured," September 25, 2008, brooklyn.news12.com/story/34794291/elderly-driver-jumps-curb-5-injured.

26. Women have long been involved in fighting for streets safe from reckless drivers; see Norton 2011.

27. According to *Urban Dictionary*, the term *stroller nazi* refers to someone who "shoves their way through crowds (practically running over others) using a stroller as their weapon" (www.urbandictionary.com/define.php?term=Stroller Nazi, posted October 18, 2006).

28. sirvigo, 2008, "Park Slope Stroller Patrol is this annoying anyone but me?" Brooklynian, May 2008. www.brooklynian.com/discussion/16003/park-slope-stroller-patrol-is-this-annoying-anyone-but-me.

29. Robert, 2008, "Dawn of the Age of the Stroller Valet . . . in Park Slope." *Curbed New York*, October 6, 2008. ny.curbed.com/2008/10/6/10557796/dawn-of-the-age-of-the-stroller-valet-in-park-slope.

30. Comments are no longer available on the *Daily News* website.

31. In terms of resources, many of these women decided to stay at home with their child(ren) for an undesignated amount of time. Others left prior careers to start working in new fields, some of which catered to new mothers and their children, such as doulas, lactation consultants, childbirth educators, occupational therapists, and the like.

32. The meanings may be multiple, while the demand/request breaks with contextual conventions yet operates within gendered conventions at the same time. Sociolinguistically, one might also characterize this mitigating wordplay as a hip, intertextual politeness strategy (see Brown and Levinson 1979).

33. Surrogacy and its moral and social dilemmas are central themes throughout the plot of Fey's film *Baby Mama*.

34. When we asked some Brooklyn residents about the meaning of the name, some said that had the safety pin not been in place, one might be able to read racialized connotations into the sign, even though the safety pin was never spoken aloud when referring to the store.

Chapter 4

1. Bertha Lewis is president of the Black Institute and former president of ACORN, an affordable housing advocacy organization. See Atlas (2010) for more on Lewis' role in ACORN's activism.

2. Dowdall 2015.

3. Lewis' account also shows how different people have an array of reading practices that allow them to understand messages through multiple semiotic devices. Lewis'

grandmother keys into the notion that "luxury" doesn't just describe quality but is also a code word that excludes her community (on reading practices see Shuman 1983 and Jaworski and Thurlow 2009).

4. FCRC backed up this promise with a Community Benefits Agreement, which outlined specific public benefits, and which several local organizations signed, including Lewis, who at the time was the head of ACORN.

5. "Affordable" meant that renting those apartments would cost 30 percent of a family's income and units would be available to households making as much as $120,000 per year.

6. See also Lavine and Oder (2010) for a critical overview of the planning and public input process and the role of the courts in the context of opposition to the project.

7. The first film, *Brooklyn Matters* (2007) by Isabel Hill presented the main issues of the conflict, while a second, feature-length documentary *The Battle for Brooklyn* (2011) directed and written by Michael Galinsky and Suki Hawley, told the story of Daniel Goldstein and his partner, Shabnam Merchant, who refused to sell their condo to FCRC and were eventually evicted by eminent domain. The investigative theater group, The Civilians, wrote and performed three performances including *In the Footprint: The Battle over Atlantic Yards* (2010), which we discussed in Chapter Four. While the playwrights, performers, actors and filmmakers claimed that their work was disinterested, most viewers or audiences we spoke to came away with a better understanding of the opposition, if not open sympathy for it. Interestingly, the FCRC executives we talked to told us they did not see these shows.

8. DevelopDontDestoryBrooklyn.net (also archived as dddb.net) and NoLandGrab. org are no longer active. Journalist Norman Oder has been critically tracking the Atlantic Yards Project on his blog *Atlantic Yards / Pacific Park Report* (atlanticyardsreport. blogspot.com) since 2005 and continues to follow developments.

9. Among these were John Turturro, Steve Buscemi, Rosie Perez, Michelle Williams, and the late Heath Ledger, as well as writers Jonathan Safran Foer and Nicole Krauss. In 2006, Pulitzer Prize–winning author Jennifer Egan published an op-ed piece in the *Times*, "A Developing Story." In 2008, Chris Knutsen and Valerie Steiker edited a volume of essays and short stories called *Brooklyn Was Mine* that served to raise money for Develop, Don't Destroy Brooklyn. This anthology featured Brooklyn authors including Phillip Lopate, Alexandra Styron, Susan Choi, Lawrence Osborne, Jennifer Egan, Jonathan Lethem, Vijay Seshardi, and Dinaw Megestu.

10. Elsewhere we analyze media coverage of the initial period of the conflict (Snajdr and Trinch 2018a).

11. One important component of planning and development in New York City beyond the scope of our present study is rent control, which began in 1943 and which remains in effect throughout some parts of the city. See for example Keating and Kahn 2002.

12. See, for example, Flint (2011) and Robert Caro's (1974) classic biography of Moses, *The Power Broker*. During his long career, Moses headed up a dozen public commissions and authorities.

13. There is an extensive literature on the growth of suburbia in the United States (see e.g. Kelly 1993; Duany, Plater-Zyberk and Speck 2001; and Hayden 2004). At the same

time African American areas of the city were redlined, whereby banks practiced discriminatory lending policies that prevented investment in homeownership (See Lipsitz 2011; Hillier 2003). Not all groups experienced this transformation equally. Stanger-Ross (2009) documents how Italian Americans remained in urban areas experiencing an influx of African American migrants from the rural South and how this fueled conflict and racial tensions. One Brooklyn informant told us that "The Irish fled. The Italians stayed," when referring to her Midwood Brooklyn neighborhood's demographic changes from the 1960s to the 1980s (interview with authors, January 28, 2011).

14. Smith's paper was published in 1979. He noted that the changes started in 1959 in Society Hill, the same time period as when Bertha Lewis was there with her grandmother.

15. In the 1970 Hal Ashby film *The Landlord*, a gentrifier is depicted as a white, wealthy renovator, acting alone, to rebuild and save a brownstone building in Park Slope. The original novel by Kristin Hunter takes place in Chicago.

16. Not all areas of the city have the same property tax rates. See the website of New York University's Furman Center, furmancenter.org, for an overview of the history and politics of New York City property taxes.

17. Anthropologist Rachel Heiman (2015) provides a detailed ethnographic look at zoning in suburban communities in America.

18. See for example Angotti (2011) on city planning and Osman (2011) on the transformation of Park Slope, and Kelly Anderson's 2012 documentary film *My Brooklyn*, on the redevelopment of the Fulton Mall area.

19. The tax photos are available on the NYC Records & Information Services Digital Gallery at www1.nyc.gov/site/records/historical-records/digital-gallery.page.

20. Census data in this section are from Social Explorer (socialexplorer.com). There are different conceptualizations of the neighborhood of Prospect Heights. Community District 8, which also includes Crown Heights, places the border between the two neighborhoods along Rogers Avenue. Other sources suggest the border of the neighborhood is Washington Avenue. For our discussion, we used census tracts 129.02, 161, 163, 203, 205, 207, 215, 217, 219, 221, 223, and 225. The latter two were combined into tract 305 in 2010.

21. This smaller configuration of Prospect Heights includes census tracts 129.02, 161, 163, 203, 205, 207, and 215, which we used for our neighborhood survey.

22. See also Small (2017), who provides an overview of the accelerating pace and scope of gentrification throughout New York City's boroughs between 2000 and 2015 for CityLab, drawing on data from New York City Comptroller's report "A New Geography of Jobs: A Blueprint for Strengthening NYC Neighborhoods," available at comptroller. nyc.gov/reports.

23. See also Heiman (2015) on gates, space, and semiotics in an American suburb.

24. The term *black orbs* is Jonathan Lethem's, who wrote about this pedestrian peril in the essay "Ruckus Flatbush," in *Brooklyn Was Mine* (Steiker and Knutsen 2008).

25. The "rusted" material is certainly newly manufactured, fabricated in Indiana by the metal-cladding outfit ASI Limited (Schrader 2010).

26. Similarly, the poshness of shop signs with aesthetics that utilize the decaying industrial remnants of a prior economy—such as Brooklyn Industries' slogan (see Figure 3.7)—may be interpreted negatively by some.

27. Over ninety thousand small businesses benefit from BIDs in New York City (Toussaint 2018). While the work of BIDs varies widely, they make up a central part of neoliberal, private-based public governance initiatives throughout North America and Europe (See Zukin 2010; Houstoun 2002; Mallet 1994; Symes and Steel 2003).

28. The full text of the Landmarks Law is available through an online portal to the Charter, Administrative Code, and Rules of the City of New York (www1.nyc.gov/nyc-resources/service/4080/nyc-charter-laws-codes-and-rules). See Title 25, Chapter 3. "There are more than 39,000 landmark properties in New York City, most of which are located in 149 historic districts and historic district extensions in all five boroughs. The total number of protected sites also includes 1,430 individual landmarks, 120 interior landmarks, and 11 scenic landmarks" ("About LPC," www1.nyc.gov/site/lpc/about/about-lpc.page, accessed December 5, 2020). Out of the eighteen neighborhoods our signs data comes from, eight—Boerum Hill, Brooklyn Heights, Carroll Gardens, Clinton Hill, Ditmas Park, Fort Greene, Crown Heights North, and Park Slope—have portions of their communities landmarked.

29. Watson is disparaging of this landscape, of which he reports: "In truth it struck me as defeating their own purpose, for the glare of them was so uniform as to lose the power of discrimination" (Henkin 1998, 46).

30. Catalano's extensive body of work can be viewed on Flickr, at www.flickr.com/photos/badwsky. The large fonts and literalness of historical Old School commercial signage vividly contrasts with New School storefronts in former New York City resident and artist Julia Wertz's (2017) nostalgic illustrated history of the city.

31. Wheated's interior linguistic landscape pays homage to various Brooklyn neighborhoods and places. Their menu offers pizzas called Ditmas Park, Caton Park, Vinegar Hill, Borough Park, and Coney Island.

32. There are also many storefronts captured in web archives of past New York streetscapes from the 1910s and 1920s that, although they may include small fonts, clearly depict an Old School style of word-richness (often with texts painted on store windows). Several blogs, including *Vanishing New York* (vanishingnewyork.blogspot.com, also now a book [2018]) by Jeremiah Moss—the pen name of retail shop activist Griffin Hansbury, Kevin Walsh's *forgotten new york*, (forgotten-ny.com), and Esther Crain's *Ephemeral New York* (ephemeralnewyork.wordpress.com), provide vivid, publicly accessible, and growing records of storefronts and other artifacts of New York's past. See also hundreds of photos uploaded to the NYC Signage Pinterest page, at www.pinterest.com/exwhyzedprint/nyc-signage.

33. Information on current BIDs can be found at New York City Department of Small Business Services website, www1.nyc.gov/site/sbs/neighborhoods/bid-directory.page.

34. Other residents in the arena footprint sold their condo units to FCRC (Snajdr and Trinch 2018a). Goldstein's home was taken in order to build the basketball arena portion of the Atlantic Yards plan. Another resident, Jerry Campbell, who refused to sell

his home on Dean Street, also had his property seized through eminent domain, but for subsequent parts of the project.

35. We were not able to ask those tenants how they felt about being relocated, but our Atlantic Yards interviews with various owners and renters who were displaced for that development would suggest that people have a broad range of feelings about being moved.

36. Certain areas of Manhattan where a vacancy rate of 5 percent was the norm, now have 25 percent vacancies. See Kilganon (2018) and Vacant New York (www.vacantnewyork.com) for Justin Levinon's interactive digital map of the city's vacant storefronts.

37. In a follow-up discussion, Pintchik mentioned that city leaders were contemplating fining property owners whose storefronts were empty, because they believe property owners are warehousing their commercial properties to hold out for higher rents from bigger tenants (interview with authors, March 8, 2015). Pintchik told the *Brooklyn Sun* in 2008 that he received fifteen calls in one week from businesses wanting to rent one of his buildings across from what at the time was just the proposed site for the Barclays Arena (Hope 2008).

38. In 2010, Walgreens bought Duane Reade, New York City's local chain pharmacy, which was founded in 1960.

39. For a nuanced analysis of the different segments of consumption (corporatization and life-style), driving gentrification in various Brooklyn neighborhoods, see Benediktsson, Lamberta, and Larsen (2015).

Chapter 5

1. The press release was published by *Eater New York* and is available at ny.eater.com/2017/7/24/16019934/summerhill-crown-heights-press-release-nyc (Serena Dai, "Here's That Press Release Summerhill Sent about Its Bullet Hole Wall, in Full," July 24, 2017).

2. *Merriam-Webster*, s.v. "oasis (n.)," accessed December 12, 2019, www.merriam-webster.com/dictionary/oasis.

3. See also sociologist Erving Goffman (1959) on the concept of face and its relationship to public interaction.

4. *Gothamist* reported that Brennan responded to protestors when they pleaded "Talk to us Becca!" by saying "I would love to. I said call me! Let's get coffee," and continued to sit at a table in front of her store (Whitford 2017b). More press coverage of this second demonstration is available at Emma Whitford, "Furious Crown Heights Residents Confront 'Bullet Hole' Bar Owner: 'Our Only Demand Is for Her to Close,'" *Gothamist*, Aug. 21, 2017, gothamist.com/news/furious-crown-heights-residents-confront-bullet-hole-bar-owner-our-only-demand-is-for-her-to-close.

5. This meeting was held at a Repair the World community center on Nostrand Avenue and, according to participants we spoke with, included about one hundred people (60 percent black, 10 percent Latino, and 30 percent white).

6. A video of the meeting can be found on a Twitter post by @OurBKSocial (August 25, 2017): "ICYMI: Becca Brennan, Summerhill (Crown Heights) bar owner's remarks on the backlash of the 'bullet-ridden wall' inside her establishment." twitter.com/OurBKSocial/status/901103875368910849.

7. Stephens, who had everything the media reported about Brennan remarkably well committed to memory, told us in March of 2019 that Brennan had joked with a *Gothamist* reporter that she should go get some paper bags to serve the rosé in (see Whitford 2017a).

8. Only one self-identified West Indian man, who said he owned a deli in another part of Brooklyn, seemed to disagree with the sentiments everyone else expressed. Essentially, he said if the community is so worried about violence, it was going after the wrong person with what he kept referring to as "two fake bullet holes." He argued that rather than worrying about "two fake bullet holes," the community should focus on the West Indian Day Parade, where, he claimed, there is always senseless gun violence, or on clearing the brothel next to his store. He seemed to be bothered by the community taking a law-abiding store owner to task. People then attempted to explain that his argument was invalid. We wondered if his defending stance toward Brennan was an attempt to stake a claim on his own rights to do law-abiding business his way.

9. We are referring to McIntosh's working paper titled "White Privilege and Male Privilege: A Personal Account of Coming to See Correspondences through Work in Women's Studies." A shorter, often quoted version appears under the title "White Privilege: Unpacking the Invisible Knapsack," published in 1989.

10. For example, McIntosh points out how, at the time she was writing this essay, the African experience in America, beginning with slavery, was barely taught in schools. Never were students asked to contemplate slave owners as damaged or immoral people, and in fact, people who were slaves "were seen as the only group at risk of being dehumanized" by the system of slavery (McIntosh 1988, 4).

11. The phrase was coined by French poet and dramatist Emile Augier in the 1855 play *Le Marriage d'Olympe*. We thank Johanna Lessinger for this reference.

12. In addition to a large African American and West Indian community, Crown Heights has a substantial Orthodox Jewish population. One of our Atlantic Yards informants, the Reverend Herbert Daughtry, in his 1997 book *No Monopoly on Suffering: Blacks and Jews in Crown Heights (and Elsewhere)*, has documented in detail a series of violent incidents against Crown Heights residents and other people of color in Brooklyn, as well as the history of the complicated relationship between Orthodox Jewish and African American and West Indian residents. Pritchett (2002) also provides a historical perspective on the development of gangs and conflict in nearby Brownsville.

13. Colon goes on to say that such a move "isn't just mean, it's also incredibly obnoxious. Like the kind of thing that Judge Smails did in *Caddyshack*, except you're wearing skinny jeans and a Peter Gabriel tour t-shirt from 1982 instead of golf stuff" (Colon 2013b).

14. Chris Crowley (2018), writing for *New York Magazine*'s Grub Street, noted other businesses that used the word *crack* to sell food, including Michigan-based gastropub HopCat which offered "crack" fries.

15. Stephens told us that, although she was raised outside of Brooklyn, her father was born and grew up in East New York.

16. This anti-establishment spirit extends to oppose the gentrification process itself. For example, Brooklyn publisher Akashic Books, whose titles include *Brooklyn Noir 1*, and *Brooklyn Noir 2*, prominently displays its slogan "Reverse Gentrification of the Literary World" in a banner on its website.

17. Posters referring to Summerhill as racist had gone up on walls and lampposts around Crown Heights before this first event. They had the word *Summerhill* written in the store's font and repeated vertically four times on an 8½-by-11-inch page with various unflattering and accusatory words (for example "Summerhill / Racist"; "Summerhill / Gentrifier," and "Summerhill / Colonialist." There were other signs in this format that appeared with quotations of things Brennan had presumably said: "I was tired of walking to Franklyn Street." All accused Brennan of being laden with superiority and white privilege. The online publication *Gothamist* wrote a short story about the posters reporting that a thirty-one-year-old white woman, who wished to remain anonymous, took credit for putting the signs up, saying, "It is up to white people to call white people on their shit" (Whitford 2017b).

18. "Becky" is a slang term—popularized by Beyoncé in the song "Sorry"—for a white woman perceived to be racist (Goldberg and McShane 2017).

19. Many New School Brooklyn shops prefer to display the small Visa or Mastercard signs on their cash registers inside the store.

20. Anthropologist Setha Low noted that the Flatbush Food Co-op's new signage in this case is also likely to be dialoguing directly with the super-gentrified Park Slope Food Co-op's notoriously strict rules that prohibit nonmembers from shopping there (Personal communication, Public Space Research Group, CUNY Graduate Center, March 3, 2017). Low's read indicates Brooklyn insiderness because one must know a lot about Brooklyn to get this index.

21. For additional examples and discussion of Old School appropriation and mimicking of the corporate, see Snajdr and Trinch 2018b.

22. A West-Indian deli owner told us that there is a difference between bodegas, delis, markets, and groceries. Other New Yorkers agree, although the definitions vary from person to person.

23. To reporter Elizabeth Segran's question about how the name might "come off as culturally insensitive," one of the founders said, "I'm not particularly concerned about it. . . . We did surveys in the Latin American community to understand if they felt the name was a misappropriation of that term or had negative connotations, and 97 percent said 'no.' It's a simple name and I think it works" (Segran 2017). There is no mention of which Latin American community was surveyed or how the people in it were asked to respond. See for example Dávila's (2008) work on how corporations market to Latin American and Latinx identities in the global economy.

24. It could also refer to the female warriors from Greek mythology, after which the Spanish soldier Francisco de Orellana named the world's largest river in 1541.

25. Recently, our son—who is now seventeen years old—and his football teammates

began to frequent a bodega near their school after practice and before hopping on the subway to come home. Our son told us that not only will the guy behind the counter and at the grill make them any sandwich they want, the cook also gave him and his friends the honor of naming the sandwiches.

26. This remark is a reference to how Peralta Supermarket's security cameras once helped solve a spate of local assaults in the area (Hagan, personal communication).

27. This line was written by the film star Foxy Brown, who grew up in the neighborhood and who elaborated in her note that "You always treated me like Inga even when I became 'Foxy Brown.' Ok. Now I'm gonna cry, so good luck in everything you do. Love Always and Forever [signed] Inga 'Muñeca.'"

28. American Heritage Dictionary, 5th Edition (2011) s.v. "finished,"

29. See also Colon (2013a) who helped to promote the effort online. When McCarthy's online petition at change.org closed, it had gathered 3959 signatures.

30. One prominent mural, on the side of a Fort Greene building housing a restaurant called Habana-Outpost, depicts Wallace wearing a beret, his image embellished with Che Guevera-esque flourish and the name "Comandante Biggie." See donyc.com/p/biggie-smalls for a list of Wallace murals and accompanying photographs of the artwork.

31. Harriot (2018) goes on: "[White people] will go to a party and ask to change the music. . . . They will open an artisan kale-cupcakery that uses locally sourced, farm-raised ingredients but won't hire kids from the neighborhood or use the mom-and-pop cleaners down the street to launder their tablecloths."

32. For examples of this archive, see the *Atlantic Yards / Pacific Park Report* blog, atlanticyardsreport.blogspot.com. An older archive, NoLandGRab is no longer active, but has been archived. Patti Hagan's nondigital archive also exists and is in need of preservation.

Conclusion

[unnumbered note]Matter - def (n.) physical substance; an affair or situation under consideration; a topic (*American Heritage Dictionary*, 5th edition. 2011).

1. The cover can be viewed at www.newyorker.com/magazine/2019/04/01.

2. Brooklyn Bagels stayed open for not quite two years, closing in 2017. As of this writing, the retail space is an empty storefront with a sign up that reads "for rent."

3. Ethnonyms are polysemous, after all, and their meaning still depends on who uses them. Even in Smith and Eisenstein's study (2016, 96), an informant remembers being talked to by a nun in Catholic school who said, "What are you doing back there, you dumb Syrians?"

4. These problematic and relational gendered positions of subjection and dominance are complicated and not new. See, for example, historian Amy Kaplan's (2005, 23–53) work on manifest domesticity and the role of nineteenth-century white women writers in co-constructing narratives of empire and nation building.

5. Aiello (2011) and Heiman (2015) show how elements of the built environment can be exclusionary and sources of community conflict as public semiotics.

6. For more in-depth research on this topic see Levinson (2018).

7. See Code of Virginia, § 15.2-1812, Memorials for War Veterans (law.lis.virginia.gov/vacode/title15.2/chapter18/section15.2-1812). Media coverage of this controversy is extensive. One counter protest, rallying against demonstrators gathering in support of unshrouding the statue and promoting white supremacy, resulted in the death of thirty-two-year-old Heather Heyer.

References

Abel, Elizabeth. 2010. *Signs of the Times: The Visual Politics of Jim Crow*. Berkeley: University of California Press.

Abu-Lughod, Janet. 1994. *From Urban Village to East Village*. New York City: Blackwell.

Acosta, Viarlenis. 2017. "Policy Memorandum: Storefront Awning Regulations." Class post for Communication in Public Settings course, Baruch College, May 30, 2017. blogs.baruch.cuny.edu/paf9103ura/?p=2789.

Agha, Asif. 2011. "Commodity Registers." *Journal of Linguistic Anthropology* 21, no. 1: 22–53.

———. 2004. "Registers of Language." In *A Companion to Linguistic Anthropology*, edited by Alessandro Duranti, 23–45. New York City: John Wiley & Sons.

———. 2001. "Register." In *Key Terms in Language & Culture*, vol. 11, edited by Alessandro Duranti, 212–13. New York City: Wiley-Blackwell.

Aiello, Giorgia. 2011. "From Wound to Enclave: The Visual-Material Performance of Urban Renewal in Bologna's Manifattura delle Arti." *Western Journal of Communication* 75, no. 4: 341–66.

Anderson, Benedict. 1991. *Imagined Communities: Reflections on the Origin and Spread of Nationalism*. London: Verso.

Anderson, Kelly, dir. 2012. *My Brooklyn*. New York City: New Day Films.

Angotti, Tom. 2011. *New York for Sale: Community Planning Confronts Global Real Estate*. Boston: MIT Press.

Ashby, Hal, dir. 1970. *The Landlord*. United Artists. DVD, 2010, 20th Century Fox Home Entertainment.

Atkinson, Rowland. 2003. "Introduction: Misunderstood Savior or Vengeful Wrecker: The Many Problems and Meanings of Gentrification." *Urban Studies* 40, no. 12: 2343–50.

Atlas, John. 2010. *Seeds of Change: The Story of ACORN, America's Most Controversial Anti-poverty Community Organizing Group*. Nashville, TN: Vanderbilt University Press.

Austin, John L. 1962. *How to Do Things with Words*. Oxford, UK: Oxford University Press.

Bagli, Charles. 2009. "Atlantic Yards Developer Releases New Arena Plan." *New York Times*, September 9. www.nytimes.com/2009/09/10/nyregion/10atlantic.html.

Bailey, Benjamin. 2000. "Communicative Behavior and Conflict between African-American Customers and Korean Immigrant Retailers in Los Angeles." *Discourse & Society* 11, no. 1: 86–107.

Bakhtin, Mikhail M. 1986. *Speech Genres and Other Late Essays*. Translated by V. W. McGee, edited by Caryl Emerson and Michael Holquist. Austin: University of Texas Press. Original work published in 1979.

Barni, Monica, and Carla Bagna. 2010. "Linguistic Landscape and Language Vitality." In *Linguistic Landscapes in the City*, edited by Elana Shohamy, Eliezer Ben-Rafael, and Monica Barni, 3–18. Bristol, UK: Multilingual Matters.

Barrett, Rusty. 2006. "Language Ideology and Racial Inequality: Competing Functions of Spanish in an Anglo-Owned Mexican Restaurant." *Language in Society* 35, no. 2: 163–204.

Basso, Keith. 1996. "Wisdom Sits in Places: Notes on a Western Apache Landscape." In *Senses of Place*, edited by Steven Feld and Keith Basso, 53–90. Santa Fe, NM: School of American Research Press.

Battistella, Edwin. 2014. *Sorry about That: The Language of Public Apology*. Oxford, UK: Oxford University Press.

Bauman, Richard. 2001. "The Ethnography of Genre in a Mexican Market: Form, Function, Variation." In *Style and Sociolinguistic Variation*, edited by Penelope Eckert and John R. Rickford, 57–77. Cambridge, UK: Cambridge University Press.

Bauman, Richard, and Charles Briggs. 2003. *Voices of Modernity: Language Ideologies and the Politics of Inequality*. Cambridge, UK: University of Cambridge Press.

Bayoumi, Moutsafa. 2008. *How Does It Feel to Be a Problem? Being Young and Arab in America*. New York City: Penguin Books.

Becker, Kara. 2009. "/r/ and the Construction of Place Identity on New York's Lower East Side." *Journal of Sociolinguistics* 13, no. 5: 634–58.

Behar, Ruth. 1993. *Translated Woman: Crossing the Border with Esperanza's Story*. Boston: Beacon Press.

Bell, Allan. 1984. "Language Style as Audience Design." *Language in Society* 13, no. 2: 145–204.

Bellafante, Gina. 2014. "As Shop Owner, Woman Sees Troubling Sides of Herself." *New York Times*, January 10, MB1. www.nytimes.com/2014/01/12/nyregion/as-shop-owner-woman-sees-troubling-sides-of-herself.html.

Benediktsson, Mike O., Brian Lamberta, and Erika Larsen. 2015. "Taming a Chaotic Concept: Gentrification and Segmented Consumption in Brooklyn, 2002–2012." *Urban Geography* 37, no. 4: 590–610.

Benito del Pozo, Paz, and Pablo Alonso Gonzalez. 2012. "Industrial Heritage and Place Identity in Spain: From Monuments to Landscapes." *Geographical Review* 102, no. 4: 446–64.

Besnier, Niko. 1991. "Literacy and the Notion of Person on Nukulaelae Atoll." *American Anthropologist* 93, no. 3: 570–87.

Biber, Douglas, and Susan Conrad. 2009. *Gender, Register and Style*. Cambridge, UK: Cambridge University Press.

Blanton, Ryan. 2011. "Chronotopic Landscapes of Environmental Racism." *Journal of Linguistic Anthropology* 21, no. 1: 76–93.

Blommaert, Jan. 2013. *Ethnography, Superdiversity and Linguistic Landscapes*. Bristol, UK: Multilingual Matters.

Bonanos, Christopher. 2004. "Is Bay Ridge the New Park Slope?" *New York Magazine*, February 13. nymag.com/nymetro/realestate/columns/n_9888.

Bondi, Liz. 1999. "Gender, Class and Gentrification: Enriching the Debate." *Environment and Planning D Society and Space* 17, no. 3: 261–82.

Bornstein, Avram. 2002. *Crossing the Green Line between the West Bank and Israel*. Philadelphia: University of Pennsylvania Press.

Bourdieu, Pierre. 1984. *Distinction: A Social Critique of the Judgement of Taste*. Cambridge, MA: Harvard University Press.

Boutin, Aimée. 2015. *City of Noise: Sound and Nineteenth-Century Paris*. Champagne: University of Illinois Press.

Boyd, Michelle. 2005. "The Downside of Racial Uplift: Meaning of Gentrification in an African American Neighborhood." *City & Society* 17, no. 2: 265–88.

Brash, Julian. 2011. *Bloomberg's New York*. Athens: University of Georgia Press.

Briggs, Charles, and Richard Bauman. 1992. "Genre, Intertextuality and Social Power." *Journal of Linguistic Anthropology* 2, no. 2: 131–72.

Brock, Mark, and Larry Walters. 1992. *Teaching Composition around the Pacific Rim*. Bristol, UK: Multilingual Matters.

Brown, Eliot. 2009. "Talking SHoP about Atlantic Yards." *Observer*, September 14. observer.com/2009/09/talking-shop-about-atlantic-yards.

Brown, Penelope, and Steven C. Levinson. 1987. *Politeness: Some Universals in Language*. Cambridge, UK: Cambridge University Press.

Bucholtz, Mary, Brendan Barnwell, and Elena Skapoulli. 2012. "Itineraries of Identity in Undergraduate Science." *Anthropology and Education Quarterly* 43, no. 2: 157–72.

Buczynski, Sandy, and Kristin Fontichiaro. 2009. *Story Starters and Science Notebooking*. Santa Barbara, CA: Libraries Unlimited.

Burrows, Edwin G., and Mike Wallace. 1998. *Gotham: A History of New York City to 1898*. Oxford, UK: Oxford University Press.

Caldiera, Teresa P. R. 2012. "Imprinting and Moving Around: New Visibilities and Configurations of Public Space in Sao Paulo." *Public Culture* 24, no. 2: 385–419.

Caro, Robert A. 1974. *The Power Broker: Robert Moses and the Fall of New York*. New York City: Alfred A. Knopf.

Chan, Shirley. 2017. "Angry Crown Heights Community Faces Off with Owner of 'Bullet Hole' Bar." *Pix11*, August 25. pix11.com/2017/08/25/angry-crown-heights-community-faces-off-with-owner-of-bullet-hole-bar.

College Board. 2017. *The Official SAT Study Guide*. New York City: College Board.

Collins, James, and Richard Blot. 2003. *Literacy and Literacies*. Cambridge, UK: Cambridge University Press.

Collins, James, and Stef Slembrouck. 2007. "Reading Shop Windows in Globalized Neighborhoods: Multilingual Literacy Practices and Indexicality." *Journal of Literacy Research* 39, no. 3: 335–56.

Collins, Patricia Hill. 1991. *Black Feminist Thought*. New York City: Routledge.

Colon, David. 2013a. "Let's Rename St. James and Fulton 'Christopher Wallace Way.'" *Brokelyn*, August 28. brokelyn.com/its-no-dream-lets-rename-st-james-and-fulton-christopher-wallace-way.

———. 2013b. "Is the $8 40 in a Paper Bag as Stupid as We Think?" *Brokelyn*, September 19. brokelyn.com/is-the-8-40-in-a-paper-bag-as-stupid-as-we-think-dumber.

Cooper, Michael. 2003. "Councilman Is Shot to Death in City Hall." *New York Times*, July 23. www.nytimes.com/2003/07/23/nyregion/councilman-is-shot-to-death-in-city-hall.html.

Crenshaw, Kimberlé. 1990. "Mapping the Margins: Intersectionality, Identity Politics, and Violence against Women of Color." *Stanford Law Review* 43, no. 6: 1241–99.

Crowley, Chris. 2018. "It's Time to Stop Calling Foods 'Crack.'" Grub Street, *New York Magazine*, December 12. www.grubstreet.com/2018/12/restaurant-chain-will-rename-its-crack-fries.html.

Curtin, Melissa. 2014. "Mapping Cosmopolitanisms in Taipei: Toward a Theorization of Cosmopolitanism in Linguistic Landscape Research." *International Journal of the Sociology of Language*, no. 228 (June): 153–77.

Daughtry, Herbert D. 1997. *No Monopoly on Suffering: Blacks and Jews in Crown Heights (and Elsewhere)*. Trenton, NJ: Africa World Press.

Dávila, Arlene. 2012. *Culture Works: Space, Value and Mobility across the Neoliberal Americas*. New York City: New York University Press.

———. 2008. *Latino Spin: Public Image and the Whitewashing of Race*. New York City: New York University Press.

———. 2004. *Barrio Dreams: Puerto Ricans, Latinos and the Neoliberal City*. Berkeley: University of California Press.

Davis, Mike. 2001. *Magical Urbanism: Latinos Reinvent the US City*. London: Verso.

Dick, Hilary Parsons, and Kristina Wirtz. 2011. "Racializing Discourses." *Journal of Linguistic Anthropology* 21, no. 1: 2–10.

Dickson, Akeya. 2014. "*Thug Kitchen*: A Recipe in Blackface." *The Root*, September 30. www.theroot.com/thug-kitchen-a-recipe-in-blackface-1790877230.

Dore, Ronald. 2008. "Financialization of the Global Economy." *Industrial and Corporate Change* 17, no. 6: 1097–112.

Dorst, John D. 1989. *The Written Suburb*. Philadelphia: University of Pennsylvania Press.

Douglas, Mary. 1966. *Purity and Danger*. London: Verso.

Douglass, G. C. C. 2012. "The Edge of the Island: Cultural Ideology and Neighbourhood Identity at the Gentrification Frontier." *Urban Studies* 49, no. 16: 3579–94.

Dowdall, George W. 2015. "Society Hill." *Encyclopedia of Greater Philadelphia*. philadelphiaencyclopedia.org/archive/society-hill.

Duany, Andres, Elizabeth Plater-Zyberk, and Jeff Speck. 2001. *Suburban Nation*. New York City: Macmillan.

Duranti, Alessandro. 2015. *The Anthropology of Intentions*. Cambridge, UK: Cambridge University Press.

Egan, Jennifer. 2007. "A Developing Story." *New York Times*, February 24. www.nytimes.com/2007/02/24/opinion/24egan.html.

Eldredge, Barbara. 2015. "The Complete List of All Things Named Brooklyn (Updated)." *Brownstoner*, November 4. www.brownstoner.com/brooklyn-life/ brooklyn-the-brand-the-complete-list-of-all-things-brooklyn.

Eliasoph, Nina. 1999. "Everyday Racism in a Culture of Political Avoidance: Civil Society, Speech and Taboo." *Social Problems* 46, no. 4: 479–502.

Ellis, Carolyn. 1995. *Final Negotiations: A Story of Love, Loss and Chronic Illness*. Philadelphia: Temple University Press.

Faegin, Joe. 2000. *Racist America: Roots, Current Realities and Future Reparations*. New York City: Routledge.

Feld, Steven. 1996. "Waterfalls of Song: An Acoustemology of Place Resounding in Bosavi, Papua New Guinea." In *Senses of Place*, edited by Steven Feld and Keith Basso, 91–136. Santa Fe: School of American Research Press.

Fernea, Elizabeth Warnock. 1965. *Guests of the Sheik*. New York City: Anchor.

Fiorvante, Janice. 1996. "If You Are Thinking of Living In/Midwood: A Rich Ethnic Mix in Mid-Brooklyn." *New York Times*, July 21, 5.

Flint, Anthony. 2011. *Wrestling with Moses: How Jane Jacobs Took on New York's Master Builder and Transformed the American City*. New York City: Random House.

Florida, Richard. 2012. *The Rise of the Creative Class—Revisited: Revised and Expanded*. New York City: Basic Books.

———. 2005. *Cities and the Creative Class*. New York City: Routledge.

Forbes, Ann Arbrecht. 1999. "Mapping Power: Disputing Claims to Kipat Lands in Northeastern Nepal." *American Ethnologist* 26, no. 1: 114–38.

Freeman, Lance. 2011. *There Goes the 'Hood: Views of Gentrification from the Ground Up*. Philadelphia: Temple University Press.

Fullilove, Mindy. 2005. *Root Shock: How Tearing Up City Neighborhoods Hurts America, and What We Can Do about It*. New York City: Ballantine.

Furman Center. 2006. *State of New York's Housing and Neighborhoods—2006*. Carolin Bhalla, project director. New York City: Furman Center for Real Estate and Urban Policy. furmancenter.org/research/sonychan/2006-report.

Gal, Susan. 2005. "Language Ideologies Compared." *Journal of Linguistic Anthropology* 15, no. 1: 23–37.

Galinsky, Michael, and Suki Hawley. 2011. *The Battle for Brooklyn*. Brooklyn, NY: RUMUR; Newtown, PA: Virgil Films & Entertainment, 2013.

Gans, Herbert. 1962. *The Urban Villagers*. New York City: MacMillan.

Geertz, Clifford. 1973. *The Interpretation of Culture*. New York City: Basic Books.

Gendelman, Irina, and Giorgia Aiello. 2010. "Faces of Places: Facades as Global Communication in Post-Eastern Bloc Urban Renewal." In *Semiotic Landscapes: Language, Image, Space*, edited by Adam Jaworski and Crispin Thurlow, 256–73. New York City: Mouton de Gruyter.

Gerend, Jennifer. 2003. "Commentary/Op-Ed: The Outrage over New York City's Storefront Awning Ticket Blitz Is Justified—But So Are the Limits." Center for an Urban Future, August. nycfuture.org/research/the-outrage-over-new-york-citys-storefront-awning-ticket-blitz-is-justified.

Glass, Ruth. 1964. *London: Aspects of Change*. London: MacGibbon and Kee.

Goffman, Erving. 1959. *The Presentation of Self in Everyday Life*. New York City: Anchor Books, Doubleday.

Goldberg, Noah, and Larry McShane. 2017. "Crown Heights Eatery Touting Bullet Holes in Wall, Serving 40 Ounces of Wine in Paper Bag Accused of Racism." *New York Daily News*, July 19. www.nydailynews.com/new-york/brooklyn/crown-heights-eatery-touting-wall-bulletholes-accused-racism-article-1.3338352.

Goodman, Amy. 2019. "Historian: Americans Must Face Violent History of Blackface amid Virginia Gov. Racist Photo Scandal." *Daily Show*, Feb. 4, 2019. Mike Burke, news director. *Democracy Now!* Video. www.democracynow.org/2019/2/4/historian_americans_must_face_violent_history.

Goodman, Barak, and Rachel Dretzin, dirs. 2003. "The Persuaders." *Frontline*, season 2004, episode 3. Aired November 9, 2003, on PBS. www.pbs.org/wgbh/pages/frontline/shows/persuaders.

Gorter, Durk, ed. 2006. *Linguistic Landscape: A New Approach to Multilingualism*. Clevedon: Multilingual Matters.

Grant, Aimee. 2016. "'I . . . don't want to see you flashing your bits around': Exhibitionism, Othering and Good Motherhood in Perceptions of Public Breastfeeding." *Geoforum* 71 (May): 52–61.

Green, Penelope. 2015. "*Thug Kitchen*: Veganism You Can Swear By." *New York Times*, October 22, D1. www.nytimes.com/2015/10/22/fashion/thug-kitchen-you-eat-vegetables-with-that-mouth.html.

Grossman, Tim. 2017. "The Bodega Effect: Lessons in Branding from the Rise and Fall of a Startup." *Entrepreneur*, September 19. www.entrepreneur.com/article/300446.

Hackworth, Jason. 2002. "Postrecession Gentrification in New York City." *Urban Affairs Review* 37, no. 6: 815–43.

Hackworth, Jason, and Neil Smith. 2001. "The Changing State of Gentrification." *Tijdschrift voor economische en sociale geografie* 92, no. 4: 464–77.

Hale, Steven. 2017. "Rebel Fail: Area Confederate General Defeated Again." *Nashville Scene*, December 27.

Harriot, Michael. 2018. "Seven Rules for White People with Black Friends." *The Root*, April 5. www.theroot.com/7-rules-for-white-people-with-black-friends-1825023173.

Hartocollis, Anemona. 2003. "The Letters and the Law: Should New York Change Its Awnings or Its Code?" *New York Times*, September 30. www.nytimes.com/2003/09/30/nyregion/the-letters-and-the-law-should-new-york-change-its-awnings-or-its-code.html.

Harvey, David. 2005. *A Brief History of Neoliberalism*. Oxford, UK: Oxford University Press.

Hayden, Dolores. 2004. *Building Suburbia: Green Fields and Urban Growth, 1820–2000*. New York City: Vintage.

Heath, Shirley Brice. 1982. "What No Bedtime Story Means: Narrative Skills at Home and School." *Language in Society* 11, no. 1: 49–76.

Heiman, Rachel. 2015. *Driving after Class: Anxious Times in an American Suburb*. Berkeley: University of California Press.

Heller, Monica. 2012. "Bourdieu and 'Literacy Education.'" In *Pierre Bourdieu and Literacy Education*, edited by James Albright and Allan Luke, 50–67. New York City: Routledge.

———. 2003. "Globalization, the New Economy and the Commodification of Language and Identity." *Journal of Sociolinguistics* 7, no. 4: 473–92.

Henkin, David M. 1998. *City Reading: Written Words and Public Spaces in Antebellum New York*. New York City: Columbia University Press.

Hill, Isabel, dir. 2007. *Brooklyn Matters*. New Day Films.

Hill, Jane. 2008. *The Everyday Language of White Racism*. Oxford, UK: Wiley-Blackwell.

———. 1998. "Language, Race and White Public Space." *American Anthropologist* 100, no. 3: 680–89.

Hillier, Amy E. 2003. "Redlining and the Home Owners' Loan Corporation." *Journal of Urban History* 29, no. 4: 394–420.

Holleran, Sam. 2017. "Graffiti, Street Art, Advertising, and the Fight for Urban Visual Space." Paper presented at What's Your Sign? Retail Architecture and the History of Signage. University of Iowa Museum of Art, Iowa City, September 9.

Hope, Bradley. 2008. "Brooklyn Family Sitting on $100M in Property, Air Rights." *Brooklyn Sun*, February 7. www.nysun.com/real-estate/brooklyn-family-sitting-on-100m-in-property-air/70892.

Hoppenfeld, Mita Shah. 2015. "Strange Fruit in the Friendly Toast: Cocktail Isn't Homage, It's Horror." *Cambridge Day*, February 9. www.cambridgeday.com/2015/02/09/strange-fruit-in-the-friendly-toast-cocktail-isnt-homage-its-horror.

Houstoun, L. O. 2002. "BIDs at Home and Abroad: BIDs Are Expanding, Diversifying, and Increasingly Being Formed Abroad." *Urban Land* 61, no. 10: 42–47.

Hurowitz, Noah. 2014. "Patrick Stewart Wants to Ban Strollers in Park Slope." *New York*, April 18. nymag.com/intelligencer/2014/04/patrick-stewart-brooklyn-strollers.html.

Hustwit, Gary, producer and director. 2007. *Helvetica*. Film First. Available at vimeo.com/ondemand/helvetica3.

Hymes, Del. 1974. *Foundations in Sociolinguistics: An Ethnographic Approach*. Philadelphia: University of Pennsylvania Press.

Ihaza, Jeff. 2017. "A Conversation with Brooklyn's Most Controversial Restaurant Owner." *Outline*, August 31. theoutline.com/post/2197/a-conversation-with-brooklyn-s-most-controversial-restaurant-owner.

Irvine, Judith, and Susan Gal. 2000. "Language Ideology and Linguistic Differentiation." In *Regimes of Language: Ideologies, Polities and Identities*, edited by Paul Kroskrity, 35–84. Santa Fe, NM: School of American Research Press.

Jackson, John L., Jr., 2005. *Real Black: Adventures in Racial Sincerity*. Chicago: University of Chicago Press.

Jacobs, Jane. 1961. *The Death and Life of Great American Cities*. New York City: Random House.

Jaffe, Alexandra, ed. 2009. *Stance: Sociolinguistic Perspectives*. Oxford Studies in Sociolinguistics. Oxford, UK: Oxford University Press.

Jakobson, Roman. 1971. "Shifters, Verbal Categories and the Russian Verb." In *Word and Language*, 130–47. Vol. 3 of *Roman Jakobson: Selected Writings*. The Hague: Mouton Press.

Jaworski, Adam, and Crispin Thurlow. 2009. "Taking an Elitist Stance." In *Stance: Sociolinguistic Perspectives*, edited by Alexandra Jaffe, 195–227. Oxford Studies in Sociolinguistics. Oxford, UK: Oxford University Press.

Jaworski, Adam, and Simone Yeung. 2010. "Life in the Garden of Eden: The Naming and Imagery of Residential Hong Kong." In *Linguistic Landscapes in the City*, edited by Elana Shohamy, Eliezer Ben-Rafael, and Monica Barni, 153–81. Bristol, UK: Multilingual Matters.

Jeffries, Lesley. 2007. "Journalistic Constructions of Blair's Apology for the Intelligence Leading to the Iraq War." In *Language and the Media*, edited by Sally and Astrid Enslin, 48–69. New York City: Continuum.

Johnstone, Barbara. 2009. "Pittsburghese Shirts: Commodification and the Enregisterment of an Urban Dialect." *American Speech* 84, no. 2: 157–75.

———. 1990. *Stories, Community and Place: Narratives from Middle America*. Bloomington: Indiana University Press.

Kaplan, Amy. 2005. *The Anarchy of Empire and the Making of U.S. Culture*. Cambridge, MA: Harvard University Press.

Kasinitz, Philip. 1988. "The Gentrification of 'Boerum Hill.'" *Qualitative Sociology* 11, no. 3: 163–82.

Keating, Dennis, and Mitch Kahn. 2002. "Rent Control in the New Millennium." *Race Poverty and the Environment* 9, no. 1: 30–33.

Kelly, Barbara M. 1993. *Expanding the American Dream: Building and Rebuilding Levittown*. Albany: State University of New York Press.

Kilganon, Corey. 2018. "The Empty Storefronts of New York: A Panoramic View." *New York Times*, September 6. www.nytimes.com/interactive/2018/09/06/nyregion/nyc-storefront-vacancy.html.

Kittay, Eva. 1987. *Metaphor: Its Cognitive Force and Linguistic Structure*. Oxford, UK: Clarendon.

Kuntzman, Gersh. 2007. "Battle over Arena Bagels!" *Brooklyn Paper*, May 19. www.brooklynpaper.com/battle-over-arena-bagels.

Kurgan, Laura, Eric Cadora, David Reinfurt, Sarah Williams, and Leah Meisterlin. 2006. "Million Dollar Blocks." Spatial Information Design Lab, Graduate School of Architecture, Preservation and Planning, Columbia University, September 15–October 28. spatialinformationdesignlab.org/projects.php%3Fid%3D16.

Kwong, Peter. 1997. *Forbidden Workers: Illegal Chinese Immigrants and American Labor*. New York City: Free Press.

Lacy, Paul. 2008. *Brooklyn Storefronts*. New York City: W. W. Norton.

LaFrance, Marianne, and Clara Mayo. 1978. "Cultural Aspects of Nonverbal Communication." *International Journal of Intercultural Relations* 2, no. 1: 71–89.

Lamarre, Patricia. 2014. "Bilingual Winks and Bilingual Wordplay in Montreal's Linguistic Landscape." *International Journal of the Sociology of Language*, no. 228 (June): 113–51.

Landry, Rodrigue, and Richard Y. Bourhis. 1997. "Linguistic Landscape and Ethnolinguistic Vitality." *Journal of Social Psychology* 16, no. 1: 23–49.

Lane, Anthony. 2011. "The Fun Factory." *New Yorker*, May 16, 74–87. www.newyorker.com/magazine/2011/05/16/the-fun-factory.

Lavine, Amy, and Norman Oder. 2010. "Urban Redevelopment Policy, Judicial Deference to Unaccountable Agencies, and Reality in Brooklyn's Atlantic Yards Project." *Urban Lawyer* 42, no. 2: 287–373.

Leahy, Michael. 1999. *If You're Thinking of Living In: All About 115 Great Neighborhoods In and Around New York*. New York City: New York Times Company.

Lecuna, Vicente. 2017. "Modern Dreams, Sinister Spaces." In *Mall to Prison: El Helicoide's Downward Spiral*, edited by Celeste Olalquiaga and Lisa Blackmore, 174–83. New York City: Urban Research.

Leeman, Jennifer, and Gabriella Modan. 2010. "Selling the City: Language, Ethnicity and Commodified Space." In *Linguistic Landscapes in the City,* edited by Elana Shohamy, Eliezer Ben-Rafael, and Monica Barni, 182–98. Bristol, UK: Multilingual Matters.

———. 2009. "Trajectories of Language: Orders of Indexical Meaning in Washington, DC's Chinatown." In *Reshaping Cities*, edited by Michael Guggenheim and Ola Soderstrom, 167–88. London: Routledge.

Lees, Loretta. 2003. "Super-Gentrification: The Case of Brooklyn Heights, New York City." *Urban Studies* 40, no. 12: 2487–509.

Lethem, Jonathan. 2006. "Brooklyn's Trojan Horse: What's Wrong with the Buildings Frank Gehry Wants to Put in My Neighborhood?" *Slate*, June 19. www.slate.com/articles/arts/culturebox/2006/06/brooklyns_trojan_horse.html.

Levinson, Sanford. 2018. *Written in Stone: Public Monuments in Changing Societies*. Durham, NC: Duke University Press.

Levitt, Theodore. 1983. "The Globalization of Markets." *Harvard Business Review*, May-June: 2–20.

Levy, Marc. 2015. "Creator of 'Strange Fruit' Cocktail Explains Origins, Asks Severed Ties of Friendly Toast." *Cambridge Day*, March 23. www.cambridgeday.com/2015/03/23/creator-of-strange-fruit-cocktail-explains-origins-asks-severed-ties-of-friendly-toast.

Ley, David. 1996. *The New Middle Class and the Remaking of the Central City*. Oxford, UK: Oxford University Press.

Liebow, Elliot. 1967. *Tally's Corner*. Boston: Little, Brown and Co.

Lipsitz, George. 2011. *How Racism Takes Place*. Philadelphia: Temple University Press.

Loewen, James. 2018. *Sundown Towns: A Hidden Dimension of American Racism*. New York City: New Press.

Lott, Eric. 2013. *Love and Theft: Blackface Minstrelsy and the American Working Class*. London: Oxford University Press.

Lou, Jackie Jia. 2016. *The Linguistic Landscape of Chinatown: A Sociolinguistic Ethnography*. Bristol, UK: Multilingual Matters.

———. 2007. "Revitalizing Chinatown into a Heterotopia: A Geosemiotic Analysis of Shop Signs in Washington, DC's Chinatown." *Space and Culture* 10, no. 2: 170–94.

Low, Setha. 1993. "The Cultural Meaning of the Plaza." In *The Cultural Meaning of Urban Space*, edited by Robert Rotenberg and Gary McDonogh, 75–94. Westport, CT: Bergin & Garvey.

Mahar, William John. 1999. *Behind the Burnt Cork Mask: Early Blackface Minstrelsy and Antebellum American Popular Culture*. Champagne: University of Illinois Press.

Malinowski, David. 2017. "Reviewing History and Race in the Built Environment on a U.S. University Campus." Paper presented at the Annual Meetings of the American Anthropological Association, Washington, DC, December 2.

Mallett, William J. 1994. "Managing the Post-Industrial City: Business Improvement Districts in the United States." *Area* 26, no. 3: 276–87.

Martin, Emily. 1990. "Toward an Anthropology of Immunology: The Body as a Nation State." *Medical Anthropology Quarterly* 4, no. 4: 410–26.

Massey, Douglas, and Nancy Denton. 1993. *American Apartheid*. Cambridge, MA: Harvard University Press.

Mathews, T. J., and Brady Hamilton. 2016. "Mean Age of Mothers Is on the Rise: United States, 2000–2014." *NCHS Data Brief*, no. 232 (January): 1–8.

Mathews, Vanessa. 2018. "Reconfiguring the Breastfeeding Body in Urban Public Spaces. *Social & Cultural Geography* 19, no. 1: 1–19.

Matoesian, Gregory M. 1993. *Reproducing Rape*. Chicago: University of Chicago Press.

Matos, Joseph, and Nancy Dillon. 2014. "Breastfeeding Moms Nurse Babies on A Train for 'Breastfeeding Subway Caravan.'" *New York Daily News*, August 8. www.nydailynews.com/new-york/breastfeeding-moms-nurse-babies-train-breast-feeding-subway-caravan-article-1.1897575.

Matsuda, Mari J., Charles R. Lawrence III, Richard Delgado, and Kimberlé Williams Crenshaw, eds. 1993. *Words that Wound: Critical Race Theory, Assaultive Speech, and the First Amendment*. Boulder, CO: Westview Press.

Matsumoto, Nancy. 2012. "The Farm on Adderley: Sometimes Pigs Do Fly." *Edible Brooklyn*, no. 26 (Summer): 9–12. www.ediblebrooklyn.com/2012/the-farm-on-adderley.

McDonald, Jamie. 2012. *New York Originals: A Guide to the City's Classic Shops & Mom-and-Pops*. New York City: Universal.

McElhinny, Bonnie. 2016. "Reparations and Racism, Discourse and Diversity: Neoliberal Multiculturalism and the Canadian Age of Apologies." *Language & Communication*, no. 51 (November): 50–68.

McIntosh, Peggy. 1988. "White Privilege and Male Privilege: A Personal Account of Coming to See Correspondences through Work in Women's Studies." Working paper 189, Wellesley Centers for Women, Wellesley, MA. nationalseedproject.org/Key-SEED-Texts/white-privilege-and-male-privilege.

Mele, Christopher. 2000. *Selling the Lower East Side*. Minneapolis: University of Minnesota Press.

Mertz, Elizabeth. 2007. *The Language of Law School*. New York City: Oxford University Press.

Milroy, James, and Lesley Milroy. 2012. *Authority in Language: Investigating Standard English*. New York City: Routledge.

Modan, Gabriella Gahlia. 2017. "New Urban Chic: The Semiotic Landscape of Gentrification in US Cities." Paper presented at City Talk Symposium, University of Bern, Bern, Switzerland, December 11.

———. 2007. *Turf Wars: Discourse, Diversity and the Politics of Place*. Malden MA: Blackwell.

Mollenkopf, John H. 1983. *The Contested City*. Princeton: Princeton University Press.

Mookherjee, Nayanika. 2006. "'Remembering to Forget': Public Secrecy and the Memory of Sexual Violence in the Bangladesh War of 1971." *Journal of the Royal Anthropological Institute* 12, no. 2: 433–50.

Mooney, Jake. 2008. "Brooklyn for Sale." *New York Times*, June 22. www.nytimes.com/2008/06/22/nyregion/thecity/22disp.html.

Moss, Jeremiah. 2018. *Vanishing New York: How a Great City Lost Its Soul*. New York City: Dey Street Books.

Murphy, Doyle. 2014. "Park Slope Breastfeeding Boutique Boing Boing Set to Close as Owner Heads for Haiti." *New York Daily News*, August 18. www.nydailynews.com/new-york/brooklyn/pioneering-park-slope-baby-store-boing-boing-close-article-1.1905330.

Murray, James T., and Karla L. Murray. 2011. *Storefront: The Disappearing Face of New York*. New York City: Ginko Press.

Myrick, Richard. n.d. "Food Truck Names That Should Be Banned. Really?" Mobilecuisine.com. mobile-cuisine.com/trends/food-truck-names-that-should-be-banned-really, accessed December 18, 2018.

Naples, Nancy. 2012. *Community Activism and Feminist Politics: Organizing across Race, Class and Gender*. New York City: Routledge.

Napolitano, Len. 2013. *Nose, Legs, Body! Know Wine Like The Back of Your Hand*. Templeton, CA: Wineology Press.

Neal, Mark Anthony. 2002. *Soul Babies: Black Popular Culture and the Post-Soul Aesthetic*. New York City: Routledge.

Nerlich, Brigitte, and David Clarke. 2001. "Ambiguities We Live By: Towards a Pragmatics of Polysemy." *Journal of Pragmatics* 33, no. 1: 1–20.

New York City Small Business Services. 2012. *Storefront Improvements: A Guide for Commercial Districts*. New York City: City of New York. www.nyc.gov/html/sbs/downloads/pdf/neighborhood_development/storefront-guide.pdf.

New York State Division of Local Government Services. 2015. *Municipal Control of Signs*. James A. Coon Local Government Technical Series. Albany: New York State Department of State.

New York State Small Business Development Center. 2004. *What's Your Signage? How On-Premise Signs Help Small Businesses Tap into a Hidden Profit Center*. Albany: New York State Small Business Development Center. www.nyssbdc.org/resources/Publications/Whats_Your_Signage.pdf.

Norton, Peter. 2011. *Fighting Traffic: The Dawn of the Motor Age in the American City*. Cambridge, MA: MIT Press.

Nowak, Glenn. 2017. "Meta-Signage around the Mega-Resorts of Las Vegas." Paper presented at What's Your Sign? Retail Architecture and the History of Signage. University of Iowa Museum of Art, Iowa City, September 9.

NYUSPS UrbanLab. 2018. "Brooklyn's Lead Developer Shares Lessons in Place Branding." *Medium*, May 21. medium.com/@NYUurbanlab/brooklyns-lead-developer-shares-lessons-on-place-branding-78e912afb4b1.

Ocejo, Richard. 2017. *The Masters of Craft: Old Jobs in the New Urban Economy*. Princeton, NJ: Princeton University Press.

———. 2011. "The Early Gentrifier: Weaving a Nostalgia Narrative on the Lower East Side." *City & Community* 10, no. 3: 285–310.

Ochs, Elinor. 1990. "Indexicality and Socialization." In *Cultural Psychology: Essays on Comparative Human Development*, edited by James Stigler, Richard Schweder, and Gilbert Herdt, 287–308. Cambridge, UK: Cambridge University Press.

Ortner, Sherry. 1972. "Is Female to Male as Nature Is to Culture?" *Feminist Studies* 1, no. 2: 67–87.

Oser, Alan. 1999. "Developer Buys Former Plant of *Daily News* in Brooklyn." *New York Times,* April 17. www.nytimes.com/1999/04/17/nyregion/developer-buys-former-plant-of-daily-news-in-brooklyn.html.

Osman, Suleiman. 2011. *The Invention of Brownstone Brooklyn: Gentrification and the Search for Authenticity in Postwar New York*. New York City: Oxford.

Ouroussoff, Nicolai. 2009. "New Yards Design Draws from the Old." *New York Times*, September 9. www.nytimes.com/2009/09/10/arts/design/10yards.html.

Pagliai, Valentina. 2011. "Unmarked Racializing Discourse, Facework, and Identity in Talk about Immigrants in Italy." *Journal of Linguistic Anthropology* 21, no. s1: E94–E112.

Papen, Uta. 2015. "Signs in Cities: The Discursive Production and Commodification of Urban Spaces. *Sociolinguistic Studies* 9, no. 1: 1–26.

———. 2012. "Commercial Discourses, Gentrification and Citizen's Protests." *Journal of Sociolinguistics* 16, no. 1: 56–80.

Pardess, Rebecca. 2012. "10 L.A. Restaurants and Trucks with Double Entendre Names." KCET, May 17. www.kcet.org/food/10-la-restaurants-and-trucks-with-double-entendre-names.

Patch, Jason. 2008. "'Ladies and Gentrification': New Stores, Residents and Relationships in Neighborhood Change." In *Gender in an Urban World*, edited by Judith N. DeSena, 103–26. Research in Urban Sociology, vol. 9. Bingley, UK: Emerald Group Publishing.

Patrick, Peter L. 1995. "Recent Jamaican Words in Sociolinguistic Context." *American Speech* 70, no. 3: 227–64.

Paulston, Christina B. 1994. *Linguistic Minorities in Multilingual Settings*. Amsterdam: John Benjamins Publishing.

Pavlenko, Aneta, and Alex Mullen. 2015. "Why Diachronicity Matters in the Study of Linguistic Landscapes." *Linguistic Landscape* 1, no. 1/2: 114–32.

Payne, Bob. 2011. "The Informer: The 15 Best Places to See Right Now." *Conde Nast Traveler*, March 15. www.cntraveler.com/stories/2011-03-15/the-informer-the-15-best-places-to-see-right-now.

Paz, Octavio. 2002. "The Sons of La Malinche." In *The Mexico Reader: History, Culture, Politics*, edited by Gilbert Joseph and Timothy Henderson, 20–27. Durham, NC: Duke University Press.

Peyser, Andrea. 2003. "Bad Sign for Biz: City Fining Shops for 'Wordy' Awnings." *New York Post*, May 12. nypost.com/2003/05/12/bad-sign-for-biz-city-fining-shops-for-wordy-awnings.

Philips, Susan U. 1975. "Literacy as a Mode of Communication on the Warm Springs Indian Reservation." In *Foundations of Language Development*, vol. 2, edited by Eric H. Lenneberg and Elizabeth Lenneberg, 367–82. New York City: Academic Press.

Polasek, Patrick M. 2014. "A Critical Race Review of *Grand Theft Auto V*." *Humanity and Society* 38, no. 2: 216–18.

Pritchett, Wendell. 2002. *Brownsville, Brooklyn: Blacks, Jews and the Changing Face of the Ghetto*. Chicago: University of Chicago Press.

Purnell, Brian. 2013. *Fighting Jim Crow in the County of Kings*. Louisville: University Press of Kentucky.

Rahman, Muhammad, and Vikas Mehta. 2017. "Letter Forms as Communicative Urban Artifacts for Social Narratives." *Interdisciplinary Journal of Signage and Wayfinding* 2, no. 1. doi.org/10.15763/issn.2470-9670.2017.v2.i1.a18.

Reichl, Alexander. 1999. *Reconstructing Times Square: Politics and Culture in Urban Development*. Lawrence: University Press of Kansas.

Remnick, Noah. 2017. "Notorious B.I.G., Brooklyn Street Bard, Gets Official City Tribute at Last." *New York Times*, August 2. www.nytimes.com/2017/08/02/nyregion/christopher-wallace-notorious-big-tribute-brooklyn.html.

Roberts, Sam. 2011. "Slower Racial Change Found in Census of City." *New York Times*, July 29. www.nytimes.com/2011/07/29/nyregion/census-finds-slight-stabilizing-in-new-york-city-racial-makeup.html.

——. 2007. "In Surge in Manhattan Toddlers, Rich White Families Lead Way." *New York Times*, March 23. www.nytimes.com/2007/05/17/us/17census.html.

Robinson, Linton H. 1996. *Mexican Slang: A Guide*. Bueno Books: California.

Rodriquez, Jason. 2006. "Color-Blind Ideology and the Cultural Appropriation of Hip-Hop." *Journal of Contemporary Ethnography* 35, no. 6: 645–68.

Rodríguez-San Pedro Bezares, Luis E., and Ángel Weruaga Prieto. 2011. *Elogios triunfales: Origen y significado de los* Vítores *Universitarios Salmantinos* [Triumphant praise: Origin and meaning of the *Vítores* of the University of Salamanca]. Salamanca, Spain: Universidad Pontificia de Salamanca.

Rosner, Helen, and Serena Dai. 2017. "New 'Instagrammable' Crown Heights Restaurant Brags about Fake Bullet Holes: Summerhill Checks Off All the Gentrification Red Flags." *Eater New York*, July 18. ny.eater.com/2017/7/18/15989954/summerhill-crown-heights-nyc-gentrifying-bar.

Rotenberg, Robert. 1993. "On the Salubrity of Sites." In *The Cultural Meaning of Urban Space*, edited by Robert Rotenberg and Gary McDonogh, 17–30. Westport, CT: Bergin & Garvey.

Sagalyn, Lynne B. 2003. *Times Square Roulette: Remaking the City Icon*. Boston: MIT Press.

Santora, Marc. 2006. "Circumstances Made Him a Hero, and Then Cost Him His Life." *New York Times*, September 5. www.nytimes.com/2006/09/05/nyregion/05slay.html.

Sassen, Saskia. 2001. *The Global City*. Princeton, NJ: Princeton University Press.

Schieffelin, Bambi, Katherine Woolard, and Paul Kroskrity. 1998. *Language Ideologies: Practice and Theory*. New York City: Oxford University Press.

Schlictman, John Joe, Jason Patch, and Marc Lamont Hill. 2017. *Gentrifier*. Toronto: University of Toronto Press.

Schrader, Stuart. 2010. "Weathering Deindustrialization." Paper presented at the Annual Meeting of the American Anthropology Association, New Orleans, LA, November 19.

Scollon, Ron, and Susie Wong Scollon. 2003. *Discourse in Place: Language in the Material World*. London: Routledge.

Searle, John. 1969. *Speech Acts: An Essay on the Philosophy of Language*. Cambridge, UK: Cambridge University Press.

Segran, Elizabeth. 2017. "Two Ex-Googlers Want to Make Bodegas and Mom-and-Pop Corner Stores Obsolete." *Fast Company*, September 13. www.fastcompany.com/40466047/two-ex-googlers-want-to-make-bodegas-and-mom-and-pop-corner-stores-obsolete.

Seiler, Cotten. 2008. *Republic of Drivers: A Cultural History of Automobility in America*. Chicago: University of Chicago Press.

Senison, Heather. 2016. "Brooklyn Most Expensive Place to Live in US: Bloomberg." amNewYork, February 1. www.amny.com/real-estate/brooklyn-most-expensive-place-to-live-in-u-s-bloomberg-1-11416734.

Shohamy, Elana, Eliezer Ben-Rafael, and Monica Barni, eds. 2010. *Linguistic Landscapes in the City*. Bristol, UK: Multilingual Matters.

Shostak, Marjorie. 1981. *Nisa, the Life and Words of a !Kung Woman*. Cambridge, MA: Harvard University Press.

Shuman, Amy. 1983. "Collaborative Literacy in an Urban Multiethnic Neighborhood." *International Journal of the Sociology of Language*, no. 42 (January): 69–81.

Sieber, R. Timothy. 1987. "Urban Gentrification, Ideology, and Practice in Middle-Class Civic Activity." *City & Society* 1, no. 1: 52–63.

Sieber, Tim, Graca I. Cordeiro, and Ligia Ferro. 2012. "The Neighborhood Strikes Back: Community Murals by Youth in Boston's Communities of Color." *City & Society* 24, no. 3: 263–80.

Silverstein, Michael. 2003. "Indexical Order and the Dialectics of Sociolinguistic Life." *Language and Communication* 23, no. 3: 193–229.

———. 1976. "Monoglot 'Standard' in America: Standardization and Metaphors of Linguistic Hegemony." In *The Matrix of Language: Contemporary Linguistic Anthropology*, edited by Donald Brenneis and Ronald Macauley, 284–306. Boulder, CO: Westview Press.

Slater, Tom. 2006. "The Eviction of Critical Perspectives from Gentrification Research." *International Journal of Urban and Regional Research* 30, no. 4: 737–57.

Small, Andrew. 2017. "The Gentrification of Gotham." *CityLab*, April 28. www.citylab.com/life/2017/04/the-Gentrification-of-gotham/524694.

Smith, Andrea L., and Anna Eisenstein. 2016. *Rebuilding Shattered Worlds: Creating Community by Voicing the Past*. Lincoln: University of Nebraska Press.

———. 2013. "Thoroughly Mixed yet Thoroughly Ethnic: Indexing Class with Ethnonyms." *Journal of Linguistic Anthropology* 23, no. 2: 1–22.

Smith, Neil. 2002. "New Globalism, New Urbanism: Gentrification as a Global Urban Strategy." *Antipode* 34, no. 3: 427–50

———. 1996. *The New Urban Frontier: Gentrification and the Revanchist City*. London: Routledge.

———. 1979. "Toward a Theory of Gentrification: A Back to the City Movement of Capital, Not People." *Journal of the American Planning Association* 45, no. 4: 538–48.

Smitherman, Geneva. 2000. *Black Talk: Words and Phrases from the Hood to the Amen Corner*. Boston: Houghton Mifflin.

Snajdr, Edward. 2008. *Nature Protests: The End of Ecology in Slovakia*. Seattle: University of Washington Press.

Snajdr, Edward, and Shonna Trinch. 2018a. "When the Street Disappears: Eminent Domain, Redevelopment and the Dissociative State." *PoLAR: Political and Legal Anthropology Review* 41, no. 1: 21–43.

———. 2018b. "Old School Rules: Generative Openness in the Texts of Historical Brooklyn Retail Signage." *Interdisciplinary Journal of Signage and Wayfinding* 2, no. 2: 12–29.

Springer, Kimberly. 1999. *Still Lifting, Still Climbing: Contemporary African American Women's Activism*. New York City: New York University Press.

Staeheli, Lynn, and Don Mitchell. 2007. "Locating the Public in Research and Practice." *Progress in Human Geography* 31, no. 6: 792–811.

Stanger-Ross, Jordan. 2009. *Staying Italian*. Chicago: University of Chicago Press.

Steiker, Valerie, and Chris Knutsen, eds. 2008. *Brooklyn Was Mine*. New York City: Riverhead Books.

Stewart, George. 1982. *Names on the Land*. New York City: New York Review of Books Classics.

Storey, Samantha. 2007. "The Park Slope Parent Trap." *New York Times*, July 8. www.nytimes.com/2007/07/08/realestate/08cov.html.

Street, Brian. 1984. *Literacy in Theory and Practice*. Cambridge, UK: Cambridge University Press.

Street, Brian, and Niko Besnier. 1993. "Aspects of Literacy." In *Companion Encyclopedia of Anthropology*, edited by Tim Ingold, 527–62. London: Routledge.

Strunk, William, and E. B. White. 1999. *The Elements of Style*, 4th ed. New York City: Pearson.

Susser, Ida. 2012. *Norman Street*, 2nd ed. New York City: Oxford University Press.

Suttles, Gerald. 1968. *The Social Order of the Slum*. Chicago: Chicago University Press.

Symes, Martin, and Mark Steel. 2003. "Lessons from America: The Role of Business Improvement Districts as an Agent of Urban Regeneration." *Town Planning Review* 74, no. 3: 301–13.

Taylor, Candacy. 2016a. "The Roots of Route 66." *Atlantic*, November 3. www.theatlantic.com/politics/archive/2016/11/the-roots-of-route-66/506255.

———. 2016b. *Route 66: Road Trip*. Berkeley, CA: Perseus Books.

Taylor, Kate, Mary Hanbury, and Dennis Green. 2018. "Amazon's Growth Could Threaten These 10 Industries." *Business Insider*, June 28. www.businessinsider.com/amazon-is-killing-these-7-companies-2017-7.

Thompson, Andrew. 2012. "Signs and Billboards: What's Legal and What's Not?" *CityLaw*, Dec. 19. www.citylandnyc.org/signs-and-billboards-whats-legal-and-whats-not.

Thug Kitchen. 2014. New York City: Rodale Books.

Thurlow, Crispin, and Giorgia Aiello. 2007. "National Pride, Global Capital: A Social-Semiotic Analysis of Transnational Visual Branding in the Airline Industry." *Visual Communication* 6 no. 3: 305–44.

Thurlow, Crispin, and Adam Jaworski, eds. 2011. *Semiotic Landscapes: Language, Image, Space*. London: Bloomsbury Academic.

Topousis, Tom. 1999. "Pol: City Yawning at Illegal Awnings." *New York Post*, November 21.

Toussaint, Kristin. 2018. "Report: 93K Small Businesses Benefited from NYC's Business Improvement Districts." *Metro*, April 16.

Trinch, Shonna. 2003. *Latinas' Narratives of Domestic Abuse: Discrepant Versions of Violence*. Philadelphia: John Benjamins Publishing.

Trinch, Shonna, and Edward Snajdr. 2018. "Mothering Brooklyn: Signs, Sexuality and Gentrification Undercover." *Linguistic Landscape* 4, no. 3: 214–37.

Turner, Julia. 2006. "Where Do 'Baby-Daddies' Come From? The Origin of the Phrase." *Slate*, May 7. slate.com/human-interest/2006/05/a-brief-history-of-baby-daddies.html.

Upadhye, Janet. 2013. "Biggie Smalls Too Fat to Have Corner Named for Him, Committee Member Says." *DNAinfo*, October 16. www.dnainfo.com/new-york/20131016/clinton-hill/biggie-smalls-too-fat-have-corner-named-for-him-cb-member-says.

Urciuoli, Bonnie. 2011. "Discussion Essay: Semiotic Properties of Racializing Discourses." *Journal of Linguistic Anthropology* 21, no. 1: 113–22.

Vaughn, Melissa, Brendan Vaughn, and Michael Harlan Turkell. 2010. *The New Brook-lyn Cookbook: Recipes and Stories from 31 Restaurants that Put Brooklyn on the Map*. New York City: William Morrow Cookbooks.

Walker, Ameena. 2017. "The Notorious B.I.G. Mural in Bed-Stuy Will Come Down." *Curbed New York*, May 19. ny.curbed.com/2017/5/19/15662140/brooklyn-biggie-smalls-mural-destroyed.

Wall, Glenda. 2001. "Moral Constructions of Motherhood in Breastfeeding Discourse." *Gender & Society* 15, no. 4: 592–610.

Walley, Christine J. 2013. *Exit Zero: Family and Class in Postindustrial Chicago*. Chicago: University of Chicago Press.

Warde, Alan. 1991. "Gentrification as Consumption: Issues of Class and Gender." *Environment and Planning D Society and Space* 9, no. 2: 223–32.

Warner, Michael. 2002. "Publics and Counterpublics." *Public Culture* 14, no. 1: 49–90.

Waterston, Alisse. 2014. *My Father's Wars: Migration, Memory, and the Violence of a Century*. New York City: Routledge.

———. 2013. "Autoethnography." In *Theory in Social and Cultural Anthropology: An Encyclopedia*, edited by R. Jon McGee and Richard L. Warms, 36–38. New York City: Sage Publications.

———. 1999. *Love, Sorrow and Rage*. Philadelphia: Temple University Press.

Waterston, Alisse, and Barbara Rylko-Bauer. 2006. "Out of the Shadows of History and Memory: Personal Family Narratives in Ethnographies of Rediscovery." *American Ethnologist* 33, no. 3: 397–412.

Wells, Pete. 2018. "10 of the Best New N.Y.C. Restaurants (For Now). *New York Times*, November 15. www.nytimes.com/2018/11/15/nyregion/best-new-nyc-restaurants.html.

Wertz, Julia. 2017. *Tenements, Towers & Trash: An Unconventional Illustrated History of New York City*. New York City: Black Dog & Leventhal Publishers.

Wharton, Rachel. 2012. "Ample Hills Creamery Survives Its Own Success." *Edible Brooklyn*, no. 26 (Summer): 4–6. www.ediblebrooklyn.com/2012/ample-hills-creamery.

White, Monica M. 2011. "Sisters of the Soil: Urban Gardening as Resistance in Detroit." *Race/Ethnicity: Multidisciplinary Global Contexts* 5, no. 1: 13–28.

Whitford, Emma. 2017a. "New Crown Heights Restaurant Proudly Advertises Cocktail Next to 'Bullet Hole-Ridden Wall.'" *Gothamist*, July 18. gothamist.com/food/new-crown-heights-restaurant-proudly-advertises-cocktail-next-to-bullet-hole-ridden-wall.

———. 2017b. "Crown Heights 'Bullet Hole' Bar Owner Apologizes for Being Insensitive." *Gothamist*, July 19. gothamist.com/food/crown-heights-bullet-hole-bar-owner-apologizes-for-being-insensitive.

———. 2017c. "Crown Heights Bar Owner Plasters Over Controversial 'Bullet Hole' Wall." *Gothamist*, September 20. gothamist.com/2017/09/20/summerhill_crown_heights_wall.php.

Wilder, Craig Steven. 2000. *A Covenant with Color: Race and Social Power in Brooklyn 1636–1990*. New York City: Columbia University Press.

Wilkerson, Isabel. 2010. *The Warmth of Other Suns*. New York City: Random House.

Williams, Mary Elizabeth. 2009. *Gimme Shelter*. New York City: Simon and Schuster.

Wilson, Claire. 2005. "Near Prospect Park, a Touch of Greenwich." *New York Times*, May 1.

———. 2003. "Ditmas Park and Ditmas Park West." *New York Times*, November 2.

Wortham, Stanton, Elaine Allard, Kathy Lee, and Katherine Mortimer. 2011. "Racialization in Payday Mugging Narratives." *Journal of Linguistic Anthropology* 21, no. 1: 56–75.

Wu, Tim. 2015. "Urban Blight Comes to the West Village." *New Yorker*, May 24. www.newyorker.com/business/currency/why-are-there-so-many-shuttered-storefronts-in-the-west-village.

Yeh, Rihan. 2009. "We're Mexican Too: Publicity and Status at the International Line." *Public Culture* 21, no. 3: 465–93.

Zenfell, Martha Ellen, ed. 2002. *Insight Guide: New York City*. New York City: Langenscheidt Publishers.

Zukin, Sharon. 2010. *Naked City: The Death and Life of Authentic Urban Places*. New York City: Oxford University Press.

———. 1989. *Loft Living*. New Brunswick: Rutgers University Press.

———. 1987. "Gentrification: Culture and Capital in the Urban Core." *Annual Review of Sociology* 13 (August): 129–47. doi.org/10.1146/annurev.so.13.080187.001021.

Zukin, Sharon, and Ervin Kosta. 2004. "Bourdieu Off-Broadway: Managing Distinction on a Shopping Block in the East Village." *City & Community* 3, no. 2: 101–16.

Index

Bold page numbers refer to tables, figures, and illustrations.

geo-discursivity, 73–74

Gimme Shelter (Williams), 107

Goldstein, Daniel, 2, 175–76, 219, 252n7, 254n34

Gone with the Wind (1939), 188

Good Times (1974), 94, 248n6

Gosh, Amitav, 74

Gothamist, 4, 184–85, 190, 202

Gowanus, 82–83

Grace Hopper College, 233

graffiti, 10, 12, 20, 89, 242n8

Grand Theft Auto, 191–92

Green, Victor Hugo, 242n10

Greenlight Bookstore, 75

Green Line, 10

Grub Street (*New York Magazine*), 256n14

Guzman Business Services, **34**, 35, 38–40

Habit boutique, 103, 141–42

Hackworth, Jason, 27

Hagan, Patti, 2, **147**, 149, 177, 212–14, **213**, 227

Hamlet (Shakespeare), 32, 245n24

Harriot, Michael, 218–19, 258n31

Hawley, Suki, 252n7

Heath, Shirley Brice, 67, 85

Heiman, Rachel, 253n17

Helvetica typeface, 64. *See also* typography

Henkin, David M., 168

Heyer, Heather, 259n7

Highline, 150

Hill, Isabel, 252n7

Hill, Jane, 95–96, 98, 105–6, 139, 142, 247n16

Hill, Marc Lamont, 28

Hindy, Steve, 87

Hipsqueak boutique, 47, 226

Hispanics. *See* Latinos/Latinx

historic preservation
    landmark properties and districts, 172, 244n11, 254n28

historic preservation (*continued*)
    Landmarks Preservation Commission (LPC), 165–72, **170**, 195
    and zoning, 165, 168, 172

Holiday, Billie, 98–99, 247n19

homosexuality, 104

Hood, John Bell, 233

HopCat gastropub, 256n14

"Horror in Red Hook, A" (Lovecraft), 74

housing prices, 7, 112, 114, 121, 162, 216, 252n5

Hudson Yards, 150

Huebner, Roselyn, 84–85

humor
    racialized, 188–91, 195–96, 199, 235–36
    and wordplay, 80, 82–84, 89, 91, 105, 107, 116, 139

Hunter, Kristin, 253n15

Hurston, Zora Neale, 94

hybrid signs, 117, 204–5

identity
    and ethnicity, 30, 56–57, **57**, 62–63
    intersectional, 28, 104
    and language, 9–11, 15, 21, 76, 102, 244n16
    and non-gentrifier immigrants, 26
    and place, 10, 78
    and signage, 55–57, **56**, 61–62, 224–25, 229, 244n16
    and women, 30, 195–96

Ihaza, Jeff, 195, 197–99

imagined community, 10, 83–84

immigrants and immigration
    Brooklyn as center of, 17, 26, 61, 107, 119–20, 150–51, 168, 178, 250
    and commerce, 204, 210, 219
    and inner city decay, 150–51
    and non-gentrifying newcomers, 26–27, 54, 107
    and role of women, 119–20

inclusion, 63, 234, 236

Picket Fence restaurant, **90**, 90–91, 94, 248n26

Pintchik, Michael, 136, 154, 172–74, **173**, 176, 179

Pipa restaurant, 246n1

place and place-making
    and corporate development, 146, 150, 180–81
    and culture of place, 10, 13–14
    and indexicality, 16–17
    and language, 3–4, 9–11, 13–14, 211–12, 234–35
    and signage, 13–14, 29–30, 70–71, 80–93, 107, 194–95, 215, 224, 231
    and written texts, 77–78

Plan B store, 103

Poe, Edgar Allan, 29, 67, 236

Poehler, Amy, 137

polysemy
    and available meanings, 78–80, 90
    and dominant groups, 83–84, 104–5, 193–95, 225
    and offensive meanings, 113, 231, 247n17, 256n14, 257n18
    and place-making, 80–81
    and racial meaning, 96–99, 235–36
    in signage, 46–49, 64, **84**, 251n32
    and taboo meanings, 80–81, 98, 117–18, 137, 247n18

positionality, 25, 79, 243n18

poverty, 91–92, 163, 191–93, 197

privilege
    and gentrifiers, 19, 105, 140, 215, 218–19, 256n9
    and public texts, 230–31
    and Summerhill controversy, 30, 187–94, 197, 201–3, 257n17
    white privilege, 12, 191–94, 197, 201–2, 210, 215, 218, 233–35, 256nn9–10
    See also McIntosh, Peggy

Prospect Heights, 147–58, 162, 172, 177, 220, 253n20

Protestantism, 26, 103–5. *See also* religion

public, definition of, 242n11. *See also* Warner, Michael

public-private partnership, 148, 150–53. *See also* corporate development

public schools, 83, 122–30, 133–34, 153, 160, 250n21. *See also* education

public space, 117, 140, 228, 233–34

public texts, 7–12, 20, 89, 168–69, **169**, 218, 242n8

"Purloined Letter, The" (Poe), 67, 236

race and racism
    and credit, 18, 92, 192, 252–53n13
    and memorializing black culture, 216–17
    and neighborhood transition, 150–51, 158
    and neoliberalization, 19
    and segregation and Jim Crow, 11–12, 151, 242nn9–10
    and sexual stereotypes, 105, 110–13, 117–19, 136–39
    and signage, 55–57, 92–94, 99, 103–4, 112–13, 235–36
    and sincerity theory, 62, 97
    and Summerhill restaurant controversy, 187, 197
    and white privilege, 12, 191–94, 197, 201–2, 210, 215, 218, 233–35, 256nn9–10
    See also African Americans; ethnicity; Latinos/Latinx; privilege

Ratner, Bruce, 3, 146, **148**, 152, 176

real estate
    and gentrification and neighborhood perception, 84, 107, 156–57, 161–62, 216
    and reinvestment, 20, 172–73, 176, 179
    See also affordable housing; rent gap

Red Hook, 82–83

Seshardi, Vijay, 252n9
sex
    and New School signage, 80, **81**,
        102–4, 118, **118**, 234, 236
    and racial stereotypes, 105, 110–13,
        117–19, 136–39
    and taboos, 117, 122–23, 136,
        140–42, 154
Shakespeare, William, 32, 64, 245n24
Shelter restaurant, 102
SHoP architectural firm, 161
Shostak, Marjorie, 115
signage
    and branding, 64, 67, 87–90, 101–2,
        205–6, **206**, 208
    corporate, 66, 180
    and gender, 102–3, 105, 116–18, **118**,
        140–43
    and identity, 55–57, **56**, 61–62,
        224–25, 229, 244n16
    and indexicality, 14–17, 96–98, 100,
        104–5
    and place-register, 29–30, 205, 212,
        213, 215–16, 224–26
    as political devices, 11–12, 224
    and public nature of, 16, 70–71, 232
    and regulation of, 50–54, 165–68,
        166, 227–28
    as social acts, 11, 224
    and social hierarchy, 76, 224–25,
        242n8
    styles of, 8, 33–35, 45–46, 50, 66, 180,
        207, 224–36
    and transitional neighborhoods,
        7, 20, 23, 159, 162–63, 204–5,
        254n26
    types of, **36**, 44–46, **45**, 50–52, 167,
        207, **207**
sign makers, 50–54, 167–68
Silverstein, Michael, 14–15, 55
sincerity theory, 62–63, 76, 97, 100, 102,
    187. *See also* race and racism
slumming, 192

small business
    and Atlantic Yards project, 22, 175
    and gentrification, 46, 115–16, 153,
        172, **173**, 176–78, 187–90, 226
    regulation of, 50–51, 165–68,
        171, 208
    research on, 22–23
    sustainability of, 175, 178, 181,
        254n27, 254n33
Smith, Andrea, 61–62, 69
Smith, Betty, 74
Smith, Neil, 7, 20, 27, 103–4, 151, 153,
    215–16, 235
Smitherman, Geneva, 94–96, 98, 112–13
social hierarchy, 15, 76, 224–25, 242n8
social justice, 128
social media. *See* internet and social media
Society Hill (Philadelphia), 145–46, 151
socioeconomic status
    and mobility, 27, 178, 225–26, 229
    and privilege, 90–91, 94
    and research methods, 25, 54
    and signage semiotics, 54–56, 106–7,
        110, 143, 242n8
sociolinguistics
    and language appropriation, 96,
        137, 139
    and New School Distinction-
        Making Signage, 66–67, 81, 93,
        99, 113, 251n32
    and Old School Vernacular Signage,
        16, 29, 55, 61, 77
    and place-making, 21, 70, 146,
        224–26
    and signage as social acts, 11, 16, 22,
        29, 35, 232
Sofreh restaurant, 226
Sophie's Choice (Styron), 74
Spanish language, 38–39, **39**, 95–98, **96**,
    105, 139, 226, 247n17. *See also* lan-
    guages other than English
speech acts, 186, 224, 231
speech as action, 23

CPSIA information can be obtained
at www.ICGtesting.com
Printed in the USA
LVHW071553231221
707028LV00007B/155

9 780826 522788